Markets Don't Fail!

Markets Don't Fail!

Brian P. Simpson

LEXINGTON BOOKS
Lanham • Boulder • New York • Toronto • Oxford

LEXINGTON BOOKS

A division of Rowman & Littlefield Publishers, Inc.
A wholly owned subsidiary of The Rowman & Littlefield Publishing Group, Inc.
4501 Forbes Boulevard, Suite 200
Lanham, MD 20706

PO Box 317
Oxford
OX2 9RU, UK

British Library Cataloguing in Publication Information Available

Library of Congress Cataloging-in-Publication Data

Simpson, Brian P., 1966–
  Markets don't fail! / Brian P. Simpson.
    p. cm.
  Includes bibliographical references and index.
  ISBN 0-7391-1034-9 (cloth : alk. paper) — ISBN 0-7391-1364-X (pbk. : alk. paper)
  1. Capitalism. 2. Comparative economics. 3. Externalities (Economics) 4. Public
goods. I. Title.
HB501.S594 2005
330.12'2—dc22   2005002155

Printed in the United States of America

⊖™ The paper used in this publication meets the minimum requirements of American
National Standard for Information Sciences—Permanence of Paper for Printed Library
Materials, ANSI/NISO Z39.48–1992.

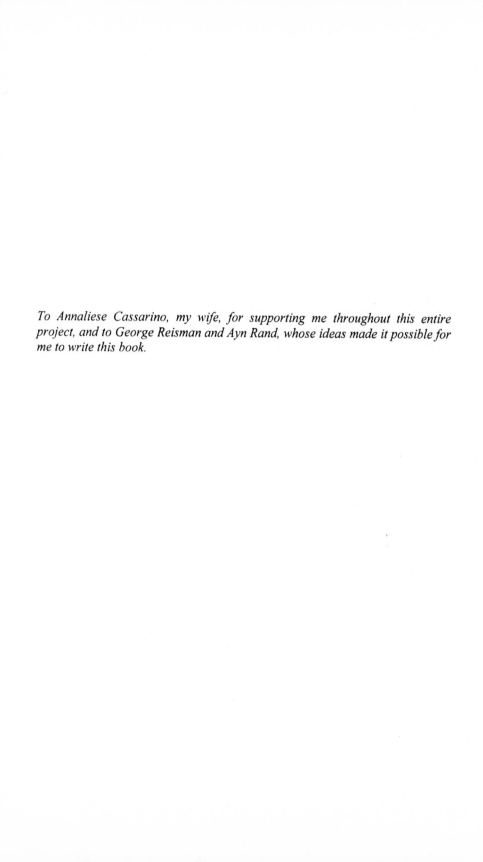

To Annaliese Cassarino, my wife, for supporting me throughout this entire project, and to George Reisman and Ayn Rand, whose ideas made it possible for me to write this book.

Contents

Preface

Markets Don't Fail! has its origins in the "microeconomics" classes I have been teaching since I received my Ph.D. in economics. In all of the contemporary economics textbooks that I am generally required to use there is typically at least one chapter that addresses topics concerning "market failure." From these topics come the chapter titles of this book. Understanding that it would be intellectually dishonest to let the students go away from my classes with the belief that markets actually do fail, I devised a method to use the false material in the textbooks as a means of telling the truth. Hence, from the very first economics class I taught, I have always presented the topics on "market failure" in the following manner: first I present the arguments against the market (showing what the claims against the market are), then I proceed to show what is wrong with these claims (thus refuting the false ideas put forward), and finally I show why markets actually succeed. I present other false claims in the contemporary economics textbooks (and there are many of them) using a similar format.

The material in *Markets Don't Fail!* provides a strong antidote to the arguments typically presented in contemporary economics textbooks. It has proved quite effective in dispelling the myths of market failure in my own classes. Now that these ideas exist in the form of a book, they represent an even more powerful way to counteract some of the false claims emanating from modern economics textbooks. Now students can spend hours reading and thinking about the arguments presented here and come to a thorough understanding of them. This is something that cannot be done through class lectures alone.

Markets Don't Fail! would make a great supplemental book in any class that uses a contemporary, mainstream economics textbook. It would even serve as a good companion textbook in graduate level courses. Most graduate students in economics have never heard of the arguments refuting the claims of market failure and probably take the idea of market failure as an axiom. This book will help change that.

Although this book would be excellent as a companion to the mainstream textbooks, it does not have to play this subordinate role. It could be used in conjunction with other books on free market economics to provide more rigorous training to students on sound economic ideas. It goes well beyond virtually all other free market economics books because it provides important moral and epistemological arguments in defense of the market.

Although this book concentrates primarily on economic topics, as the above statement indicates, it goes much deeper than economics in providing arguments against market failure and for market success. When one claims that something is a success or failure, one is using some standard upon which to base his judgment. Much of this book involves exposing the invalid standards of judgment upon which the claims of "market failure" are based and providing valid standards upon which to judge the market. The book gets to the fundamental, philosophical reasons why the claims of market failure are false and why markets actually succeed. It provides a major integration of philosophy and economics. If one does not understand at this point why the philosophical arguments are important, one will come to a greater understanding of why as one reads the book. Here I will simply say that by going deeper, the book provides a more comprehensive, rigorous, and logically consistent defense of the free market.

This book is an invaluable tool for those who want to gain a better understanding of the free market and the ideas that are used to attack it.

Brian P. Simpson
La Jolla, CA
February, 2005

Acknowledgments

I want to make one general reference to a book that has been so instrumental in my understanding of economics that it would be far too repetitive for me to reference it on every separate occasion that is necessary (although I still do reference it on a few occasions when it is absolutely essential). That book is *Capitalism: A Treatise on Economics* by the economist George Reisman. I draw from *Capitalism* when discussing capitalism and socialism, monopoly and competition, the antitrust laws and predatory pricing, externalities, regulation, environmentalism, economic inequality, and how to implement a capitalist society.

I would like to thank the following people who made helpful comments on earlier versions of the manuscript of this book: Andrew Bernstein, Harry Binswanger, William Decker, Onkar Ghate, John McCaskey, John Ridpath, and Charles and JoAnn Simpson. I would also like to thank George Reisman for providing detailed comments on the entire manuscript. Finally, I would like to thank John Lewis for doing a thorough review of the book for the publisher and also for providing detailed comments on the entire manuscript.

Introduction

The theme of this book, as the title explicitly states, is that markets do not fail. The critics of the free market are wrong because their assaults on the market are based on inappropriate standards of judgment and flawed economic arguments. For instance, critics of the market use invalid concepts and a false code of morality to judge the market. Further, in their economic arguments they fail to take into account the long-run effects of government interference in the market. Of course, if I used this book to prove merely that markets do not fail, my task would be incomplete. I focus on the fact that markets do not fail in order to answer as explicitly, tersely, and clearly as possible all the critics of the market who write of alleged examples of market failure. Most of the claims economists make concerning market failure will be addressed in the following chapters.[1] In the process, I show that if one uses a proper standard of judgment and sound economic arguments, one will come to the conclusion that markets do not fail, but actually succeed.

Free markets exist where people voluntarily produce and trade goods and services. Because they are based on voluntary trade, and because individual rights must be protected to establish and maintain a free market, they provide an environment where all individuals are free from the initiation of physical force and thus are free to use their minds to think, act on their own rational judgment, and produce the values their lives require. Voluntary trade is beneficial to all those who participate in it because all parties to a trade gain from the trade. The fact that all parties gain is the reason why trade occurs in the first place.

The political/economic system that establishes and maintains a free market is known as laissez-faire capitalism. This is the only social system consistent with the requirements of human life and thus is the *only* moral social system. Social systems that yoke or chain the individual to the collective—whether socialism, fascism, military dictatorship, absolute monarchy, the welfare state or mixed economy, and systems based on race and nationality, among others—are

1

systems that initiate physical force against the individual and prevent him from performing the tasks his life requires. These systems stand in opposition to the requirements of human life and thus are immoral. Why this is the case will become clear as one reads the book.

It is governments, not markets, that fail. When governments do not protect the existence of a free market (which means, when governments fail to protect individual rights, including private property rights), this leads to a lower rate of economic progress, a lower standard of living, misery, poverty, and, when taken to its logical and consistent end, death and destruction on a massive scale. Likewise, when governments preserve the free market, human life flourishes. This has been proven time and time again throughout the history of mankind. The twentieth century is rife with examples that illustrate this principle. All one must do is recall the differences between such countries as the USSR and the United States, East and West Germany, or North and South Korea. In all of these cases, the governments that established political/economic systems that are the exact opposite of a free market, and forced the individual to live for the state (the former country in each example), caused a lower standard of living and murdered millions of people. The governments that followed more capitalistic policies (the latter country in each example) made possible a much higher standard of living and allowed human life to thrive to the degree that they followed such policies.

The latter two pairs of countries are as close as one can get to an economic and political experiment, where a country is split in two and each half follows a different path. The results of each experiment are unequivocal. Capitalism succeeds and collectivism (here in the form of socialism and communism) fails. I will show that capitalism succeeds at allowing human life to flourish *because* it is consistent with the requirements of human life, while collectivism leads to the destruction of human life *because* it is inconsistent with those requirements.

Other examples from the twentieth century of the destructive nature of collectivist political/economic systems include Vietnam, Nazi Germany, Cuba, China, India, Mexico, virtually all African nations, the Middle East, and most South American nations. In each case the result has been the same. To the degree that a country's government has followed anti-capitalistic policies, the result has been less freedom, a lower standard of living, and greater destruction of human life.[2]

The nations in the world whose governments have followed more capitalistic policies are the industrialized nations and the rapidly developing nations of East Asia (for example, Hong Kong prior to its control reverting back to China). Here the results are also unequivocal. The more capitalistic the government, the greater the freedom, the higher the standard of living, and the more human life has been able to flourish.

Going back a little further in history, the rise of Great Britain as an economic power in the eighteenth century is another great example of the success of capitalism. Great Britain rose as an economic power because of the freedom that existed within it and its colonies. Further back, the initial European settlements in America provide yet another example. Those settlements that used collectivist systems stagnated or failed, while those that provided greater individual freedom prospered.[3]

In order to establish and maintain a free market governments must be limited to protecting individual rights. To do this they must be limited to protecting people from domestic criminals (with the police), from foreign aggressors (with the military), and from contract violations (with the courts). Whenever a government engages in activities such as income redistribution, regulation, or the granting of special favors, it violates individual rights. These types of government policies lead to pressure-group warfare, an inefficient use of resources, a decrease in the satisfaction and well-being of individuals in the economy, and greater government control of people's lives.

This book will show that the arguments claiming market failure fail to provide a critique of the market. The only thing these arguments prove is that some people accept false ideas and use these ideas to mistakenly claim that markets fail. I will defend the market against attacks concerning monopoly and the antitrust laws, predatory pricing, "externalities," the regulation of safety and quality, environmentalism, economic inequality, "public goods," and asymmetric information. Not only will I defend the market from an economic standpoint, I will provide a moral and epistemological defense of the market as well. The first step in doing this is to provide a description of the nature of three types of political/economic systems: capitalism, socialism, and the mixed economy (or welfare state).

Notes

1. One particular issue, the belief that a free market would create periodic recessions and depressions, will not be addressed in this book. This is because a thorough treatment of the topic (including the refutation of various theories of the trade cycle, such as "sticky" price theory and real business cycle theory, which claim that such cycles are a naturally occurring phenomenon in a free market) would require a book as long, if not longer, than this one. I may in the future undertake the writing of such a book. Until then, one can turn to such works as Ludwig von Mises, *Human Action: A Treatise on Economics*, 3rd ed. (Chicago: Contemporary Books, Inc., 1966), 441-448 and 550-571 and George Reisman, *Capitalism: A Treatise on Economics* (Ottawa, Ill.: Jameson Books, 1996), 511-517 and 938-940 to gain an understanding of how recessions and depressions are the result of government intervention into the free market (particularly, government intervention in money and banking).

Further, in this book, I deal with general arguments made against the market. However, there are a number of events specific to one period in time which are often used as the basis to claim that markets fail. One such event is the California electricity crisis in 2000-2001. I do not address such events in this book because I want to focus on refuting the general arguments made against the market, which can apply to any time period. By refuting these, the way is paved to address specific, concrete events that are used to claim that markets fail. The ideas presented in this book can be used to help understand why, in concrete cases such as the California electricity crisis, it was not a case of market failure but one of government failure. For a good explanation of how the California state government created the electricity crisis in that state, see Jack Wakeland, "California's Green Brownout, Part 1," *The Intellectual Activist* 15, no. 3 (March 2001): 15-30 and "California's Green Brownout, Part 2," *The Intellectual Activist* 15, no. 5 (May 2001): 11-31. Also, see George Reisman, "California Screaming, Under Government Blows," 2000, <http://www.capitalism.net/GovernmentBlows.htm> (25 Aug. 2004) and "News Report: California's Blackouts Caused by Demons," 2002, <http://www. capitalism.net/articles/News%20Report%20California's%20Blackouts%20Caused%20by %20Demons.html> (25 Aug. 2004).

2. In the last two decades or so, China has made reforms in some areas of its economy, which have moved it slightly toward capitalism. This has made it possible for China to achieve a greater rate of economic progress.

3. For more on European settlements in America, see Edward Eggleston, *A History of the United States and Its People* (Lake Wales, Fla.: Lost Classics Book Company, 1998), 29, 30, 39, 65, and 66.

Chapter One

Capitalism, Socialism, and the Mixed Economy

Introduction

To understand why markets do not fail, it is essential to have a basic understanding of the nature of a free market and the nature of the opposite type of political/economic system. Once this base has been established, it will be easier to see where the arguments against capitalism go wrong. Although I present descriptions of three types of political/economic systems in this chapter, two of them (socialism and the mixed economy) do not have any fundamental differences between them. They are both collectivist systems; that is, systems that subordinate or sacrifice the individual to some group or collective (whether the state, "society," the "public good," future generations, etc.). Therefore, these two systems should be regarded as the same in terms of fundamental characteristics. The only difference between them pertains to the degree to which they sacrifice the individual to the collective. As I will show, socialist societies sacrifice the individual to the collective to a much greater degree than do mixed economies. Nonetheless, I include a separate section on the mixed economy because so much confusion exists between it, capitalism, and socialism.

Capitalism

There are many terms that are synonymous with capitalism. These include "laissez-faire capitalism," the "free market," and a "market economy." I regard all of these as equivalents but will mainly use "capitalism."

Two fundamental characteristics of the political/economic system known as capitalism are that it has private ownership of the means of production and bans the initiation of physical force from all human relationships.[1] The former characteristic is well known and does not require much explanation. It simply means that private individuals, as opposed to the government, own and use property to produce wealth for their own benefit. The latter characteristic is not so well known and does require elaboration.

To initiate physical force means to start or be the first one to use force. It means, for example, to act like a criminal. Because capitalism bans the initiation of force, this implies that all criminal activity, such as rape, murder, robbery, etc. is banned. However, it also implies that the initiation of force by the government is banned. Individual criminals are not the only ones that initiate force against others. Governments, when they engage in confiscatory taxation, impose regulations (such as worker health and safety regulation or environmental regulation), or enforce a minimum wage, initiate physical force. When governments do this, they are acting in a criminal manner.

For example, when the government imposes a minimum wage, it forcibly prevents employers from paying—and workers from receiving—a wage lower than what the government deems acceptable. If an employer and employee agree on a wage that is less than the minimum wage, no one—neither the employer nor the worker—has used force against the other. Both sides have agreed to the wage *voluntarily*. Therefore, when the government forcibly prevents such a trade from taking place, it is *initiating* physical force against employers who would like to pay a lower wage and workers who are willing to accept a lower wage.[2] If one does not believe the government uses physical coercion in this situation, one need only remember that the fines and other forms of punishment that the government uses to get people to obey minimum wage laws, and similar dictates, are enforced by *armed* agents of the government. Just like the criminal, who initiates force against his victim, the government also initiates force and thus acts in a manner similar to the criminal.

Under capitalism, freedom is protected. Freedom means the absence of (or freedom from) the initiation of physical force. Much of the focus of freedom is on the absence of the initiation of force by the government. For example, the freedom of the press refers to the freedom to publish written works without being stopped by the government, and the freedom of speech refers to the freedom to speak without being stopped by the government. The reason why so much focus is on freedom from the government's initiation of force is because in any civilized, or even semi-civilized, society private criminals represent only a very small minority of the population and do not constitute a large threat to one's freedom. As long as the government acts in a proper manner, it is easy to deal with such criminals. It is only governments that can initiate physical force on a massive scale (and often have throughout mankind's history), and therefore the focus of banning the use of such force is mainly on it.

Freedom under capitalism does not mean "freedom" from the facts of reality or the "freedom" to do whatever one feels like doing. For instance, it does not mean one is free to jump to the moon with nothing but the power of one's unaided legs. This would violate the laws of nature and no one is able to do that. Likewise, freedom does not mean one is free to commit crimes against others. This would be a violation of the victims' freedom.

Capitalism protects individual rights, including private property rights. "A 'right,'" as defined by the novelist and philosopher Ayn Rand, "is a moral principle defining and sanctioning a man's freedom of action in a social context."[3] In other words, rights are an application of moral principles to a society of men. Moral principles tell individuals what is right and wrong for them to do and thus are used to guide human action. Moral principles provide necessary guidelines that help individuals make the right choices in their own lives. They make it possible for individuals to further their lives and happiness. Such principles would be necessary to guide the actions of a man even if he was alone on a deserted island. For instance, they would be necessary to help a man decide that it is right for him to kill an animal and eat it and wrong for him to let it live while he starves. However, moral principles are also necessary to determine what actions by a man are proper and improper among a group of men (i.e., in a society of individuals). Rights perform this function. They secure each man's freedom by restricting the actions of individuals to those that do not initiate physical force against other men. The recognition and protection of individual rights makes peaceful coexistence among men possible.

The most basic right is the right to life. This means that a man has the freedom to take all the actions required to further and enjoy his own life. All other rights, including the right to liberty, the pursuit of happiness, and private property rights, follow from the right to life.[4] For example, if one has the right to his own life, he must be free to do what is necessary to further his own life (i.e., he must have liberty). Furthermore, he must be able to produce the material values his life requires and thus be free to acquire property, use it to engage in production, and dispose of it when necessary (i.e., he must have private property rights). In addition, he must be free to experience the results of successfully furthering his life and well-being (i.e., he must be free to pursue his own happiness).[5] Capitalism provides protection for these and all rights.

Freedom, the protection of individual rights, and banning the initiation of physical force are inextricably linked. In order to secure the protection of individual rights, one must protect the individual from the initiation of physical force, and therefore one must protect individual freedom. The only way to violate a man's rights or freedom is to initiate force against him. For example, when a man steals your wallet he is violating your right to your own property (i.e., the right to the money you have earned). He is also violating your right to your own life, liberty, and the pursuit of happiness. By taking money that you have spent a part of your life earning, he is telling you, in effect, that you cannot spend your life pursuing your own goals and values, but that you must serve his desires. This takes away your freedom to do what is best for you according to your own rational judgment and prevents you from reaping happiness as the reward for your achievements. The same violation of a person's rights occurs when the government initiates physical force to, for example, expropriate income from an individual through confiscatory taxation. Here, instead of a private individual violating a person's freedom, the government does.

There are many confusions today with respect to the concept "rights" and to better understand the nature of capitalism, socialism, and the mixed economy I will address some of the more common confusions. One confusion pertains to the question, "To whom do rights belong?" The answer to this question is that only *individuals* possess rights; there are no group "rights." For example, there are no rights of black people or white people, no workers' rights or employers' rights, and no men's rights or women's rights. Rights apply to individuals as such and protect all individuals from the initiation of force regardless of what group to which they might belong.

Connected with this issue is the fact that there are no rights to things that other men must provide. For instance, there is no right to a job, a "decent" wage, or healthcare. In all such cases, in order to give some group (whether healthcare users or workers) an alleged right to something, one must violate the rights of others. For example, to give someone an alleged right to a job or a certain level of wage, one must initiate force against employers to make them provide the job or pay the wage. Or, in order to guarantee someone healthcare, one must initiate force against taxpayers to make them pay for the healthcare and/or force doctors and other healthcare workers to provide the healthcare at levels of compensation they might consider unacceptable. Rights are rights to action, not rewards from others. It is a contradiction in terms to say that someone has a "right" to something if, in the very act of providing it, the rights (i.e., the freedom) of others must be violated in order to provide that thing. To say that someone has a "right" to something that someone else must provide is equivalent to making the absurd claim that someone has a "right" to violate the rights of others.

So-called group rights are actually special privileges given to one group, by the government, at the expense of others. Group privileges represent a violation of individual rights. Further, giving some groups special privileges at the expense of others represents an act of sacrificing some individuals (whether employers, taxpayers, or healthcare workers in the examples given) to those people who are receiving the special privileges. It is immoral to sacrifice some people to others because it stands in opposition to human life. Actual rights protect all individuals (and therefore all groups of individuals) from being sacrificed to anyone.[6]

Rights are not special privileges bestowed upon us by the government. Rights derive from our nature as human beings; they stem from the fact that we are beings who possess reason (i.e., a conceptual faculty). Man's possession of reason gives him rights because reason makes rights necessary and possible. The possession of reason makes rights possible because reason enables man to think in terms of principles and ideas, including moral principles and ideas. Since rights are types of moral principles, man's possession of reason is what makes it possible for him to understand and act on the concept "rights." In addition, man needs rights because reason is his basic tool of survival and if he is to be able to use this tool he must be free from the initiation of physical force. For instance, if men are to protect themselves from the elements, they must use reason to gain all the knowledge required to build shelter. To do this, they need to understand the principles of civil engineering, carpentry, plumbing, electrical work, and so on. A man cannot put forth the effort to acquire the requisite knowledge and skills (let alone use the knowledge and skills) if someone forcibly prevents him from doing so. Without the protection of his rights, man is prevented from using his reason to further his life and happiness. In other words, man needs rights because his survival depends on it.[7]

To state the need for rights in a slightly different way, because we possess reason our actions must be guided by (proper) moral principles and ideas in order to survive.[8] Rights provide this guidance in a social setting. Rights allow individuals to live their lives unassaulted by others. They allow individuals to be free from the initiation of force so they can perform the tasks their lives require. For instance, humans must produce wealth and be able to keep what they produce in order to survive. Private property rights ensure an individual's ability to keep what he produces (or they ensure his ability to keep the income he earns from trading what he produces). If one is not allowed to keep what one produces, but is forced to give it to others, then one is enslaved to those to whom one is forced to give the product of his effort. The enslavement of men stands in opposition to their survival.

Since governments do not bestow rights upon us, what is the function of a government? A government is an institution that has a legal monopoly on the use of force in a given geographic region. A government employs force, or the threat of force, to achieve its ends. Whether a government is protecting individual rights by protecting the citizens of a country from criminals or whether it is violating individual rights by expropriating funds from the citizens of a country through confiscatory taxation, it is using force to achieve its goals. A proper government uses force *only* in retaliation against those who initiate force. Therefore, a proper government consists of the police, the military, and the courts. As I stated in the introduction, the police are used to protect people from domestic criminals (including those who commit acts of fraud), the military is used to protect people from foreign aggressors, and the courts are used to protect people from contract violations and provide an objective means of determining guilt or innocence for those accused of crimes. Contract violations and fraud represent special instances of the initiation of force. Both are indirect forms of force. In both cases, someone is attempting to take something from you against your will. He is not physically assaulting you to do so, but he is doing it against your will. For example, if a television repairman tells you he must take your television set to his shop to repair it, but instead of bringing it back to you, he fixes it and sells it, he has committed an act of fraud against you and is guilty of using force, indirectly, against you because he has taken your television set without your consent. In this situation, you give as much permission to the repairman to sell your television and keep the proceeds as you give to a criminal who breaks into your home to steal your television.

The result is the same in both cases: your property is taken from you against your will.

When dealing with the government's use of force, one must keep clearly in mind the difference between the government's *initiation* of force and its use of force in *retaliation* against those who initiate force. In the case where the government retaliates with force, it is acting in a manner that is consistent with the requirements of human life because it is protecting individual rights, and therefore it is proper for the government to act in such a manner. In the case where the government is initiating force, it is acting in a manner that stands in opposition to the requirements of human life because it is violating individual rights, and this is therefore improper.

So capitalism has private ownership of the means of production, bans the initiation of physical force from all human relationships, and thus protects freedom and individual rights. If people cannot initiate force against each other under capitalism, how are they supposed to deal with each other? The answer: they deal with each other through voluntary trade. As I have emphasized (and will continue to do so since it is crucial to understand this point to be able to evaluate markets appropriately), voluntary trade is to *everyone's* advantage. Each person who participates in a trade gains from it. The fact that people gain from a trade is the reason why they engage in trade in the first place. If they did not stand to gain, if they only stood to break even or lose from the trade, they would not engage in it. For example, the reason why I trade with the grocer and give up, say, $20 to buy food is because I consider the food I will obtain more valuable than the money I give up. Likewise, the reason why the grocer gives up the food to acquire the $20 is because he considers the money more valuable than the food. Both parties gain in this transaction. The trade is a "win-win" situation. Both sides are better off by virtue of the fact that the trade has taken place. This is how trade *creates* value.

Through voluntary trade, people can benefit enormously from the division of labor that exists under capitalism. In a division of labor society, people produce little or none of what they consume and rely on the labor of others to produce most or all of what they consume. In such a society, by specializing in one area and becoming more knowledgeable in that area, each person is able to raise his productivity much more than he would be able to had he not specialized. By engaging in voluntary trade, individuals can benefit from the knowledge gained by others. In essence, you specialize and become more knowledgeable at the job you perform and trade with someone else who has become more knowledgeable in his line of production. In this way, a society of men can tremendously raise their standard of living from what it would have been had they not specialized.

The major benefit of the division of labor under capitalism is the multiplication of knowledge. Through the division of labor, a group of men can radically increase the sum of knowledge they possess, concerning the production of wealth, relative to the same group of men living in a self-subsistent society, where each man produces everything he consumes (which is the opposite of a division of labor). In a self-subsistent society, each man performs essentially the same tasks. Each man grows his own crops, hunts to obtain his own meat, builds his own shelter, makes his own clothes, etc. Therefore, whether a self-subsistent society consists of just one man or one-million men, the total knowledge possessed by such a society is essentially equivalent to the knowledge possessed by any one individual. However, in a division of labor society, the knowledge available is multiplied by the number of specializations practiced by all individuals. If there are one-million men working in one-thousand specializations, the knowledge possessed by this society has increased one-thousand fold relative to the self-subsistent society. The knowledge in a division of labor society is equal to the knowledge possessed by the doctor, the engineer, the mechanic, the plumber, the farmer, the computer programmer, and so on. Instead of needless duplication of the knowledge individuals gain, as occurs in a self-subsistent society, the division of labor society makes far better use of each individual's mind by enabling each person to specialize in different fields and thus gain different types of knowledge. Hence, such a society vastly increases the amount of knowledge that a group of men can possess concerning the production of wealth and thus radically improves their ability to produce wealth.

Capitalism makes it possible for a division of labor society to exist and flourish. It allows people to be free to use their minds to think, act on their own rational judgment, produce the values their lives require, and trade with others. People are free to gain skills, get a job, live where they choose, and save or consume their wealth.

The profit motive provides people with an incentive to produce under capitalism. To the extent that people want to earn high profits and become wealthy, they must produce goods that people want to buy. The profit motive also leads to a movement of goods to those regions of the economy where demand is high and away from those regions where demand is low. This occurs because profits will be higher in those regions where demand is high and lower in those regions where demand is low. The profit motive also leads to a movement of factors of production to those industries where the rate of profit is high and away from those industries where the rate of profit is low or negative.[9] These movements from low profit to high profit areas of the economy occur because, other things being equal, businessmen want to earn the highest rate of profit possible. This means they invest in those industries and regions where they can earn a high rate of profit and avoid those industries and regions where the rate of profit is low or negative. These movements coordinate production by ensuring that businesses will produce the goods that are in high demand, while avoiding the production of goods in low demand. It also provides the incentive to ship the goods to those regions where demand for them is the greatest. The profit motive under capitalism leads to a growing abundance of goods and services for everyone. It leads to the greatest prosperity and the highest standard of living that is possible *for everyone.*[10]

Implicit in the above is the vital role the price system plays in coordinating production under capitalism. The price system plays an important role because profits are calculated in terms of prices. Profits equal the difference between the prices businesses pay for the factors of production they purchase and the prices at which they sell the goods they produce with those factors of production. It is the fluctuation of prices in response to changes in supply, demand, and costs of production that performs the coordinating function under capitalism. Buyers of goods, in essence, bid up the prices of goods for which they have more demand (by buying more of them), thus making it more profitable to produce these goods, and bid down the prices of goods for which they have less demand (by abstaining from purchasing them), thus making it less profitable to produce these goods. This is how buyers are able to get the goods they value the most.

The price system coordinates the plans of each individual in a capitalist society with the plans of other individuals so that there is a harmony among the plans. Everyone plans his activities based on the prices he receives as a seller and the prices he pays as a buyer. For instance, when producers decide to expand or contract their businesses, they do so in response to changes in profitability and these changes are communicated through the price system and are coordinated with the plans of consumers, whose spending patterns are influencing the fluctuation in prices and profits. The price system also helps producers determine which factors of production to use. For example, if the price of wood rises relative to the price of aluminum, home manufacturers will be led to use more aluminum in the homes they build and less wood. Workers also plan using the price system when they decide what skills to gain or where to get a job based on wages (which is the price of labor) and the cost of living (i.e., the prices of housing, food, transportation, and so on) in various locations. Consumers also plan their purchases based on fluctuations of prices. The price system tells buyers which goods are relatively more scarce and which are relatively less scarce. For instance, if some consumers decide to eat more beans and less corn, then the price of beans will rise relative to the price of corn. These actions, in turn, will be coordinated with the actions of other consumers who, based on the higher price of beans and the lower price of corn, decide to include more corn and less bean in their diets.

One sees above the importance of the price system and the profit motive. Prices and profits integrate an enormous amount of information in the economy. They integrate the actions of hundreds-of-millions—even billions—of people. Without them, chaos would ensue in the economy.

Both the price system and the profit motive rest on the protection of individual rights. If individual rights are not protected, people will have neither the ability nor the selfish incentive to use their property to produce goods in response to the profit motive; set prices based on demand, supply, and costs; or bid the prices of goods up and down based on their valuations of such goods.

Capitalism is based on the morality of rational self-interest. That is, capitalism is a political/economic system that recognizes that it is a virtue for individuals to act in their own rational self-interest. Capitalism says, in essence, that your life belongs to you, and you are free to live it to pursue your own happiness. Capitalism is moral (and benevolent) because it is consistent with the requirements of human life—because it is consistent with the ethical theory of egoism. In fact, capitalism is the *only* moral social system because it is the only system that is consistent with the requirements of human life.[11] It is the only system that protects each individual so he can live his life to pursue his own rational self-interest. Further, capitalism is to everyone's advantage. No matter what your race, gender, income level, intelligence, etc. it is to your advantage to live in a capitalist society because capitalism protects the rights of all individuals and makes possible an ever growing supply of wealth and thus a continuously rising standard of living for everyone.

There are no pure capitalist countries that have ever existed or that currently exist today.[12] However, nineteenth-century America came the closest. It was the freest nation to have ever existed, despite some anti-capitalistic elements present in its political system. Because of that freedom, America witnessed a very high rate of economic progress during that time period. Further, the very high standard of living that exists in America today has been built upon the freedom that existed in the past and the remnants of freedom that still exist today in America thanks to the existence of that better past.

One place that, until recently, had a substantial amount of freedom was Hong Kong, which was a British colony until 1997. As a result of that freedom, Hong Kong witnessed a very high rate of economic progress. Unfortunately, since 1997, control of Hong Kong has been turned over to Communist China. If China maintains the freedom that was established and upheld by the British, this territory will continue to achieve high rates of economic progress. Otherwise, economic progress will decline.

An Important Discussion on Moral Theory:
Egoism versus Altruism

The Nature of Morality, Egoism, and Altruism

The moral judgments in the section on capitalism require elaboration on the ethical theory that underlies them. While this book is not a treatise on ethics, in order to better understand the nature of a free market, and the nature of its antithesis, I will provide an exposition of two diametrically opposed ethical theories: egoism and altruism.[13] The moral judgments in the previous section are based on an acceptance of the validity of the ethical theory of egoism. This ethical theory says that one's only moral concern should be to pursue one's own rational self-interest. This means that each individual should act to sustain and further his own life and happiness.

Why is it moral to act egoistically? To answer this question one must first answer more fundamental questions concerning what is morality and whether men need morality (and if they do need it, why do they need it). These are some of the questions that will be answered in this section.

Morality provides man with a code of values to guide his choices and actions. Because human beings are alive—and can die—they must pursue values. If they are to survive, they must pursue the things that are necessary to sustain and further their lives (i.e., food, clothing, shelter, knowledge, etc.). If an entity was not confronted with the alternative of life or death, it would have no need to pursue values. For instance, a rock has no need to pursue values. Its existence does not depend on any action it must take to obtain things such as food, clothing, shelter, knowledge, or anything else. It can remain in existence as long as it is left alone (i.e., it is not pulverized or worn away by wind and sand). However, a man cannot survive through inaction. If a man does nothing—if he does not at least put some food into his mouth and eat it—his life goes out of existence. A man must take some action to sustain his life. If a man does not pursue values—if he does not pursue that which is necessary to sustain his life—he dies. Hence, life gives rise to the need to pursue values.

However, a man must *choose* to take the necessary actions to further his life. Men do not have automatic knowledge about what they must do to sustain and further their lives. They must make the choice to attempt to acquire such knowledge. Even if they have the appropriate knowledge, there is no guarantee that they will act consistently on such knowledge and take the necessary actions to further their lives. Again, they must choose to take such actions. It is morality that provides man with the knowledge and guidance he needs for self-preservation. Morality provides man with a code of values to determine what is right and wrong, or good and bad, for his life. Therefore, men need morality for their own survival.

What is it that determines what a man should do to sustain his life? For example, what determines whether he should attempt to live on land or underwater? What determines whether he should eat pizza or arsenic? The answer: the nature of his life. Human life has a specific nature and therefore has certain requirements; it requires a specific course of action in order for it to be preserved. In other words, some things can further a man's life and some can destroy it. This implies that human life must be the standard of value if it is to be sustained. The nature of human life is the standard by which one determines whether something is of value or disvalue. That which is for man's life is of value; that which is against it is of disvalue.

More specifically, it is the *individual* human life that is the standard which determines whether something is of value or disvalue. If a man wants to survive, he must choose to further *his own* life; he must choose to take the necessary actions, based on the nature of human life, to further his own existence. This is the basic choice reality gives each man: to act to further his own life or not. Because of this, in order to survive, each individual must be the beneficiary of his own actions. In moral terms, the choices that a man makes which are consistent with the requirements of his life are moral choices. The choices that a man makes which are inconsistent with the requirements of his life are immoral.

The man who chooses to sustain and further his life and happiness is an egoist. The egoist acts to sustain and further his life and happiness in a long-range manner through the use of his mind. This is, in the simplest terms, what it means to act in one's rational self-interest. So, why is it moral to act egoistically? It is because that is what human life requires. If morality provides man with knowledge and guidance for self-preservation, and self-preservation requires that man act to sustain and further his own life and happiness, then it is moral to act egoistically.

Of course, a man can choose not to act egoistically. He can ignore the requirements of his life and make choices that are harmful or destructive to his life. For instance, he can choose to consume poison. However, if he does this—if he makes choices inimical to his life—it will lead to his own destruction. A man cannot survive by engaging in self-destructive activities.

A man may also choose to act in a manner destructive to his own life by acting in accordance with a code of morality that stands in opposition to the requirements of his life. For example, he may choose to act altruistically. Altruism is the exact opposite of egoism. Altruism says an individual should not act in his own rational self-interest, but should place the interests of others above his own. It says he should sacrifice himself to others. To sacrifice means to give up a greater value for a lesser value or a non-value.[14] Since life requires the pursuit and attainment of values, sacrificing oneself to others is harmful to one's life. For instance, life requires that I eat a certain amount of food. However, according to altruism, one should give up the food one possesses and give it to others. If one acted consistently on this idea, and gave up all his food, it would quickly lead to the destruction of one's life.

One might think that acting in a self-sacrificial manner is harmful only if one acts consistently (i.e., on principle) in such a manner. One might think that as long as one acts to further his life most of the time, acting altruistically only on occasion and making only minor sacrifices will not actually destroy a person's life. While this may be true in most cases, it does not deny the destructive nature of the morality of altruism. The first thing to consider in this matter is that one altruistic action can ruin—and even end—a person's life. For example, I once read a newspaper article about a man who took an ex-convict, who was a complete stranger to the man, into his home to help the ex-convict out after he was released from jail. The ex-convict had been in jail for murder. The ex-convict eventually murdered this man too. This man lost his life due to only one act of sacrifice.

The second thing to consider in this matter is that *to the degree* that a man acts altruistically, he acts to achieve his own destruction. If he acts altruistically only to a small degree (such as by giving up only one meal a week to feed an indigent person), he will harm his ability to survive only a small amount. If he acts altruistically to a great degree (such as by giving up seven meals a week), he will significantly harm his ability to live. If he acts in an altruistic manner on principle (such as by giving up all his meals), he will destroy his own life. *Only by avoiding acting in an altruistic manner, on principle, can one avoid acting in a self-destructive way.* One must avoid acting altruistically to be able to further one's life and well-being. Or, stated in a positive manner, one must act egoistically to further his own life and well-being.

The Morality of Rational Self-Interest and Capitalism

Under capitalism, there is a harmony of men's rational self-interests in which the success of each man promotes the well-being of all men. An example of this principle is the success of a productive genius like Bill Gates. As Bill Gates grows richer, other individuals benefit because they obtain better computer software. Under capitalism, a person can grow rich only by providing goods and services that people value and only by getting people to buy those products *voluntarily*. Hence, the only way for Bill Gates, or any lesser producer, to grow rich or earn an income is to produce and sell something that people judge to be worth buying. Everyone is made better off in the process and there is no conflict between the success of one person and the rational self-interest of any other person in a capitalist society.

In fact, it is in one's self-interest that those with whom one trades become as rich as possible. In a capitalist society, most of the wealth that people possess is tied up in the production of goods and services. Most wealth exists in the form of factories, machinery and equipment, inventory, etc. Hence, the more wealth that a person possesses, the more goods and services he is capable of producing. The more goods and services he is capable of producing, the more he has to offer in trade. The more a man has to offer in trade, the more that is available for people to buy from him. This makes anyone who trades with him better off.

The principle that there is no conflict between men's rational self-interests in a capitalist society applies even to those who might "lose" in a specific instance of competition. For example, there is no conflict of self-interest between competing producers who are vying for the patronage of the same customers. It is true, for instance, that if a customer chooses to buy a product from producer A instead of from producer B, that A has gained a customer at the expense of B. However, this does not mean there is a conflict of self-interest between the two producers. To understand why, one must consider what, in fact, is in a person's self-interest. One must think about this issue in relation to the business that a business owner earns, and one must also consider the wider context of competition and how, in general, it is of benefit to everyone.[15]

First, one must keep in mind that competition requires freedom and, as has been shown throughout this chapter and will be shown throughout the rest of this book, freedom is an indispensable requirement of human life. Further, the existence of freedom implies that one deal with others in a voluntary manner. Therefore, one must *earn* a customer's business by offering him something he considers worth buying over the other choices that exist. No business owner has a right to an individual's business, as the discussion on individual rights in the section on capitalism makes clear. If one does not earn a customer's business, then one does not deserve his business. It is not in one's rational self-interest to take the unearned.[16]

Second, one must understand that the competition referred to here is *economic* competition. This type of competition involves competing to *produce* and trade wealth, not to *consume* a fixed supply of goods that exist (like animals in the jungle competing to consume a fixed supply of food and shelter). Hence, economic competition leads to a growing abundance of wealth for all individuals who engage in it. In other words, economic competition is not a so-called zero-sum game; it is not a case of one person taking wealth from another person. It is a "positive-sum game"; it is a case of one person or company creating a good or service and trading it with others. Therefore, the more economic competition that takes place the more wealth that is available in the economic system and the wealthier people will be.

Third, to the extent that producer B in the example above has obtained any wealth at all through legitimate means (i.e., through voluntary trade), he has done so (or those he has inherited it from have done so) by successfully competing against others. Therefore, he has no legitimate complaint against competition because he would not have any wealth to begin with if the freedom to compete did not exist.

Fourth, producer B benefits from the day he is born, long before he engages in his first act of economic competition (and gets his first job or opens a business), from all the wonderful products that have been brought into existence through the competition that has taken place before his lifetime. For example, competition in the automobile industry has improved the quality of automobiles and made them more affordable. Because of this, the purchasing power of the income of B's parents (and his income when he begins to earn one) is higher than it otherwise would be. They can buy far more goods, and far higher quality goods, with their income due to the existence of economic competition. This is of enormous benefit to B.

Finally, B will benefit from all the products that will be brought into existence throughout his lifetime from the competition that will take place during that time. So the "loser" in economic competition is really not a loser at all. Clearly he gains from competition. His standard of living is raised. This shows that it is in one's self-interest to engage in economic competition and expose oneself to the chance of "losing" in a specific instance of it to reap the enormous benefits of competition throughout time and throughout the economic system.

Myths of Egoism and Altruism

There are many myths concerning egoism and altruism, and I will dispel two of them here to help one gain a better understanding of these two moral theories. One myth is the belief, adhered to by many people, that to be selfish one must sacrifice others to oneself. However, this is not true. Sacrificing others to oneself is just a variation on the theme of sacrifice and is the exact opposite of acting selfishly. Based on this false standard, it is often said that a criminal acts selfishly when he steals wealth from others for his own gain. However, it is not in one's rational self-interest to steal from others. It is in one's self-interest to respect the rights (i.e., the freedom) of others and engage in voluntary trade with them. This is how an individual benefits from the talents and abilities of others. An individual produces what he is capable of producing and trades with others to obtain what they are capable of producing. Each person in the trade benefits from the talents and abilities that the other person brings to the trade.

By stealing from others, a criminal does not benefit from the talents and abilities of others, but causes others to set their talents and abilities *against* him. They use their abilities to try to stop the criminal. If the criminal is caught, which becomes more likely to the extent he engages in criminal activities, he will be punished. Therefore, to the extent a person engages in such activities, he throws away the gains from voluntary trade. A person may be able to get away with a crime without being caught; however, as with acting altruistically, to the degree he engages in criminal activity, he harms his ability to sustain and further his life and happiness. If he does not get caught committing a crime, he still sets people's talents and abilities against him and may have to spend a significant amount of effort evading authorities. This is not in his self-interest. If a person commits crimes regularly he will either be caught or will spend his entire life running from the authorities. In this case, he will completely throw away the benefits of voluntary trade. Clearly, this is not in his self-interest.

More importantly, human beings do not survive by theft; they survive by production. Human beings must produce the values their lives require in order to survive.[17] To the extent that individuals engage in criminal activities, they undermine the type of society that makes production possible. Hence, they undermine the type of society on which their standard of living rests and thus on which their very lives depend. To see this as clearly as possible, one need merely imagine the standard of living of a society comprised totally of criminals. The people in such a society would starve very quickly. All the individuals would either spend their time and efforts committing crimes against others or protecting themselves from others. No time would be spent producing the values on which people's lives depend. Furthermore, no one would have an incentive to produce anything in such a society for fear of having what they produced stolen by others. Hence, nothing would be produced. Obviously, this is not in anyone's self-interest.

By sacrificing his victim, the criminal also sacrifices his own interests. He sacrifices long-term gains simply to snatch some loot in the short run. It is not in a person's self-interest to act in this manner—a range-of-the-moment manner. It is in a person's self-interest to act in a long-range—or rational—manner. A man's life exists for the long run and he must plan, live, and further his life over its entire course. If a man is to live and enjoy his *life*, he cannot pursue activities that lead to short-run gratification at the expense of his long-run well-being. Doing this is irrational and not in one's self-interest.

The above applies in general, not just with respect to economic relationships. It is not in a person's self-interest to sacrifice others in economic and non-economic matters. Whether the sacrifice involves stealing from someone or, say, betraying a friend's confidence, to the degree that one sacrifices others, he acts against his own interests. For instance, in the case of revealing a friend's secret, an individual will undermine his ability to have close relationships with his friends and, if taken far enough, undermine his ability to have any friends at all.

The belief that acting selfishly means sacrificing others to oneself is an altruist fallacy. Embracing the altruist code of morality leads people to believe that the only alternative to, and therefore the opposite of, sacrificing oneself to others is sacrificing others to oneself, and that this is what it means to be selfish. However, sacrificing oneself and sacrificing others are fundamentally similar because both involve an act of sacrifice and both lead to the same result: the destruction of human life. Hence, they are not opposites; they are simply two variations on the same lethal theme: the theme of sacrifice. The opposite of both of these is to engage in no act of sacrifice. That is, it is to neither sacrifice oneself to others nor sacrifice others to oneself. This is what it means to act in one's rational self-interest. The selfish person acts independently of others and deals with others in a voluntary manner in all his relationships. The selfish person trades value for value with others, which is to each person's advantage. No act of sacrifice is involved in this.[18]

Another fallacy with regard to these ethical theories is the belief that altruism means simply to show kindness toward others. However, this is not what altruism refers to. Throughout its history, altruism has meant to place the interests of others above one's own interests. It has meant to subordinate or sacrifice one's interests to the interests of others (i.e., to sacrifice oneself to others). To sacrifice oneself to others is very different from merely showing kindness toward others.[19] It is often in a person's self-interest to show kindness toward others. For example, if you value others (such as friends or family members), then it is in your interest to show kindness toward them. If you value others, you derive a personal—selfish—pleasure from their existence. Those whom you value make your life more enjoyable and you should therefore want to see them succeed in their lives. You should want them to be happy, and it should make you happy that they are happy. Therefore, being kind to the people you value *is* selfish. It is consistent with a person furthering his own life and happiness. If you claim to value others but do not derive pleasure from their existence and their happiness, then you do not actually value them. A person who acts in his own rational self-interest does show kindness toward others, when it is appropriate.[20]

The selfish man is not a hermit. He is not indifferent to the existence of other people. He recognizes that the existence of other people is valuable to him in many ways. For instance, the selfish man recognizes that the existence of other producers is to his self-interest because he can gain access to what they produce by trading with them. It is therefore in the selfish man's interest to deal with and show kindness toward such individuals. Further, it is in the selfish man's interest to seek out people who share common values (i.e., friends) because, as stated in the previous paragraph, sharing experiences with friends makes life more enjoyable. Therefore, the selfish man seeks out such people and shows them kindness and affection. The selfish man also knows the value of a romantic relationship because he knows that this type of relationship can greatly enhance the enjoyment of his life. Therefore, the selfish man seeks out such a relationship and shows kindness and affection to his lover.

More on the Nature of Egoism and Altruism

Egoism recognizes the fact that human life has many requirements and that to sustain and enjoy one's life, one must focus on the attainment of values. Egoism recognizes that the attainment of values is beneficial to human life and that it should be rewarded and extolled. Altruism focuses on the giving up of values. It focuses, not on the achievement of the things necessary to further one's life and well-being, but on the abnegation of these things. This is why altruism is destructive to human life and egoism is beneficial to it.

If a man swallows poison and therefore acts in a manner inconsistent with his nutritional requirements, he will destroy himself. Likewise, if he embraces a poisonous moral code he will destroy himself. This is exactly what one does if one embraces a code of morality based on sacrifice, in either of its variations. Of course, the exact opposite is true if one follows a code of morality that is consistent with the requirements of human life. This is exactly what a man does when he acts in his own rational self-interest. Here, he improves his ability to survive.

The individual human life must be the standard of a proper code of morality because one's life is the source of everything one values. Without your life, *you* have no values, because there is no you. Based on this, one can see that practicing a code of moral values such as altruism, which is destructive to human life, is a deadly contradiction. It says that people are supposed to follow a code of moral values that destroys the source of everything they value— including the code of morality! In order for a code of moral values to be beneficial to human life—in order for it to provide a guide to human action which makes possible the furthering of human life and happiness—it must be consistent with the requirements of human life. Such a code is the moral code of egoism. As stated by the novelist and philosopher Ayn Rand, the purpose of morality is not to teach people to suffer and die (as altruism does), but to enjoy life and live (as egoism does).[21] One can see from this discussion that the altruist code of morality is the morality of death because that is what it leads to if one puts it into practice. Likewise, egoism is the morality of life because that is what it leads to if one puts it into practice.

Although the majority of people today believe in altruism, this does not make it a valid code of morality. An idea does not become true simply because the majority of people believe in it. If this was a correct theory then the earth must be flat and it must also be the center of the universe because at one time the majority of people believed in these theories. These theories, of course, are false. An idea is false if it does not correspond to the facts of reality, regardless of how many people believe in it. Likewise, an idea is true if it does correspond to the facts of reality, regardless of whether only a few people believe in it. All true ideas come into existence through the mind of one individual and thus start out being accepted by only a minority of people. Only after years or decades of convincing others does the idea become accepted by the majority. If the human race is to have a bright future, eventually a majority of people will come to embrace egoism as the only valid code of morality.

* * *

So now one can understand the moral judgments I made in the section on capitalism. Having a sound understanding of ethics is indispensable to fully understanding the nature of capitalism, socialism, and the mixed economy. Specifically, it is necessary to understand their moral status. It is also indispensable when evaluating many of the claims concerning market failure.

Socialism

In stark contrast to capitalism is the economic system of socialism. Socialism is characterized by government ownership of the means of production and requires massive amounts of the initiation of physical force to implement. In other words, it requires a massive violation of individual rights to create and maintain a socialist society. It involves expropriating all wealth from individuals. It requires that the government tell people where to work, where to live, what profession to go into, whether or not one can go to school and where, etc. The government must control what people can do because if it is to control production, it cannot own the material assets needed to produce but allow workers to live where they want and work in professions of their own choosing. If the government does not control people's actions, people might decide to live and work in areas of the economy that are not consistent with the government's economic plan. Therefore, the government must control people's lives in order to attempt to coordinate production.

Socialism must be implemented and sustained through violent political means. It requires a political system such as communism (or a similar system). Communism is a totalitarian system of government in which a single ruling party controls the government. Socialism requires the evil means of communism because one must be willing to spill a great deal of blood to implement and sustain a socialist society. If one does not believe a large amount of blood must be spilled to establish and maintain a socialist society, think of what it would require to implement socialism anywhere in the world that some semblance of freedom exists, such as in the United States. If the state controls all people and property under socialism, are people going to voluntarily give up control of their property and hand it over to the state? Are they going to give up the ability to choose a profession and choose where to live? Are they going to give up their freedom or the right to their own lives? Of course not. Massive amounts of force must be used to implement and sustain a socialist society. That is why socialism has existed only in countries where the governments have been willing to use the necessary force to create it, such as in Nazi Germany, Communist Russia, Cuba, and China, among a few others.

Socialism leads to misery and poverty. This is the case because one has no freedom under socialism and no profit motive or price system exists, so there is no incentive to produce, no coordination of production, and no ability to calculate profit and loss. Furthermore, socialism leads to poverty because it uses a system of central planning, where a small ruling elite (those in charge of the government) decide what, how, where, and for whom goods should be produced. This system leads to chaos in production because it is impossible for a small group in charge of the government to have all the knowledge that people acting in the economy have about their particular area of production. Central planning fails to take advantage of the intellectual division of labor. Imagine the chaos that would ensue if a small group of government bureaucrats in Washington, D.C. attempted to coordinate the production and distribution of goods throughout the U.S. economy, which has hundreds-of-millions of people acting within it and, perhaps, hundreds-of-thousands of goods being produced and sold. The bureaucrats would have to know what goods need to be produced, how to produce them, when to produce them, how much to produce and in what varieties, where they need to be distributed, what methods of distribution to use, etc. It is impossible for a small group of people to possess such a vast amount of knowledge. Central planners would have to be omniscient deities to plan an entire economy. Therefore, any such attempt to plan an economy must lead to disaster (and actually has in practice).[22]

Socialism is based on the altruist code of morality. Altruism says it is a virtue for the individual to sacrifice himself to others. Socialism merely provides a specific cause to which the individual is supposed to sacrifice himself. Under socialism, people are told to sacrifice themselves for the good of the state, the race, the nation, future generations, and so on. In practice, socialism has succeeded tremendously in sacrificing people. Literally hundreds-of-millions of people have been sacrificed on the altar of socialism. It has been estimated that almost one-hundred million people have starved, been murdered, or been worked to death in labor camps under socialist regimes that have existed, and still exist, around the world.[23] This figure does not include the suffering of the hundreds-of-millions of people who have been forced to live in abject poverty and misery under socialist dictatorships. Based on this, it is clear that both in theory and in practice socialism is destructive to human life.

Socialist countries that have existed around the world (some of which were already mentioned) include the former USSR and the Eastern European countries that the USSR controlled. Nazi Germany, Communist Cuba, China, North Korea, and Vietnam are other examples.[24] All of these countries have met a similar fate under socialism. Massive violations of individual rights and a miserably low standard of living were, and are, the norm.

Some might wonder why I have not included Sweden, which is often thought to be a socialist nation, in my list of socialist countries. I have not because it is not a socialist country. It can be described by the next economic system to be discussed.

The Mixed Economy

The two components of the mixed economy (also known as the welfare state or a hampered market economy) have been described above. The mixed economy is a mixture of capitalist and socialist elements. It is an attempt to mix some freedom (the capitalist component) with government controls (the socialist component).

A mixed economy produces economic inefficiency and a lower standard of living to the extent that controls exist. Controls under the mixed economy replace or inhibit the benevolent effects of voluntary trade, the price system, and the profit motive, with government force. Because of this, the mixed economy undermines the ability to produce wealth. For the same reasons that complete government control of the economy under socialism is economically harmful, partial controls in the mixed economy are harmful. Socialism is destructive for all the reasons discussed in the previous section and these reasons are why socialist policies in a mixed economy are destructive. Socialist policies do not magically become good because they exist within the context of a mixed economy. The greater the degree of government controls in the mixed economy; i.e., the greater the degree of socialist elements that exist within a mixed economy, the greater the economic inefficiency and stagnation that result. Government controls in a mixed economy might not cause outright economic stagnation; the economy may still be able to progress forward if the controls are limited enough. However, to the degree that controls exist, the rate of economic progress will be lower. If the controls are great enough, they will cause economic stagnation or regression.

Many people think that the mixed economy combines the best of the two economic extremes. They think it combines what they consider to be good about capitalism (such as the incentive to produce an abundance of wealth), but allows the government to intervene with socialistic policies (such as to redistribute income) to act for "the good of society." Based on what has been said above, however, it should be apparent that this statement is completely false. *There is nothing morally or economically good about socialism or socialistic elements in a mixed economy.* When the government interferes in the market to, for instance, redistribute income or enact worker and product safety legislation, it violates individual rights and thus acts in a manner that is inconsistent with the requirements of human life.[25]

The government cannot act for "the good of society" by implementing socialistic policies. When the government initiates physical force it benefits some members of society *at the expense of others*. For example, when the government redistributes income, it gives income to some people *by taking it from others*. Whenever the government initiates force, someone is being sacrificed. Believing it is good for the government to initiate force to sacrifice some people to others is based on an acceptance of the validity of the morality of sacrifice. However, as was shown above, the morality of sacrifice, in any of its variations, is destructive because it stands in opposition to the requirements of human life. It does not matter whether a more virulent form of sacrifice is being implemented through socialism or a milder form is being implemented through the mixed economy. Either way it is destructive to human life.

The only way for the government to act for the good of *every* member of society, and thus truly act for "the good of society," is to protect individual rights (which means, to implement only capitalist policies). This is true because only when the government does this do all members of society benefit from the government's action. Only then is each individual protected from the initiation of physical force and thus left free to further his own life and well-being. Only then is no member of society sacrificed to any other member.

A mixed economy is a transition economy. It is an economy either in transition from capitalism to socialism or vice versa, depending on what ideas are becoming more prevalent in a culture, influencing the direction in which a country is moving.[26] Capitalism and socialism are incompatible economic systems because of the incompatible ideas, such as the diametrically opposed moral ideas, that underlie them. Capitalist and socialist elements cannot remain together forever in the same country. For example, the United States was a much more capitalist society during the latter half of the nineteenth century, when it had only a relatively small amount of government intervention. However, over the last century or so, as the altruist code of morality has become more consistently accepted in America and any existing elements of egoism have disappeared as a result, the United States has drifted more toward socialism and away from capitalism. The United States was a much freer country in the nineteenth century. There are many statist controls that exist today (such as minimum wage laws, worker health and safety regulation, environmental legislation, welfare, among many others) that did not exist a century ago. Step-by-step, more socialist controls have been implemented throughout the last century and continue to be added to this day. Many other countries have followed a similar pattern.

If the mixed economy is not rejected on principle (and capitalism accepted on principle) an economy will drift toward socialism or some other form of dictatorship. This occurs because once the principle of freedom has been rejected in favor of some controls, the door is open for greater violations of freedom. At this point, some other principle, besides the protection of individual rights, guides people's actions. When this occurs, people will clamor for the different types of government controls they want implemented. The result is an endless series of cries, by various groups, for controls in a growing number of areas of people's lives. This leads to more and more violations of people's freedom and is exactly what we see happening in the United States today.

For example, both conservatives and liberals call for more controls (whether controls on embryonic stem-cell research by conservatives or more welfare handouts by liberals, among many others). Neither the liberals nor the conservatives are advocates of capitalism. Both advocate different versions of the mixed economy (disagreeing only on what is to be controlled).

The only debate that takes place in a mixed economy, barring a move toward capitalism, concerns which areas of people's lives should be controlled next. Debate about whether any controls should exist at all completely disappears. This occurs because once the principle of protecting freedom has been rejected, the only question remaining is which freedoms are to be taken away. The only way to head toward capitalism is to accept the idea that individual rights should be fully protected (i.e., that they should be protected *on principle*) and therefore that we should have no controls.[27]

Economically, the drift toward dictatorship occurs because previous rounds of controls by the government create problems whose solution appears to be further rounds of controls. In other words, controls breed more controls. For example, after the government implements rent controls and makes it unprofitable to be a landlord, the government then finds it necessary to provide public housing to people because a large number of landlords have left the rental housing business and there is now a shortage of housing. Or, after the government subsidizes farmers to grow certain agricultural commodities it finds there is an overabundance of these commodities and therefore must forcibly restrict how much of the commodities farmers can grow. These examples could be multiplied many times over. Of course, the real solution to the problems created by one round of controls is not further rounds of controls, but the elimination of all controls.

All of the Western, industrialized nations (including the United States, Germany, Japan, Canada, Britain, and France) are mixed economies. Some have more socialistic elements (such as France) relative to others, but they must still be considered mixed economies since there is some freedom and many privately owned companies producing wealth in them. Albeit, in some of the countries the companies are heavily regulated; nonetheless, there are still significant elements of capitalism that remain in these countries. Even Sweden is a mixed economy. The means of production are not completely owned and controlled by the government in Sweden. There are still substantial amounts of private production that take place in that country and a largely market driven price system that exists.

Conclusion

Based on the above comparison of the three types of political/economic systems, one can see there is a link between protecting individual rights and creating economic prosperity. This highlights a fundamental link between economics and politics. When the government violates individual rights, it creates economic inefficiency and economically harmful results. Likewise, to the degree that a government protects individual rights, it promotes economic efficiency and a higher rate of economic progress.[28] This is why the highest rate of economic progress is achieved under capitalism and the lowest rate is achieved under socialism. The mixed economy lands somewhere in the middle, closer to socialism the greater the degree of controls that exist within an economy or closer to capitalism the greater the degree of freedom that exists within an economy.

Finally, as one can see throughout this discussion, and as will be shown throughout the remaining chapters of the book, capitalism is not only economically superior to socialism and the mixed economy, it is also morally superior. In fact, as stated previously, capitalism is the *only* moral social system. It is the only system consistent with the requirements of human life because it is the only system that completely bans the initiation of physical force from all human relationships. It is the only system that recognizes that each individual has a right to his own life and that each individual must be free to produce the values his life requires and pursue his own happiness. In a word, capitalism is the only *egoistic* social system.

Notes

1. See Ayn Rand, *Capitalism: The Unknown Ideal* (New York: Signet, 1967), 19 for more on this definition.

2. One might wonder why a worker would accept a lower wage. He might if he was competing with other workers and the choice was to accept a lower wage or lose the job to another worker.

3. Ayn Rand, *The Virtue of Selfishness* (New York: Signet, 1964), 110.

4. Rand, *The Virtue of Selfishness*, 110.

5. See Leonard Peikoff, *Objectivism: The Philosophy of Ayn Rand* (New York: Meridian, 1991), 352 for more on the connection between the right to life and the derivative rights.

6. Why it is immoral to sacrifice some groups to others will be made clear in the section titled "An Important Discussion on Moral Theory: Egoism versus Altruism," in this chapter.

7. For a thorough discussion on the nature of rights and their connection with our ability to think at the conceptual level, and with morality, see Ayn Rand, *Atlas Shrugged*, 35th anniversary ed. (New York: Signet, 1992), 976-977, *The Virtue of Selfishness*, 108-117, and *Capitalism*, 17-18.

8. Why this is so is discussed in this chapter in the section titled "An Important Discussion on Moral Theory: Egoism versus Altruism."

9. Factors of production are resources used to produce other goods. They include capital goods and labor. Capital goods include all the machines, buildings, land, and physical assets that businesses use to produce goods.

10. For more on the coordinating function of profits, see the section titled "The Nature of Competition" in chapter 2.

11. For an explanation of this and the preceding statement, see the section titled "An Important Discussion on Moral Theory: Egoism versus Altruism," in this chapter.

12. One might wonder why this is the case. It is because in order for a pure capitalist country to exist, the right philosophical base must first be established in a culture. This includes, most fundamentally, the wide acceptance of the right moral and epistemological ideas. These ideas include an egoistic moral philosophy and recognition of the fact that reason is man's only means to knowledge and basic tool of survival. These ideas have never been fully integrated into any culture. Nineteenth-century America came the closest to fully and consistently accepting the right ideas and that is why it was the closest any country has ever come to a pure capitalist society. For a discussion on egoism in this book, see the section titled "An Important Discussion on Moral Theory: Egoism versus Altruism" in this chapter. For a discussion on reason in this book, see the section titled "Environmentalism and the Abandonment of Reason" in chapter 6. For a discussion on the link between reason, egoism, and capitalism, see Ayn Rand, *For the New Intellectual* (New York: Signet, 1961), 81-82; *The New Left: The Anti-Industrial Revolution*, Revised edition (New York: Signet, 1975), 227-229; and *Philosophy: Who Needs It* (New York: Signet, 1982), 62-63. Also see Leonard Peikoff, ed., *The Voice of Reason: Essays in Objectivist Thought* (New York: Meridian, 1989), 89 and Harry Binswanger, ed., *The Ayn Rand Lexicon: Objectivism from A to Z* (New York: Meridian, 1986), 410.

The fact that capitalism has never been fully realized in any country should not be taken as evidence that it is impossible or impractical to establish a capitalist society. It is both possible and practical. For a discussion on how to achieve a capitalist society, see the "Epilogue." The practicality of capitalism (i.e., its ability to succeed, when put into practice, at making it possible for human life to flourish) has been established in this chapter and will be discussed in greater detail throughout the book. Further, the fact that many people are opposed to capitalism does not make it impractical. This simply shows that many people believe in impractical political/economic systems (i.e., they believe in systems that, if put into practice, would fail because the systems would make it harder or impossible for human life to flourish). Impractical systems will be discussed in this chapter and throughout the book.

13. My presentation of egoism and altruism is *very* brief. I present it only as a tool for showing why markets do not fail, but in fact succeed. I owe my understanding of the nature of egoism and altruism to Ayn Rand. For a more thorough discussion on these topics see her, *The Virtue of Selfishness*, vii-xii, 13-70, and 112; *Atlas Shrugged*, 930-933 and 942-952; *Philosophy*, 61; *For the New Intellectual*, 54, 73, and 80-82; and

Capitalism, 195-196. Also, see Peikoff, *Objectivism*, 206-220 and 229-234 and Binswanger, *The Ayn Rand Lexicon*, 4-11, 429-432, and 446-452.

14. Rand, *The Virtue of Selfishness*, 50.

15. In this paragraph I use the term "self-interest" synonymously with "rational self-interest." I will also use the term "selfish" synonymously with "rational self-interest." I will do this throughout the book.

16. See Rand, *The Virtue of Selfishness*, 57-66 for more on this.

17. Before something can be stolen, it still must be produced. Therefore, even criminals cannot escape the fact that human survival depends on production.

18. For more on this, see Ayn Rand, *The Fountainhead* (New York: Signet, 1952), 682-683 and *The Virtue of Selfishness*, 34.

19. The attempt to equate altruism with kindness is an attempt to make altruism appear harmless and even benevolent. Likewise, the equation of selfishness with being unkind to others is an attempt to make it appear harmful and malevolent. However, these interpretations do not provide a valid understanding of what altruism and selfishness mean.

20. I say when it is appropriate because a selfish person does not show kindness randomly. This would be self-destructive. For instance, if I show kindness randomly it would be equally likely that I show kindness to my mother or Osama bin Laden. Showing kindness or affection is appropriate in many relationships; however, the degree of kindness or affection you show should be based on the value, or potential value, that others represent to you.

21. Rand, *Atlas Shrugged*, 932.

22. For more on "planning" in a socialist society see, Ludwig von Mises, *Human Action: A Treatise on Economics*, 3rd ed. (Chicago: Contemporary Books, Inc., 1966), 691-695, 698-701, and 703-705. Also, see F. A. Hayek, *Individualism and Economic Order* (Chicago: The University of Chicago Press, 1948), 77-91.

23. Stéphane Courtois et al., *The Black Book of Communism: Crimes, Terror, Repression*, trans. Jonathan Murphy and Mark Kramer (Cambridge: Harvard University Press, 1999), 4.

24. Nazi Germany was a little different than the communist countries, but it was still a socialist country. In Nazi Germany, socialism was merely implemented in a slightly different way than in the communist countries. The Nazis maintained the facade that property was privately owned (by allowing individuals, as opposed to government officials, to run the day-to-day operations of businesses), while the communists openly nationalized the means of production. However, under Nazism, the government dictated what to produce, how to produce it, what prices to charge, and to whom to sell. Hence, property was not, in fact, privately owned but was controlled (and thus effectively owned) by the government. The results of the Nazi variety of socialism were the same as the results of the communist variety: massive violations of individual rights, mass murder, and a low standard of living. For more on the Nazi variety of socialism, see Mises, *Human Action*, 717-718.

Those who think Nazi Germany was able to achieve a significant productive capability—on its own—through its form of socialism should think again. The only reason the Nazis were able to achieve any significant amount of production at all was due to the fact that in the decades prior to the rise of the Nazis, Germany had been an industrialized, mixed (not socialist) economy and had achieved a substantial productive capability, which the Nazis then seized and used for their own purposes. If they could not have taken advantage of the productive capability achieved under previous (more capitalist) German governments, the productive capability under the Nazis would have been far lower. For a discussion on the mixed economy, see the next section.

25. Just how worker and product safety legislation and the redistribution of income are destructive to human life will be shown in chapters 5 and 7, respectively.

26. The type of ideas that determine the direction in which a country is heading are more fundamental, philosophical ideas (primarily moral and epistemological ideas), not economic ideas. For a discussion of the influence of philosophy on a culture, see Rand, *Philosophy*, 1-11.

27. For more on this, see Peikoff, *Objectivism*, 373-377.

28. This link will become clearer with each chapter of the book that one reads.

Chapter Two

Monopoly

Introduction

The first claim against the market that I will refute is the assertion that a free market leads to large firms gaining monopoly power. This "monopoly power" allegedly leads to greater economic inefficiency, a lower productive capability, higher prices, and a lower standard of living in the economy. Hence, it is said the government must step in to restore competition. I will show that this claim is based on an invalid view of competition and monopoly, and more fundamentally, on the false ethical theory of altruism and an invalid understanding of concepts. I will also show that the free market allows for the maximum amount of competition that is possible in any industry and that deviating from a free market, with some form of government intervention in the name of allegedly increasing competition, actually decreases the intensity of competition that exists in the economy and thus reduces the level of economic efficiency, causes a lower productive capability, higher prices, and a lower standard of living.

Economic versus Political Monopoly

There are two concepts of monopoly that exist and one provides a good understanding of monopoly while the other provides a poor understanding of monopoly. The concept accepted by most people today is the one that is deficient, and it is the acceptance of this invalid concept of monopoly that leads people to (incorrectly) believe that monopolies arise out of the free market. The concept of monopoly accepted by most people today is known as the economic concept of monopoly. This concept says a monopoly exists when there is only one supplier of a good in a given geographic region.[1] The concept that provides a sound understanding of monopoly is known as the political concept of monopoly. This says that monopolies arise when the government initiates physical force to reserve a market or a portion of a market to one or more sellers.

The economic concept of monopoly focuses on the number and size of firms in an industry. It says the smaller the number of firms in an industry, and the larger those firms are, the more monopoly power that exists in that industry. It says monopoly power can arise naturally out of the market simply by firms becoming big. The political concept focuses on the restriction of competition by the government and says monopoly power can be held by many small producers against just one or a few large producers, or can be held by one large producer against other, smaller producers.[2] It says as long as a firm is being helped by the government in some way—no matter what its size—then that firm has monopoly power.

The problem with the economic concept is that it leads to confusion because it can be used to say that no firm is a monopoly or all firms are monopolies, depending on how broadly or narrowly one defines a good. It can also be used to say a firm both is and is not a monopoly. In other words, the economic concept of monopoly leads to blatant contradictions. Based on this concept, it is arbitrary whether a firm is a monopoly or not.

For example, if one defines a good by brand name (such as Coke or Pepsi), every firm is a monopoly. This is so because each firm is the only seller of its brand name product. However, if one broadens his definition of a good and, continuing with the same example, considers the good "soft drink" or, expanding it further to "beverage," then neither Coca-Cola nor Pepsi-Cola is a monopoly and no other firm is a monopoly either. This is the case because all producers of beverages compete with each other. Producers of soft drinks, juices, bottled water, coffee, tea, and even tap water compete against each other. This example can be applied to any industry.[3]

Depending on how one defines a good, what one person says is a monopoly and what another says is a monopoly could be quite different. One could say that no business is a monopoly and all businesses are monopolies, all at the exact same time. Because of this contradiction, the economic concept is meaningless and invalid.[4] It is a subjective concept because it can be used in an arbitrary manner to say whether a monopoly exists or not. It does not provide one with an objective method of determining which firms are, in fact, monopolies.

In the discussion on the antitrust laws in chapter 3, I will show in more detail just how arbitrarily the economic concept of monopoly is applied. As a preview to that chapter I will say that even when numerical indexes, such as the market share of a firm, are used to determine whether a firm is a monopoly (based on the economic concept), the claim is still arbitrary because the specific numerical value used to indicate the existence of a monopoly is arbitrary. For instance, if it is decided that firms with an 80 percent or more market share in an industry are monopolies, what rational basis is there for using 80 percent instead of 75 percent or 85 percent? There is no rational basis. It is arbitrary.[5] This method must be arbitrary because it is based on a concept that is arbitrary and subjective. In antitrust cases, determining whether a company is a monopoly or not is based on the subjective feelings and arbitrary declarations of the judge who presides over the case, or the economists whose numerical technique the judge depends upon to determine whether a monopoly exists.[6]

There is no confusion over who is a monopolist based on the political concept. Any producer or producers that are given special privileges by the government to produce in a specific geographic region are monopolists. Whether they are given special privileges through government issued licenses (such as for doctors, electricians, beauticians, etc.), tariffs, quotas, exclusive franchises (such as electrical utilities), subsidies, or government owned enterprises (such as the U. S. Post Office), they are monopolists. The political concept is a valid concept because it does not lead to subjective and arbitrary conclusions about who is a monopolist. Based on this concept, one can objectively determine who is a monopoly because one can actually identify which firms are and are not monopolies without any contradictions.[7] One cannot arbitrarily say that no firm is a monopoly and all firms are monopolies based on the political concept. Firms either have monopoly power or they do not.

As one can see, based on a proper understanding of what a monopoly is, it is clear that *monopolies do not arise naturally out of the market. The only time a monopoly exists is when the government interferes with the market* using the initiation of force to give some firm or firms monopoly power. In this chapter I will show that it is only when a firm possesses monopoly power based on the political concept that the standard negative effects associated with monopoly arise. Only then do economic inefficiency, a lower productive capability, higher prices, and a lower standard of living result. These things occur because only then is competition actually restricted.

An Important Epistemological Discussion: The Nature of Concepts

Before showing the effects of political monopolies, I will provide a discussion on the nature of concepts. I do this because some readers might not understand my statements in the previous section concerning the invalidity of the economic concept of monopoly and the validity of the political concept of monopoly. The discussion in this section will help the reader gain a better understanding of monopoly and of concepts in general.[8]

Concepts are mental tools used to classify and categorize concretes of a certain kind. For instance, the concept "man" is used to identify and classify beings of a certain kind: beings whose most fundamental characteristic is the possession of reason (or the ability to think at the conceptual level). In general, concepts are used to classify and categorize entities, actions, relationships, attributes, etc. We perform such classifications and categorizations for a specific purpose: to be able to apply the knowledge we gain about *some* concretes in a category to *every* concrete in a category. For instance, we use the knowledge gained and subsumed under the concept "man," such as that he has ten fingers, ten toes, walks upright, has a pair of lungs, a heart, a conceptual faculty, etc. and apply this to all men. This allows us to, among other things, retain an enormous amount of data concerning a large number of concretes and thus allows us to economize on the use of our mental capacity. We do not have to treat every concrete that we come upon as a completely new phenomenon. Once a specific concrete has been conceptualized, we can apply the knowledge gained about that concrete in general to specific instances of it.

A simple example of how concepts enable us to economize on our mental space is the act of counting. Without numerical concepts, one would have to hold in his mind at one time a number of specific entities corresponding to the number he was trying to retain in his mind. For instance, the number nineteen, instead of one concept, would be /////////////////. It is impossible to retain this in one's mind at one time, let alone distinguish it from ///////////////////, or retain nineteen million entities in one's mind. Without counting, man would be limited to retaining, perhaps, five or six objects at best. Without mathematical concepts, a growing number of entities quickly blurs into an unretainable sum.[9]

Further, once the concept "nineteen" has been understood, it can be applied to a potentially limitless number of concretes. For instance, whether one is dealing with nineteen cows, nineteen cats, nineteen computers, nineteen dollars, etc., if one understands the concept "nineteen," one has gained knowledge about a concrete that can be used to understand the world better and improve one's ability to act successfully in it. For example, understanding numerical concepts in general (and certain mathematical principles) can make the difference between knowing whether a business venture will make a profit or loss. Therefore, the more concepts one understands, the more knowledge one gains (and the more potential knowledge one can gain on the basis of those concepts), and the greater one's ability will be to act successfully in the world.

In order to achieve the crucially important cognitive purpose above, a concept should group existents based on their fundamental similarities and differences. Those existents that are fundamentally similar should be grouped together, while those that are fundamentally different should be grouped separately. A fundamental characteristic of a concrete is one that explains all the other characteristics, or the largest number of other characteristics, of that concrete. For example, the possession of reason is the fundamental or distinguishing characteristic of man because it is the one characteristic that explains virtually all the things that man is capable of doing but that other living beings are incapable of doing. For instance, the possession of reason explains why man can count, follow a recipe, play a board game, read a book, read engineering drawings, build a skyscraper, learn calculus, invent the computer, write a symphony, etc.[10] By classifying concretes based on their fundamental similarities and differences, concepts enable man to obtain a deeper and clearer understanding of reality.

In contrast to the above, grouping fundamentally different things together based on non-essential characteristics is very harmful when forming concepts because it leads to greater confusion, not a clearer understanding of reality. This is so in the case of having a proper understanding of monopoly and it is true of having a proper understanding of anything else. As an example, think of the confusion that would arise if a horse and a dog were grouped together under the same concept based on some non-essential characteristic, such as that they both have tails. This new "concept" could be called a "dorse."

By classifying these beings together, one is saying they are fundamentally the same and thus should be subsumed under the same term. However, there are significant differences between these two animals and to treat them as being the same one would have to ignore these differences. One would have to ignore differences whose recognition would help one gain a better understanding of these animals. For instance, one would have to ignore the fact that one animal is a carnivore and the other is an herbivore. By ignoring the significant differences, one would make it more difficult to, for example, determine what to feed these animals, how to care for them in general, and how to distinguish them from other animals that have some of the same characteristics. Confusion about how to care for these animals would result because the same basic principles of care and nutrition would not apply to the "same" animal. One would have to remember different principles apply to the "same" animal and which principles apply to what members of this "species." For example, instead of remembering that dogs eat meat and horses eat hay, one would have to remember that the "dorses" that bark eat meat and the "dorses" that whinny eat hay. Confusion about how to distinguish them from other animals would arise because, for instance, one would have a difficult time classifying other animals that have tails. Would other animals that have tails also be classified as "dorses"? If so, think of the added confusion this would lead to in trying to determine how to care for these animals and distinguish them from each other. If not, on what basis does one say they are not "dorses" (since they have tails) and on what basis did one subsume horses and dogs under the same term in the first place?

The above criticism applies to the economic concept of monopoly. This concept also classifies fundamentally different things together as if they were the same. That is why the concept is invalid.

The economic concept of monopoly groups together firms that have achieved their dominant positions through voluntary trade (i.e., by out competing their rivals) with firms that have achieved their dominant positions through the government's initiation of physical force (i.e., by the government protecting them from competition). It does so on the basis of the non-essential characteristic that these two types of firms are both large. By doing this, it ignores how these firms came to acquire their dominant positions.

These two types of firms should not be grouped together because the ways in which the companies have achieved their dominant positions are diametrically opposed to each other. The case based on voluntary trade is a part of competition and the one based on the government's use of force is an act of restricting competition. That is, the former case is a part of the rivalrous act of firms building a product and trying to get individuals to voluntarily buy it. This is what competition in a free market is all about. The latter act prevents one or more firms from building and selling a product (or even just makes it harder for them to do so). This is why it represents a restriction of competition and therefore creates monopoly power.

Because monopoly is a concept used to identify situations where competition is absent or restricted, one cannot use it to identify situations that are the result of competition, such as when firms achieve dominant positions by producing and selling better products. By grouping together situations that are the result of competition with situations that are the result of restrictions of competition, the economic concept obliterates a crucial difference and leads people to inappropriately identify when monopolies do or do not exist (i.e., when competition is actually restricted or not). To repeat, economic competition is the rivalrous act of sellers competing, within the context of voluntary exchange, to produce and sell a product. Anything that results from this process does not create monopoly power because it is part of the *competitive* process.

A proper concept should not obliterate, ignore, or even push into the background fundamental distinctions between concretes. In this case, it should not obliterate the distinction between actions that violate individual rights and actions that respect individual rights. But this is what is done when firms that achieve dominant positions through voluntary trade are classified with firms that are given dominant positions through the government's use of force. By subsuming both types of firms under the same concept, the situations are evaluated as being fundamentally the same when, in fact, they are not.

The fundamental distinction between respecting and violating individual rights cannot be stressed too strongly. One type of action is pro-human life and the other is anti-life. When the government respects individual rights, and thus firms are able to engage in production and voluntary trade, the government is acting in a manner consistent with the requirements of human life and therefore helps human life to flourish. It does this by enabling the firms' owners to further their own lives, and by making it possible for firms to produce goods from which individuals can potentially benefit and leaving people free to decide which goods are worth buying. When the government violates individual rights it is acting in opposition to the requirements of human life and is thus acting to destroy it. The government does this here by preventing the owners of firms from using their property to pursue their own rational self-interest. In addition, the government prevents firms from producing potentially beneficial goods and thus prevents people from being able to decide on their own if the goods are worth buying. Respecting and protecting individual rights *are* fundamental requirements of human life because human beings require freedom from the initiation of physical force so they can do the necessary thinking and acting to further their lives and well-being. A man cannot further his life and well-being if someone forces him to go against his rational judgment.

With a "concept" like "dorse," the fundamental differences between the things classified are obvious because many of these differences are directly perceivable. Therefore, it is easy to understand that horses and dogs do not belong under the same concept and, because of the blatantly obvious differences between them, it is hard to even imagine how one could make the mistake of grouping them under the same term, or how any confusion could arise in the care of the animals. With a "concept" like "economic monopoly," the fundamental differences between the things classified are not directly perceivable. That is why it is easier for these differences to be missed or ignored and why it is easier for these fundamentally different things to be grouped under the same term. However, it is just as important to distinguish between fundamentally different characteristics when forming concepts to identify monopolies as it is when forming concepts to identify horses and dogs. In more general terms, when forming concepts, it is just as important to recognize fundamental differences that are not directly perceivable as it is to recognize fundamental differences that are directly perceivable.

I have by no means provided an exhaustive discussion of concept formation. That is a task that falls under the field of epistemology and is one that a philosopher must undertake. This is a book that primarily focuses on economic topics and should not contain a lengthy treatment on the subject of concept formation. However, some discussion was necessary to understand what I mean when I say a concept is valid or invalid. Knowledge of the nature of concepts will also help one understand why the arguments against the market are invalid and how markets actually succeed.

Perfect Competition

So, the economic "concept" of monopoly is arbitrary, groups fundamentally different things together, is invalid, and therefore leads to confusion and false conclusions. However, "economic monopoly" is also based on an improper understanding of competition to which many economists adhere. This theory of competition is known as "perfect competition." Perfect competition is a term used to describe the "ideal" form of competition that can exist in an industry. For an industry to be "perfectly competitive" it must have five characteristics.[11] First, there must be insignificant barriers to entry and exit in such an industry. For instance, it does not take much capital to enter a perfectly competitive industry. Based on this, the automobile industry could not be described as "perfectly competitive" because it takes an enormous amount of capital to produce automobiles. However, the industry comprised of street-corner vendors would qualify as perfectly competitive, based on this characteristic, because it takes very little capital to enter this industry.

Second, there must be a large number of small producers in a perfectly competitive industry. The smallness of the producers follows from the fact that these industries have insignificant barriers to entry and thus require very little capital to enter. Third, firms in a perfectly competitive industry produce standardized or identical products (also known as homogenous products). This means that all the products produced are exactly the same. Any differences in products cannot exist in a "perfectly competitive" industry because such differences might create significant barriers to entry. Some people might become loyal to one particular brand and this might be difficult for new entrants to overcome.

Fourth, "perfect information" exists in a perfectly competitive industry. This means that buyers and sellers know everything about buying, selling, and producing a product. For instance, producers know where all the inputs used to produce the product are being sold and the prices at which they are being sold. Likewise, buyers know all the places where the product is being sold and at what prices. "Imperfect information" cannot exist in a "perfectly competitive" industry because, again, this might create barriers to entry.

Fifth, perfectly competitive firms must be price takers. This means they take the prevailing market price for their product and cannot influence that price. This is supposed to occur because perfectly competitive firms are so small compared to the total market for the good, and because everyone has "perfect information" concerning the price of the good, that if a producer attempts to raise his price above the market price he will quickly lose all his business to his competitors. So he takes the highest price he can get for his product, which is the price prevailing in the market.

To the reader that has not been trained to think like a contemporary economist, it might appear obvious that, at least with respect to some of these characteristics, so-called perfect competition has very little to do with the actual nature of competition in the marketplace. Let's take a closer look at the characteristics to see the actual nature of perfect competition.

It helps in understanding any concept to concretize what the concept means or implies in reality. By doing this, one can see whether a concept makes sense based on the facts or whether a concept is absurd and meaningless. By concretizing "perfect competition" I will show that the latter applies to it.[12] First, consider the idea that all products must be the same to have perfect competition. What does this imply? For one thing, it means that there is no competition with respect to differentiation in quality and style. This means that if perfect competition is to exist firms cannot try to make their products different from or better than their rivals' products. Therefore, this concept of "competition" actually excludes one major aspect of competition. Furthermore, it would lead to a mundane and boring life for everyone if all products (including all cars, homes, cellular phones, computers, pencils, and so on) were the same. There would be no variety in the types of goods that exist. As one can easily observe, competition has the exact opposite effect.

Second, what about the idea that an industry must have a large number of small firms in order to be considered perfectly competitive? This excludes competition by companies to drive their costs down and gain a competitive edge over their rivals by achieving economies of scale. This is probably one of the most intense aspects of competition in the marketplace. If every industry were composed of a large number of small firms, costs in many industries would be higher, and this would lead to a lower productive capability and standard of living. This is the exact opposite result that is achieved by competition. Competition leads to greater efficiency, more production, and a higher standard of living.

Many industries progress through a life cycle where, when they are young, there are many small producers vying for a small number of customers. However, as innovation takes place, by some companies improving upon their methods of production, the innovative companies grow large and expand the market by means of the lower costs and prices they are able to achieve, and the companies that do not innovate are driven out of business or are acquired by the ones that expand. Therefore, as the industry matures, it ends up with only a small number of very large firms. However, this latter state of the industry is achieved through very intense competition. In fact, high capital requirements in an industry (such as the automobile industry, which went through this exact life cycle process) are indicative of very intense competition. Hence, any potential entrant must be able to compete effectively by meeting the low costs of production that the very efficient producers currently in the industry have achieved.

Third, what about the idea that an industry must have insignificant barriers to entry and exit to be perfectly competitive? This ignores a crucial distinction between two types of barriers to entry that one must consider when assessing whether competition exists: natural and government imposed barriers. Natural barriers, such as high capital requirements, brand loyalty, or knowledge about how to produce a good, are a part of competition and voluntary trade. For instance, a firm gains customer loyalty by producing a product that customers value enough that they will not easily switch to a different brand. Further, natural barriers occur as a result of achieving greater economic efficiency through the competitive process, such as by gaining economies of scale.

Government imposed barriers (such as licensing laws, exclusive franchises, tariffs, quotas, and subsidies) impede competition and voluntary trade and are achieved through the initiation of physical force. They are achieved by the government forcibly preventing some firms from competing (such as through exclusive government franchises), making it harder for some to compete (through tariffs, quotas, and licenses), or by providing an artificial advantage to some companies (through subsidies). These types of barriers restrict competition and thus create greater economic inefficiency.

By ignoring the fundamental distinction between these two types of barriers to entry, perfect competition lumps these two fundamentally different things together and says when *any* barriers exist competition is lessened. This means it lumps together industries such as the New York City taxicab business, which has substantial government barriers, and the computer hardware manufacturing business, which has high capital requirements, and says both of these industries lack competition because of the barriers. However, this could not be further from the truth. The computer hardware business is extremely competitive *because* of the high capital requirements, and thus low costs, that have been achieved in that industry. Achieving low costs has been a part of the competitive process in this industry. In contrast, competition is severely restricted in the New York City taxicab business because of the expensive medallion, required by the city government, that one must possess for each taxicab one owns. Each medallion costs around $250,000. This medallion forcibly keeps potential competitors out of the industry and thus protects existing taxicab businesses from competition.

Fourth, what about the idea that perfect information must exist for an industry to be perfectly competitive? This is blatantly absurd. This implies, for example, that before buying a book or a movie ticket, one must have already read the book or seen the movie in order for "perfect information," and thus "perfect competition," to exist. Otherwise, this is information that one lacks and therefore perfect competition cannot exist.

Perfect information implies that humans must be omniscient in order for perfect competition to exist. If perfect information actually existed, we would not have to be concerned with learning about how to organize an economy in any particular way to produce wealth because we would already know how to best organize the economic system and produce all the wealth we need. We would know all the best methods of production, where all the raw materials are, and how they can be used. We would not have to study economics or any other subject.

Part of competition is competition concerning information and knowledge. There is competition to gain knowledge about what methods of production to use, competition to gain knowledge about customers (such as using focus group studies to determine what styles they like), and competition among firms to disseminate information about themselves (such as through advertising). By assuming that we must have perfect information to have an allegedly perfect form of competition, again, a major component of competition is excluded.

Fifth, what about the idea that perfectly competitive firms are price takers? This characteristic ignores the fact that many firms *set* their prices based on costs of production they can achieve and based on what they think the demand for their products will be. Firms compete intensely by continuously driving their costs down, setting a lower price, and thus gaining a competitive advantage over their rivals. Hence, in requiring firms to be price takers, perfect competition ignores another aspect of competition.

Perfect competition does not exist anywhere in reality. Sometimes it is claimed that agricultural industries, such as wheat farming, come closest to being perfectly competitive because the products are close to being identical and the farmers take whatever prices they can get for their products in the commodity markets. However, even these industries fail to meet the standard in many ways. First, it takes a large amount of capital to get into the agricultural business (think of all the land and expensive machinery one must possess).

Second, perfect information most certainly does not, and cannot, exist in farming or any other industry (think of all the agricultural knowledge one must have to be a successful farmer). Third, because of the high capital and knowledge requirements needed to get into the farming business, there certainly are significant barriers to enter the business. Perfect competition is a Platonic concept. By this I mean it exists nowhere in reality, like Plato's mystical World of Forms (where he believed all concepts or universals are suppose to reside).

Perfect competition, far from being an ideal form of competition (or a form of competition at all), actually means the *absence* of all competition. Under perfect competition, there is no competition to differentiate one's product, no competition to gain economies of scale and drive one's costs down, and no competition to gain or disseminate information. It is not a valid concept. It is an invalid concept because it has nothing to do with actual competition and exists nowhere in reality. A concept must actually identify something that exists in order to be valid.

A good concept of competition, which I have been using in my critique of perfect competition, is one based on rivalry. This says that the verb "to compete" means to try to outdo one's competitors in production and voluntary trade. It means a firm tries to drive its costs down and set a lower price, differentiate its product, advertise, and drive its competitors out of business by getting customers to voluntarily switch to its product. This provides one with a good understanding of how competition actually takes place in an economic system.

* * *

One has seen what so-called perfect competition is and why it is invalid, but how does this relate to this chapter's discussion on monopoly? Based on the "concept" of perfect competition, competition is said to be most intense when a large number of small producers each produce an identical product. If this is taken as one's standard of competition, then an implication of perfect competition is that monopoly, which is the opposite of competition, exists when there is only one seller producing a product that is highly differentiated from other products. This is the economic "concept" of monopoly. In order to reject this invalid concept of monopoly, one must also reject perfect competition.

To fully embrace a proper understanding of monopoly—political monopoly—one must have a proper understanding of competition. That is, one must understand the competition that takes place in an economic system is a rivalrous process that occurs between producers who attempt to get people to voluntarily buy their products. The opposite of this is when competition—viz., production and voluntary trade—is restricted through the initiation of physical force. This is identified by the political concept of monopoly.

The Ethical Basis of Perfect Competition and Economic Monopoly

The ethical basis of perfect competition and economic monopoly is provided by egalitarianism and the ethical code that underlies it: altruism. Recall that altruism says it is virtuous for individuals to sacrifice themselves to others. If this is so, a society where people are equal in every way is desirable. For example, if I possess a greater amount of wealth than other individuals, according to altruism, I should sacrifice myself and give my wealth to them. If I possess less wealth than others, they should sacrifice themselves and give their wealth to me. What would be the result of acting on this egalitarian version of altruism? Only when we all have an equal amount of wealth would no one be morally required to give it up.

Likewise, if I possess some greater ability than others, I should some how "give up" some of my ability and "give it" to others in order to sacrifice myself to others. Maybe, the egalitarians might say, I should hold back so I do not make others look worse and feel bad about their lack of talent. Or maybe I should spend less time developing my own talent and more time helping less talented individuals develop their skills. Others should do the same in the areas where they have superior ability. The result is a society where everyone is equally talented, and no one is superior to any other person at anything.

The type of world that would exist if everyone was exactly the same is the bizarre world of perfect competition. For instance, under perfect competition no one would have an advantage in the information he possesses because producers would all have perfect information. Likewise, everyone would produce identical products, no one would have a cost advantage because firms would all be the same small size, and all businesses would receive the same price that prevails in the market. Perfect competition is an egalitarian ideal. And if this is the competitive ideal, according to egalitarianism, then being different (especially superior) in any way would create some element of monopoly.[13] The superiority of one competitor over another stands in opposition to altruism and egalitarianism. Therefore, if one takes altruism and egalitarianism seriously (i.e., takes them to their logical and consistent end), one will end up believing it is beneficial to have all competitors exactly the same, and consider it harmful to have any one competitor rising above the rest.

Perfect competition is an attempt to wipeout the individual's role in competition. More significantly, it is an attempt to wipeout the mind's role in competition. It is competition built on a thoroughly collectivist base. It says individual differences should play no role in competition and, in fact, any differences are to be condemned as alleged monopoly power. "Producers" under perfect competition are mindless drones stamping out identical products, selflessly serving the needs of consumers, and engaging in no innovation, marketing, or any other competitive activity.[14] What this theory forgets is that *competition occurs between individuals*. Competition is based on individuals using their minds to outdo each other in production and trade. It is no wonder that it is enemies of capitalism that have more readily accepted perfect competition as a valid description of competition because capitalism is based on a political philosophy of individualism.[15] Capitalism is based on the idea that the individual is the fundamental unit of value and that each individual has a moral right to his own life and should not be forced to live for, or sacrifice himself to, some group or collective.

So it is the wide acceptance of egalitarianism, and beneath that altruism, that underlies the acceptance of the "concepts" perfect competition and economic monopoly. Therefore, ultimately, to reject perfect competition and economic monopoly, one must reject altruism and egalitarianism. These are not worthy goals to achieve, nor proper standards on which to make judgments. I have shown in chapter 1 the destructive nature of altruism and why it should be rejected. Further evidence of the destructive nature of altruism will be presented in later chapters, particularly chapter 4 on externalities and chapter 6 on environmentalism. Chapter 7, on economic inequality, will show the destructive nature of egalitarianism and also provide another example of the destructive nature of altruism.

Just as economic monopoly and perfect competition are based on altruism and egalitarianism, political monopoly and competition as rivalry are based on egoism and individualism. These latter fully recognize the role of the individual in competition by recognizing that competition takes place between individuals. They recognize that the source of production is the individual reasoning mind and that the mind requires freedom in order to be used properly. They recognize that individuals possess different skills and financial resources and that these differences are a part of the competitive process. They recognize that each individual has a right to his own life and should live it to pursue his own self-interest, which includes growing rich by outdoing others in the rivalrous process of economic competition. They recognize that when the individual is prevented from competing against others in voluntary trade (i.e., when freedom is restricted), this creates a (political) monopoly.

Barriers to Entry

To gain a better understanding of what a monopoly actually is, it will help to go through some specific examples to see what actually does and does not constitute a monopoly. To do this, I will discuss several specific types of barriers to entry and assess them based on the political concept of monopoly. As I have stated, there are two general types of barriers to entry: natural and government imposed. Natural barriers arise out of the normal operation of the market and are a part of competition; they do not create monopoly power. Government imposed barriers require the initiation of force to implement and do create monopoly power. In light of this, I will analyze patents, copyrights, and trademarks; franchises; government owned and subsidized businesses; economies of scale; individuals or firms that have sole control of a resource; and network effects.

Patents, Copyrights, and Trademarks

It must be stressed that monopoly power exists only when the government *initiates* physical force to reserve a market or a portion of a market for one or more sellers. Based on this, patent, copyright, and trademark protection does not create monopolies, even though it is often thought to do so based on the economic concept of monopoly simply because it creates entry barriers. Patents, copyrights, and trademarks protect intellectual property from being used by others without the owner's consent. Just as the government must use *retaliatory* force to protect physical property from being stolen, it must do the same with intellectual property. This is what the government does when it protects the use of inventions with patents, the use of authored works with copyrights, and the use of names (including brand names and company names) and logos with trademarks. Protecting patented devices, copyrighted material, and trademarks is similar to protecting any other property that a person owns.[16]

The primary focus of protecting intellectual property rights, as with the protection of any property rights, is to allow the property owner to be free from the initiation of physical force so that he can further his life and well-being. However, trademark protection, as a secondary consequence, also protects people from fraud. Fraud, as stated in the previous chapter, is an indirect type of the initiation of force because someone attempts to take a person's property from him against his will. With respect to trademarks, fraud is committed when someone uses a company's name or logo to obtain a person's money under false pretenses. For example, if someone sells a person software that has the Microsoft name and logo on it, yet Microsoft did not produce the software and did not authorize the use of its trademark, the individual who purchased the software has had an act of fraud committed against him because he has paid money to obtain what he thinks is a Microsoft product when, in fact, it is not. Had he known it was not a Microsoft product, he might not have purchased the software or might not have been willing to pay as much as he did for the software.

The protection of patents, copyrights, and trademarks helps to increase efficiency, quality, and the supply of goods by allowing those who are creative to profit from their creativity. Patents provide an economic incentive to bring inventions into existence that improve the productive capability and standard of living in countless ways. Patents provide this incentive by making it possible for inventors to bring their inventions to the marketplace knowing that others cannot legally copy their inventions. Copyrights provide producers an economic incentive to publish written and recorded material, create art, and so on, since these creators know that others cannot legally copy their works. Trademarks provide companies with an economic incentive to produce higher quality goods to build and maintain a good reputation, since the companies know that others cannot profit from their good reputations by using their names and logos without their consent.

An economy might gain in the short run by abolishing patents and copyrights (through the increase in the supply of goods originally under patent or copyright); however, it would lead to long-run losses. Here, the economic incentive to create inventions and written works would disappear since people would no longer be able to profit from their creations. For example, if patents on prescription drugs were abolished the production of existing drugs would increase in the short run. However, no new life-saving drugs would be discovered since pharmaceutical companies would no longer have an economic incentive to spend the billions of dollars and fifteen years necessary on average to develop such drugs. This would ultimately decrease economic efficiency, quality, the supply of goods, and thus the standard of living.

Abolishing trademarks would also decrease the standard of living by decreasing efficiency, quality, and the supply of goods. In this case, there would be no incentive to maintain high quality if goods from various producers were indistinguishable. For example, if any software maker could use the Microsoft name and logo, no matter how low the quality of its product, Microsoft would not have an incentive to produce a high quality product. Such a situation would create an incentive to produce cheap, low quality products and use a high quality producer's name and logo to take advantage of its good reputation. This would quickly lead to all products being of low quality.

The existence of a political monopoly creates results that are the opposite of that achieved by the protection of patents, copyrights, and trademarks. This provides confirmation that the protection of these three things does not create monopolies. Political monopolies decrease economic efficiency, quality, and the supply of goods because they violate individual rights by protecting producers from competition.

* * *

The above provides another example of the link between protecting individual rights, creating economic efficiency, and increasing the productive capability of the economic system; and violating individual rights, creating economic inefficiency, and decreasing the productive capability of the economic system. This link exists because protecting individual rights is what is necessary for economic competition to take place. Economic competition can only take place within the context of voluntary trade, and the latter can only exist when people are protected from the initiation of physical force (i.e., when individual rights are protected). This is what patents, copyrights, and trademarks do; they are a part of what makes competition possible.

The ultimate justification for protecting patents, copyrights, and trademarks is not to increase efficiency, quality, and the supply of goods. The ultimate

justification is to protect individual rights. Which means, the ultimate
justification is that each man has a right to his own life and thus has the right to
benefit from the creations of his own mind, and no man's creations, whether an
invention, authored work, or trademark, may be taken by someone and used
without the creator's consent. In other words, no creator (or anyone else) should
be sacrificed to any other individuals. The improvements in efficiency and the
rising productive capability that result are simply consequences of implementing
laws that are consistent with the requirements of human life.[17]

Based on a proper understanding of monopoly, not protecting patents,
copyrights, and trademarks would actually constitute a monopoly. It would be
the establishment of a monopoly of the dull and incompetent by forcibly
depriving the intelligent and competent of the benefit of their intelligence and
competence. Such a situation would constitute an act of the initiation of force by
the dull and incompetent, sanctioned by the government, to gain access to things
they could have never created and thus to obtain a portion of a market they
could have never obtained on their own through voluntary trade.

Franchises

Exclusive government franchises (such as water, natural gas, and electric
utilities), where the government grants the privilege to one producer to be the
sole provider of a good in a particular geographic region, represent cases of
monopoly power being granted to the producer who receives the franchise. This
is the case because the government initiates physical force to keep all other
producers out of the industry in that region and thus protects the exclusive
producer from competition. Therefore, this leads to all the inefficiencies and the
decrease in quality one would expect from actual (viz., political) monopolies.
This is why, for instance, that utilities are notorious for being inefficient and
providing poor service.[18]

This is *not* the case, however, with private franchises. When, for instance,
Burger King sells a franchise to an individual so that he is the sole provider of
Burger King's products in a given region, this does not constitute the granting of
a monopoly but is, in fact, a part of competition. This represents the protection
of Burger King's trademarks. Burger King's trademarks belong exclusively to
the owners of Burger King, and they have the right to license the use of their
trademarks to as many or as few individuals as they think is best. Allowing
anyone to use Burger King's trademarks, without the owners' consent, would
actually constitute a monopoly against Burger King for the reasons presented
above in the discussion on trademarks. Because the granting of private
franchises is a part of competition, one would not expect to see—and does not
see in practice—inefficiencies and a lower productive capability arising from the
granting of such franchises. These franchises are fully consistent with

improvements in efficiency and a higher productive capability, as the discussion above on trademarks shows.

Government Owned and Subsidized Businesses

Government owned and subsidized businesses (such as the U.S. Post Office and public schools) are monopolies. The initiation of physical force is used to provide funds to these organizations (through taxes) and to protect them from competition. This, of course, leads to all the standard inefficiencies and the decrease in quality one would expect due to the restriction of competition. One need only look at the inefficiency of, and low quality services provided by, the post office, public schools, and other government owned and operated businesses to verify this.[19]

Economies of Scale

Gaining efficiencies through economies of scale does not constitute a monopoly, although it is often believed to do so based on the economic concept of monopoly. This is believed to be the case because as a company grows bigger and more efficient by gaining economies of scale, it gains a larger portion of the market and comes closer to being the sole provider of a product. As stated previously, however, these types of barriers to entry, far from creating monopoly power, are actually a part of the competitive process. Economies of scale are achieved through intense competition to drive costs down through the accumulation of capital, the acquisition of knowledge, and the efficiencies in production and improvements in quality that can be gained based on this foundation. Potential entrants to an industry, if they want to compete successfully, must be able to achieve the low costs of production that those currently in the industry have already achieved.

One must recognize the fact that mass production requires large amounts of capital and knowledge. If the government provided new firms with the capital and knowledge to compete (this latter, perhaps, by requiring existing companies to provide their trade secrets to new entrants), this would constitute a monopoly of those who have not earned the capital and knowledge against those who have. The government would be initiating force against existing companies to force these companies to provide newcomers with their trade secrets or against taxpayers to provide newcomers with funds to purchase capital. This would help the newcomers gain access to a market that they could not have gained access to on their own through voluntary trade. Forcing current producers to provide knowledge would be economically harmful because those who are forced to provide knowledge to their competitors would have less incentive to acquire more knowledge in the future, since they would not be able to use it to gain a competitive edge over their rivals. This would decrease the productive capability of the economic system.

Further, the economic inefficiency that would result if the government used force to provide investment funds to those who could not raise such funds on their own should be obvious. To obtain funds through voluntarily means, companies must convince investors to provide them with funds based on the merits of the company and its investments. If companies can rely on the government to provide them with funds, they will not have to prove the financial viability of their investment projects to investors. The burden on companies of demonstrating that they are capable of producing a product that people actually want to buy, and that they can produce it efficiently enough to make a profit on the venture, will be greatly reduced. Inefficient companies that produce products for which there is little demand would have a far easier time obtaining funds. This, too, would lower the productive capability of the economic system.

Sole Control of a Resource

Gaining sole control of a resource does not constitute a monopoly if it is achieved through voluntary trade. Remember, an actual (viz., political) monopoly does not depend on having only one producer of a good; it depends on whether competition is being forcibly restricted. If someone had the foresight to buy up the total supply of a resource, this is an achievement that is based on the ability of the person buying the resource. Such an acquisition is based on voluntary trade and does not constitute a restriction of competition (in fact, it is a part of competition). Further, recognizing and developing uses for a particular resource take great ability. Such activities help to increase the productive capability of the economic system. This can be seen in the case of the aluminum industry where, up through the mid-twentieth century, Alcoa controlled much of the land that contained Bauxite ore, a chemical from which aluminum is made. Alcoa was (and is) an extremely efficient and innovative company, and without its efforts to discover ways to produce and use aluminum the development of the aluminum industry, and industries heavily dependent on aluminum (such as the aircraft industry), would probably have developed in a much slower fashion.[20] Of course, one must remember that the ultimate reason to protect the property rights of the sole owners of resources is not to improve the productive capability (although this will surely result). It is to preserve the ability of these individuals to live their lives for their own selfish pursuits.

Taking away resources from someone, if acquired through voluntary trade, and giving them to others would violate individual rights and constitute a monopoly. It would be a monopoly of those who did not have the means and ability to acquire the resources through voluntary trade against those who did. It would reserve a market or a portion of a market to those who are given the resources. This would decrease economic efficiency and the productive capability of the economic system because firms would have less incentive and ability to acquire and develop uses for resources in the future.

Network Effects

The last topic in the section on barriers to entry concerns so-called network effects (also called network externalities). These barriers to entry, like the others above, do not create monopoly power. However, there are many fallacies with regard to this subject that must be addressed.

"Network effects" are said to occur with goods whose value to the consumer increases as the number of units of the goods sold increases. They occur with respect to goods whose uses are dependent on other people possessing the goods or many users having specialized knowledge about how to use the goods. In other words, the use of some goods has a self-reinforcing effect: the more people that use them, the more likely it is that subsequent users will choose to use the same goods. For example, the telephone is a network good. It is not of very great value to a person if he is the only one who has a telephone. However, the more people that own telephones, the more valuable it is to telephone users because one is able to call a larger number of people. Computer operating systems are another example. The more people that use a particular operating system (such as Windows), the more valuable it is to users of the operating system because, among other reasons, it is easier to share files with people, it is easier to find producers of software for the system, and it is easier to find technical support for the system.

Network effects are said to lead to monopoly power because they create switching costs and allegedly lead to "lock-in effects" and "path dependency." Switching costs exist because once a particular standard is widely accepted, it is costly for users to switch to a new standard. In the case of a new operating system, this occurs, for example, because switching to a new system requires training people on how to use it. Further, it is difficult to find people that have the knowledge to train others on the new system because there is little incentive to gain the skills to train others due to the limited use of the new product. Also, one would have to purchase new software that is compatible with the new operating system and convert old files so they could be used on the new system. Therefore, people allegedly become "locked-in" to the use of the standard that was first widely accepted. Once a "network good" has achieved a large enough market share, it makes people dependent on the use of that good. Consequently, few people will allegedly be able and willing to switch from the established product to a new product (the so-called lock-in effect), and subsequent users will choose to use the established product because others have chosen to use it (so-called path dependency).

A claim of market failure specific to this argument is that people can get locked-in to an inferior standard just because it was the first one to gain a significant market share. Therefore, it is claimed that it may be impossible even for superior goods to unseat an established, but inferior, "network good." This has been alleged to occur with such goods as the typewriter, the VCR, computer operating systems, and computer software (such as spreadsheet and word processing programs), among others. Hence, the market allegedly fails because an inferior product might be widely accepted simply because it was the first one on the market or simply because the people selling it had a better marketing strategy.

The first thing to recognize with this claim of market failure is that, even if lock-in and path dependency existed, they would still not create a monopoly as long as the widely-accepted standard was established based on voluntary trade. However, it has been shown that lock-in and path dependency are really just fantasies of the enemies of capitalism and are neither based on the economic facts, nor a logical analysis of the facts. For instance, with respect to the typewriter it is claimed that the allegedly inferior QWERTY keyboard (named for the letters on the top left-hand side of the keyboard) has maintained its popularity simply because it was the first one to be widely used and that an allegedly superior late comer, the Dvorak Simplified Keyboard (or DSK), has not been widely used because of the early success of the QWERTY keyboard. The DSK was said to be superior because the arrangement of the keys allegedly made it possible to type faster. The claim by supporters of the "network effect" market failure argument is that no one learns how to use the DSK because DSK's are hard to find, and DSK's are hard to find because no one learns how to use them. However, a detailed study of the history of the keyboard shows (1) that the QWERTY keyboard faced intense competition during the late-nineteenth century, when the battle occurred to establish the standard, and it emerged from that competition as one of the better keyboards, and (2) that the DSK offers no advantage over the QWERTY keyboard.[21]

The lock-in/path dependency story in VCR's falls victim to a similar fate. Here, Beta tapes, sold by Sony, lost the battle to gain popularity with consumers to RCA's VHS tapes. The claim of market failure is that Beta tapes had the superior picture quality, but VHS prevailed because of RCA's superior marketing and selling ability. The actual case of the matter is that Beta did offer some advantages in picture quality, but also possessed a crucial disadvantage in terms of playing time. During its product development, Sony thought that the size of the tape would be a key factor in appealing to consumers, so it proceeded to make Beta tapes small, about the size of a paperback book. RCA, on the other hand, thought playing time was crucial and proceeded to develop tapes that could record an entire feature length movie, and eventually an entire football game, and more. This turned out to be the deciding factor as to why VHS prevailed. Beta's small size allowed for less tape in the cassette and thus a shorter playing time. VHS, while larger in size, provided a picture quality and playing time combination that consumers preferred. Hence, in this market too, the better product won.[22]

Other lock-in/path dependency tales fall victim to a similar fate. Whether in operating systems (where IBM's DOS prevailed over Macintosh's graphical user interface), computer applications (such as in word processing and spreadsheets, where Microsoft's Word and Excel prevailed, respectively), and other markets, the superior products have prevailed because as long as competition is not legally restricted, such competition is always intense in markets for so-called network goods.[23]

In addition, there are incentives in place for, and methods that can be used by, manufacturers of new and better standards to overcome established, inferior standards. First, the greater the superiority of a product, the more profit there is to be earned by displacing the inferior product. Hence, the more it will pay the owner of the superior product to finance any initial investment required to unseat the inferior product. Some of the methods employed by manufacturers to establish new products include offering substantial discounts to early users or rebates to buyers who turn in equipment that employs the old standard. Also, to decrease the cost of switching, manufacturers of new products can offer free or low cost support products and services to help convert users to the new product. This has actually occurred in the past. For instance, producers of new types of computers have occasionally offered to convert files to new formats, cable-television companies offered hardware and services to adapt old televisions to the new standard for an interim period, competing typewriter manufacturers were an important source of trained typists during the early years of the industry, some UHF television stations once offered free UHF indoor antennas, and some electric utilities once supplied light bulbs.

Furthermore, in markets that are rapidly expanding, which is usually the case in the early stages of markets for so-called network goods, the number of users that may have initially committed to a given standard is typically small compared to the number of future users of the good. Hence, the fact that a new standard might be incompatible with the one initially accepted is irrelevant, since there are probably a large number of potential users who have not committed to any standard yet.[24]

Finally, many of the companies that do not have the dominant product in so-called network good markets are able to survive in niche markets. This is true of companies such as Apple Computers, which has a small share of the personal computer market, and Sony, whose Beta videotapes have survived in a niche market in broadcasting. This indicates that it does not take a large amount of market share to be profitable, even in so-called network good industries. If these companies truly had superior products, they could use their small market share as a base to build upon and become the dominant product.

Although switching costs do exist, they are simply a part of the competitive process with which firms must deal. They are facts of economic reality that are not to be bewailed simply because they are not in agreement with one's arbitrary desires. One cannot wish an aspect of the nature of reality out of existence. One can only accept it. The people who bemoan the nature of competition and wish for an alternative (whether "perfect competition," the absence of switching costs, or something else) are guilty of attempting to rewrite reality. They think that reality is deficient simply because it is not as they wish it to be. They think it is perfectly valid to pine for the elimination of something that cannot be erased (i.e., to wish for an "alternative" reality).[25]

As stated above, the barrier of switching costs does not create monopoly power because it is a part of the competitive process. However, if the government was to interfere to help a firm overcome switching costs, this would create monopoly power, even if the firm it was helping had a better product and would eventually dominate the market without the government's help. Help from the government would create a monopoly of the firm with the new product against existing firms. The government would either have to initiate physical force against taxpayers to force them to subsidize the firm with the new product or the government might somehow restrict the competitive ability of existing firms. While the existence of switching costs as such does not lead to inefficiency and the acceptance of inferior standards, government intervention to help firms overcome switching costs does. If firms are subsidized, it causes the firms to be more inefficient because they can rely on funds expropriated from taxpayers to cover their costs. Hence, they will less likely be concerned with keeping their costs down. In addition, help from the government for companies with inferior products will help those companies to achieve a greater market share than they otherwise would be able to. Also, when the government helps firms with superior products, this creates a monopoly by helping those firms to achieve a dominant position in a quicker fashion than they otherwise would be able to through the competitive process.

Even though it is possible for the government to help the potential winners in competition, it is more likely that it will help the losers. This is true because, first of all, the good products and the efficient producers do not need help from the government to succeed. Therefore, it is less likely that efficient producers and producers of superior products will run to the government for help. Further, the government does not act on the profit motive and therefore does not have the appropriate incentive to determine which products are the ones with the greatest potential to succeed. Typically, government officials assist constituents who can help the officials remain in power or the officials react to the loudest and most powerful pressure group, regardless of the merits of a product or the people producing it. Therefore, failure is the norm. This has been the actual case in a number of examples where governments in undeveloped countries have protected domestic industries with import restrictions and subsidies to foster the expansion of the domestic industries, only to end up with the growing burden of maintaining inefficient producers into the indefinite future. This has been the case even in Japan, where the once exalted Ministry of International Trade and Industry (MITI) has been wrong with many of the industries, companies, and technologies that it has—and has not—supported. MITI has been a net burden on the Japanese economy. The Japanese economy has succeeded *in spite of* the existence of MITI. Japan has succeeded because of the significant elements of capitalism it possesses.[26]

In closing on my discussion on network goods, I must emphasize that I am not implying that an inferior product could never succeed over a superior product in a free market. It is possible that, on a very rare occasion, an inferior product might gain a greater market share than a superior product. Perhaps the difference between the two products is not that great and the inferior product made it to the market first or was being marketed and sold by a superior marketing team and sales force. However, if the superiority of the one product is great enough and/or the cost of switching is low enough relative to its superiority, given enough time the superior product will prevail. One must remember, though, that a part of competition is competition to market and sell a product. Firms must deal with the fact that they not only have to produce a good product to get people to buy it, they have to be good at marketing and selling the product also. Marketing and selling a product take ability and are a part of the competitive process. The key point is that the better products will tend to prevail in a free market because a free market possesses the necessary prerequisites for their success (i.e., the protection of individual rights). Hence, the market succeeds with respect to "network goods."

Barriers to Entry: Conclusion

One principle that runs like a thread throughout this entire section, and which I have mentioned in previous sections, is the link between protecting individual rights and achieving greater economic efficiency and a higher standard of living. Likewise, the link between violating individual rights and causing economic inefficiency and a lower standard of living is also demonstrated. This occurs in every case about which I have written. As I have said, this link exists because the things that production depends upon, such as the price system and the profit motive, can only exist if individual rights are protected. This principle will be demonstrated again and again throughout the book.

The Nature of Competition

Elaboration on the nature of competition in a capitalist society will help one gain a better understanding of the material in this chapter. When firms make decisions, such as decisions regarding what price to charge or how much to produce, they must take into account both existing *and potential* competition. Either a firm sells a good at the price determined by competition, or its competitors or potential competitors sell the good at the price based on competition. Firms cannot arbitrarily raise the price of a good; i.e., they cannot raise the price of a good above the costs of production plus a going or average rate of profit that prevails in the economy without eventually losing business to existing producers or new entrants.

In particular, a firm is susceptible to competition from above and below; that is, from suppliers and customers. For instance, if a food manufacturer arbitrarily raises the price of its food products, it might face competition from large food retailers and wholesalers (i.e., its customers) because the price the food manufacturer charges represents a cost to the retailers and wholesalers and, thanks to the profit motive, these firms have a powerful incentive to do whatever they can to keep their costs low so they can earn a higher profit.[27] Furthermore, the food manufacturer might also face competition from farmers (i.e., its suppliers) if it arbitrarily raises its price. It might face such competition because the increased price of food decreases the demand for the products of farmers, so they will lose revenue and profits. Hence, the profit motive provides an incentive for food manufacturers to keep the price of their food products at a point where it earns them enough to remain in the business, but not so much that it encourages new entrants or that it loses business to existing competitors.

The key to keeping prices as low as possible, and providing the incentive for them to be driven continuously lower, is for the freedom of competition to prevail. This means there must be no government intervention in the economy preventing companies from entering and exiting industries as they determine it is in their self-interest to do so. In other words, there must be no political monopolies. This is the most important factor in competitive price determination.

Even in single-firm industries, in a capitalist society, prices are driven to the cost of producing a good plus a going or average rate of profit (or rate of return on capital invested) that prevails in the economy. This occurs because first, if high prices and profits prevail in this type of industry, there is an incentive to find substitutes for the good produced by this firm. This will put a check on the price a firm can charge if it does not want to open itself up to the threat of this type of competition. It must keep its prices low enough so the rate of profit that could be earned by those who might develop substitutes is no higher than what they could earn in other industries. This will provide producers no extra incentive to develop the substitutes.

Second, if prices and profits are high, this provides the only existing firm both the means and incentive to expand its productive capacity. With high profits, the firm has a greater incentive to invest more capital in its own industry rather than any other industry because, based on the nature of the case, the rate of profit is high in this industry relative to other industries. The high profits also provide the means to expand because they can be re-invested back into the business. As the firm expands its business, it increases the supply of the good it produces and causes the prices and profits it can earn to decline. The existing firm has the incentive to expand its industry until the rate of profit comes down to the rate of profit that prevails in general (i.e., the going or average rate of profit). At this point, there is no longer a strong incentive for the firm to expand its business.

If the sole firm in an industry does not continuously provide what customers in the market demand, or does not expand its business in response to high prices and profits, it will give an incentive to new entrants to enter the industry, expand the supply, and push down the prices and profits that can be earned in the industry. No matter what the reason, as long as new entrants believe they can earn an above average rate of profit, they will have a strong incentive to enter the industry. Only when the rate of profit that can be earned is the same as in other industries will there be no added incentive to enter the industry in question.

The principle I have been explaining for the last few paragraphs is the uniformity of profit principle. This principle says the rate of profit (= [profit/capital invested] x 100) in any one industry tends to head toward a uniform or average rate of profit for all industries.[28] This occurs because, other things equal, investors want to earn the highest rate of profit possible. Therefore, if the rate of profit is high in an industry, capital is invested in that industry, which raises the denominator in the above equation, increases the supply in the industry, and lowers the price and the rate of profit. Capital will stop flowing in once the rate of profit is sufficiently low enough that it no longer provides an incentive for investors to invest in the industry. If the rate of profit is low in an industry, capital will be withdrawn from the industry, which will cause the denominator to decrease, supply to decrease, and the price and rate of profit to rise. This occurs until the rate of profit is high enough so that it no longer provides justification to investors to withdraw their capital.

Under capitalism, with the complete freedom to compete, even the largest firms must continuously innovate, reduce their costs, and improve the quality of their products to maintain their dominant position. This is the case because their dominant position was achieved, and can only be maintained, through voluntary trade. Hence, they must continuously get customers to voluntarily buy their products. No company can rest on its laurels under capitalism, not even the biggest firms.

This last point has been proven again and again throughout the history of capitalism in America. For example, during the earlier part of the twentieth century, after the Ford Motor Company had become the dominant automobile manufacturer in America, Henry Ford made a number of bad business decisions (including refusing to recognize the need to develop car models in addition to the Model T). This allowed General Motors to takeover the dominant position. Even though Ford was the dominant manufacturer, he still had to innovate and improve his products to get customers to continuously purchase them.[29]

Further, U.S. car manufacturers were threatened, and a significant amount of their market share was taken away, by the smaller Japanese car manufacturers in the 1980s, despite significant protection given to the U.S. car makers in the form of tariffs and quotas on Japanese imports. Also, the rise of Wal-Mart to top Sears as the largest U.S. retailer is another example that shows that the large, established firms cannot rest on their laurels and must continuously innovate and provide what the market demands or face the threat of losing their dominant position.

The U.S. economy is intensely competitive and would be even more competitive if the government did not grant so much monopoly power to existing producers. A few statistics will help one see the competitive nature of our economy, despite the government intervention that exists. One can only imagine how much more competitive it would be, and how much higher our standard of living would be, if the intervention did not exist. First, of the largest one-hundred manufacturing firms in 1909, only thirty-six remained on the list in 1948. Of the fifty largest in 1947, only twenty-five remained in 1972 and five failed to make the top two hundred. Further, of the firms on the *Fortune* 500 list in 1980, only about half remained in 1990, just ten years later.[30] All this illustrates the competitive nature of a capitalist, or even semi-capitalist, economy.

Based on the acceptance of "perfect competition," monopoly power is believed to have a large influence in the economy.[31] This is the case because such "competition," as previously stated, exists nowhere in reality. Therefore, it is believed that virtually the entire economy is tainted with some aspect of "monopoly." Evidence of this belief is provided by surveys that show that people think firms have great power to raise their prices significantly above their costs. These surveys show that many people think that after-tax corporate profits typically constitute about 25 to 30 percent of sales revenue. However, actual after-tax profits are only about 4 to 5 percent of sales revenue.[32]

One economist, Arnold C. Harberger, even attempted to measure the losses (in terms of the well-being of consumers) in the U.S. economy due to alleged monopoly power. These losses are supposedly caused by the higher prices that "monopolies" are able to charge and the higher profits that they are able to earn. He used the costs of production plus a going or average rate of profit as the test. A rate of profit above the average was evidence of monopoly power. He found that losses were around 0.1 percent of Gross National Product (GNP). Subsequent findings raised this number slightly. They found that losses were between 0.5 and 2 percent of GNP, with estimates closer to the lower bound being more likely. What this says is that very few losses due to alleged monopoly power have been found to exist.[33]

Of course, if one uses the costs of production plus a going rate of profit to gauge whether monopoly power exists, one will not find much. That is because, due to the profit motive and the freedom of competition, prices are driven to costs plus a going rate of profit under capitalism as dictated by the uniformity of profit principle. If the rate of profit is high, capital flows into the industry, expanding supply relative to demand and driving down the prices and profits that can be earned in the industry. If the rate of profit is low, capital flows out of the industry, decreasing supply relative to demand and increasing the prices and profits that can be earned in the industry. This is how capitalism makes it possible for producers to concentrate on producing those goods that are demanded the most and avoid producing those goods that are demanded the least. Those industries in which goods are the most highly demanded are the ones with the high prices and profits. Those industries where goods are demanded the least are the ones with the lowest prices and profits. The high profits provide the greatest incentive to expand those industries where demand is the highest, while the low profits (or losses) provide the incentive to contract those industries where demand is the lowest. This flow of capital from low profit to high profit industries occurs in all industries, regardless of the number of firms in the industry, as long as the freedom of competition exists.

Finally, even the above numbers overestimate the losses due to "monopoly." The study does not take into account the high profits earned due to businesses producing higher quality goods, achieving extraordinarily low costs of production, or better anticipating shifts in customer demand. If these were subtracted out, for all practical purposes, losses in Harberger's test due to alleged monopoly would probably be non-existent or very close to it.[34]

Conclusion

As one can see, monopolies are not created by the free market. They are created only by government intervention into the free market; they are created when the government gives some firms special privileges over others. A capitalist economy is intensely competitive and is typically more so the larger in size and the smaller in number are the firms in an industry. Hence, the claim that some firms acquire monopoly power in the market is false. Far from being a critique of the market, such claims only show that some people have an improper understanding of competition and monopoly, and accept inappropriate standards of judgment, namely, egalitarianism and the altruist code of morality. The proper action to take is not to condemn the market on inappropriate grounds, but to reject the invalid concepts that underlie the condemnation. Once people do this they will see that markets succeed in leading to the greatest amount of competition that is possible and to the greatest innovation, lowest prices, highest quality, widest variety of goods, and the highest standard of living that are possible.

Notes

1. Evidence for the wide acceptance of this definition of monopoly is provided by the fact that virtually every economics "principles" textbook defines monopoly in this way or a similar way. For example, see David C. Colander, *Microeconomics*, 5th ed. (New York: McGraw-Hill/Irwin, 2004), 264.

2. An example of many smaller sellers holding a political monopoly against one large seller occurs in the retail merchandise business against Wal-Mart. Some city and county governments have passed laws to prevent Wal-Mart from entering their regions.

The laws set a maximum limit on the size of stores (in terms of the number of square feet). These size requirements are less than what Wal-Mart needs to be efficient. The laws initiate force against Wal-Mart because they forcibly prevent Wal-Mart from entering a market with a store size it thinks is adequate. Hence, its smaller, less efficient rivals are protected from competition by Wal-Mart. So the smaller stores have a portion of the market reserved for them and thus have a political monopoly against one large seller. This would be the case even if Wal-Mart decided to enter the market with a store below the maximum legal size limit. Here, first, of course, is the main point that force is still initiated against Wal-Mart to prevent it from building the larger store. Further, however, is the fact that because Wal-Mart cannot achieve the level of efficiency it could have achieved with the larger store, it will not be as effective at competing and thus the smaller stores will be able to retain a portion of their business that they would not have otherwise been able to keep had Wal-Mart been allowed to build the larger, more efficient store. Hence, the smaller stores still have a portion of the market reserved for them through the initiation of force.

An example of one large seller holding a political monopoly against a larger number of smaller sellers is the U.S. Post Office. It has a political monopoly in the delivery of first-class mail, since it is illegal for anyone else to deliver such mail. It is likely that if this monopoly power was abolished a larger number of smaller sellers (such as United Parcel Service, Federal Express, Airborne Inc., and perhaps others) would compete in the delivery of first-class mail.

3. A contemporary economist might argue that a product must also have no close substitutes for a firm to have a "monopoly" in the production of that good. In fact, economists sometimes define a monopoly as a single seller of a good, *with no close substitutes*, in a given geographic region. Based on this they might claim my criticism of the economic concept of monopoly is not valid because it does not take into account this added provision. However, adding the clause "with no close substitutes" to the definition of an economic monopoly does not fundamentally change matters. Even with the addition of this clause, the definition still requires the acceptance of the premise that a monopoly is determined based on whether a firm is a single supplier of a good. The additional clause merely adds a proviso to be used in determining whether a firm, in fact, is a single supplier of a good (or how close it comes to being the only seller of a good). In my argument against the economic concept of monopoly, I am not quibbling over what basis should be used to determine whether a firm is a single seller of a good. I am saying that whether or not a firm is a single seller of a good should not be used, *at all*, as the standard by which one determines whether the firm is a monopoly (regardless of how one might determine whether the firm is the only seller of the good).

4. For a more detailed explanation of what makes a concept valid or invalid, see the section titled "An Important Epistemological Discussion: The Nature of Concepts," in this chapter. Also, technically, the problem with the economic concept of monopoly is not that it is an invalid concept, but that the concept "monopoly" has been defined incorrectly. Specifically, the concept has been defined based on non-essential characteristics. In order for a concept to be defined properly, it must be defined based on the essential characteristics of the concept. Nonetheless, here I treat the economic concept of monopoly as an invalid concept because the error of defining a valid concept based on non-essential characteristics is similar to the error of forming an invalid concept. Defining a valid concept based on non-essential characteristics converts the concept into the epistemological equivalent of an invalid concept. For a detailed discussion on the proper method of defining concepts (and its epistemological importance), see Ayn Rand, *Introduction to Objectivist Epistemology*, 2nd ed. (New York: Meridian, 1990), 40-54

and Leonard Peikoff, *Objectivism: The Philosophy of Ayn Rand* (New York: Meridian, 1991), 96-105.

5. One might respond to this by saying it is not a specific numerical value that determines whether a firm is a monopoly, it is that a firm gains more monopoly power as its market share grows. However, this is still arbitrary because at what level of market share does a firm begin to gain monopoly power? At 50 percent? 25 percent? If at 25 percent, then why not 20 percent or even 10 percent? At what level of market share does competition begin to diminish and monopoly begin to increase?

6. This subjectivism can be seen very clearly in the Microsoft case, where U.S. District Court Judge Thomas Penfield Jackson ruled that Microsoft is a monopolist and ordered the breakup of Microsoft, while a Federal Appeals Court came to the opposite conclusion and reversed the breakup order. This subjectivism can also be seen in contemporary economists' assessment of Microsoft. For example, see S. Charles Maurice and Christopher R. Thomas, *Managerial Economics*, 7th ed. (New York: McGraw-Hill, 2002), 482. Contemporary economists cannot agree whether Microsoft is a monopoly or not because their conclusions are based on a subjective concept of monopoly.

7. More specifically, by objective I mean based on a logical analysis of the facts of reality one can determine who is and is not a monopolist.

8. My discussion of concepts is based on Ayn Rand's theory of concepts and is extremely brief. For a detailed discussion of this theory, see her *Introduction to Objectivist Epistemology*, 10-18, 49, and 62-74 and *Atlas Shrugged*, 35th anniversary ed. (New York: Signet, 1992), 934. Also see Peikoff, *Objectivism*, 73-91, 105-109, and 113-116.

9. I owe this example to Peikoff. See his *Objectivism*, 107.

10. I owe this example to Ayn Rand. See her *Introduction to Objectivist Epistemology*, 45.

11. For a typical presentation of these five characteristics, see Roger A. Arnold, *Economics*, 5th ed. (Cincinnati: South-Western College Publishing, 2001), 501.

12. My critique of perfect competition is based on F. A. Hayek, *Individualism and Economic Order* (Chicago: The University of Chicago Press, 1948), 92-106 and George Reisman, *Capitalism: A Treatise on Economics* (Ottawa, Ill.: Jameson Books, 1996), 430-432.

13. The term used by contemporary economists to describe situations where firms have small differences between them, and thus where some monopoly power is alleged to exist, is "monopolistic competition."

14. I owe this point to John Ridpath. See his, "The Philosophical Origins of Antitrust," in *Why Businessmen Need Philosophy*, ed. Richard E. Ralston (Irvine, Calif.: Ayn Rand Institute Press, 1999), 167-181, especially 178-179.

15. These enemies include virtually all contemporary, mainstream economists, the majority of whom accept the validity of perfect competition and believe in the mixed economy or welfare state, which stands in opposition to capitalism. Economists more sympathetic to capitalism, such as "Austrian" economists, tend to reject the validity of perfect competition.

16. There are some differences between protecting intellectual property rights and physical property rights that I will not discuss here. For instance, there are time limits on the existence, and therefore the protection, of some intellectual property rights (such as patents and copyrights), while there are none on physical property rights. For a discussion on why this is necessary, see Ayn Rand, *Capitalism: The Unknown Ideal* (New York: Signet, 1967), 130-134.

17. As one can see, the ultimate justification for protecting patents and so forth is that it is the moral thing to do (because it is consistent with the requirements of human life). The fact that protecting patents and so forth raises the standard of living is just one example of the idea that there is no break between the moral and the practical, or in this case between morality and economics. What is good morally leads to success in practice. Egoism is a valid code of morality (i.e., it is moral to be egoistic) and, because of this, when implemented in politics and economics it leads to a higher standard of living and a flourishing of human life (in other words, it leads to success in practice). Likewise, what is morally wrong leads to failure in practice. Altruism is immoral and that is why it leads to failure when put into practice. Not protecting patents and so forth is an example of putting the altruist code of morality into practice because those who have the ability to create something are sacrificed to those who do not. The failure that this leads to is that it prevents each individual from using his mind to further his own life and well-being. This, of course, decreases the productive capability of the economic system and therefore the standard of living. Another example that illustrates the link between the moral and the practical (or morality and economics), and that has been given in this book, is the moral nature of capitalism and the success it leads to in practice, and the immoral nature of socialism and the failure to which it leads in practice. More examples will be provided throughout the book. For a more detailed discussion of this issue see the "Epilogue."

18. Of course, it would create a political monopoly even if the government allowed more than one producer in a given geographic region to receive a franchise.

19. The post office and public schools do not have complete monopolies. Their monopoly power is limited to a certain extent by the existence of some competitors in these industries. However, competition is restricted in both industries and subsidies are also provided to the post office and public schools. This gives them both significant amounts of monopoly power. Also, there are more fundamental reasons, besides subsidies and a lack of competition, why the quality of education today is so abysmally poor. On this, see Leonard Peikoff, ed., *The Voice of Reason: Essays in Objectivist Thought* (New York: Meridian, 1989), 209-232.

20. For more on Alcoa, see David B. Kopel, *Antitrust After Microsoft: The Obsolescence of Antitrust in the Digital Era* (Chicago: The Heartland Institute, 2001), 118-121.

21. See the carefully researched book by Stan J. Liebowitz and Stephen E. Margolis titled *Winners, Losers, & Microsoft: Competition and Antitrust in High Technology* (Oakland: The Independent Institute, 1999), 11-14 and 19-46. This book dispels many of the fallacies put forward by the "lock-in" and "path dependency" mongers.

22. Liebowitz and Margolis, *Winners, Losers, & Microsoft*, 120-127.

23. On operating systems, see Liebowitz and Margolis, *Winners, Losers, & Microsoft*, 127-129. On word processing and spreadsheets, see Liebowitz and Margolis, *Winners, Losers, & Microsoft*, 163-200.

24. On the issues in this and the previous paragraph, see Liebowitz and Margolis, *Winners, Losers, & Microsoft*, 22 and 109-112.

25. For more on the fallacy of rewriting reality, see Ayn Rand, *Philosophy: Who Needs It* (New York: Signet, 1982), 30 and Peikoff, *Objectivism*, 26-30.

26. For examples of the failure of government supported industries and firms in undeveloped countries, see Heinz Kohler, *Economic Systems and Human Welfare: A Global Survey* (Cincinnati: South-Western College Publishing, 1997), 266 and 623. On the failure of MITI, see Kohler, *Economic Systems and Human Welfare*, 403-405 and Karl Zinsmeister, "MITI Mouse," *Policy Review*, no. 64 (Spring 1993): 28-35.

27. Exactly what I describe here already exists in the food manufacturing business. Many grocery stores compete in this business. Their "store brands" provide intense competition against the brand name food manufacturers.

28. For the equation in this sentence, the term capital invested refers to the monetary value of physical capital invested.

29. For more on Ford's bad business decisions, see Edwin A. Locke, *The Prime Movers: Traits of the Great Wealth Creators* (New York: AMACOM, 2000), 126-127, 149, and 192.

30. See James D. Gwartney and Richard L. Stroup, *Microeconomics: Private and Public Choice*, 8th ed. (Orlando: Harcourt Brace & Company, 1997), 282. The *Fortune* 500 is the 500 largest U.S. corporations based on annual revenue.

31. The terms used to describe this allegedly widespread monopoly power are "monopolistic competition" and "oligopoly."

32. Gwartney and Stroup, *Microeconomics*, 281.

33. See Arnold C. Harberger, "Monopoly and Resource Allocation," *American Economic Review* 44, no. 2 (May 1954): 771-787 for his findings. See F. M. Scherer, *Industrial Market Structure and Economic Performance*, 2nd ed. (Boston: Houghton Mifflin, 1980), 464 for a reference to the subsequent findings.

34. The only actual losses due to monopoly power are those created by businesses that have been given some amount of monopoly power in the political sense, which do not necessarily show up in Harberger's test. This is the case because monopoly power tends to lead to high costs and prices, not high profits.

Chapter Three

The Antitrust Laws and Predatory Pricing

Introduction

The antitrust laws are related to the issue of market failure because it is claimed that such laws are necessary to correct alleged market failure that exists. Specifically, it is claimed they are necessary in order to control the growing monopoly power that some firms allegedly gain. Economically, the desire for these laws is based on the invalid concept of economic monopoly. More fundamentally, the desire for these laws is based on the altruist code of morality, as well as on an equivocation between economic and political power. In this chapter, I will show that the antitrust laws, far from preventing monopolies, actually create them. In order to understand how, one must have a proper understanding of monopoly (i.e., one based on the political concept), which you, the reader, now have.

Predatory pricing is related to the antitrust laws. This topic is related to these laws because one of the antitrust laws focuses on outlawing this activity. It is believed that large firms routinely engage in predatory pricing. I will show that this is not true. I will show that such behavior on the part of large firms is irrational because it is unprofitable. In order to begin this discussion, I must first explain the meaning of the term "trust."

The Antitrust Laws

What Are Trusts?

Trusts were a method of legally combining or merging corporations in the late-nineteenth century. After the Civil War, corporate law had not provided a mechanism to allow one corporation to merge with another. The trust movement performed this function. To create a trust, the shares of two or more corporations were handed over to a third-party trustee. The trustee then ran and operated the multiple corporations as one. The trust movement allowed for substantial economies of scale to be achieved and thus helped to bring about higher productivity, a higher rate of economic progress, and lower prices in the late-nineteenth century than would have otherwise been achieved. The trust movement was made possible due to the radical reduction in transportation costs that occurred with the rise of the railroad. This allowed production to be concentrated in large factories and products to be distributed across wide areas at a relatively low cost. America experienced its most rapid rate of economic progress in the late-nineteenth century, largely due to the rise of the trust.

Why Did People Want the Antitrust Laws?

As one can see, a smaller number of larger firms would come into existence as firms merged with each other through the trusts. Many people advocated the antitrust laws based on a growing fear of "economic monopolies." As we now know, nothing is to be feared by a smaller number of larger firms, as long as the freedom of competition exists. Nevertheless, these fears played a significant role in the development of the antitrust laws. Much of this fear was based on an equivocation of economic and political power. I will discuss the nature of economic and political power in more detail below to help one gain a proper understanding of these two very different types of power.

In addition, some people, such as small businesses who competed with the larger trusts, wanted to gain monopoly power (in the political sense) through the antitrust laws by restricting their larger and more efficient rivals. Others wanted to tear down those who had succeeded and obtained great wealth through the trust movement. Here, one sees the altruist code of morality at work because this is a case of wanting to sacrifice those who have succeeded to those who have not. In addition, some politicians wanted to expand their political power and gain more control over people's lives. Others feared, amazing as it may seem, that the trust movement would end with one giant corporation owning all the productive assets in the country. In essence, they feared the existence of one giant economic monopoly.

This latter justification for the antitrust laws was based on a desire to prevent what some people thought was socialism from being established in America. One giant organization owning all the productive assets does have the superficial appearance of socialism and these people thought that socialism would be achieved in this way. However, this is not a form of socialism.

Even if one firm did end up owning all the productive assets—which most certainly would not occur—this would not constitute socialism if it were gained through voluntary trade. This firm would still face the threat of potential competition under capitalism and thus could only maintain its all-embracing dominant position if it continued to innovate, drive costs and prices down, and provide the goods that customers demanded. So there is nothing to fear under capitalism even in this bizarre case because actual socialism is not achieved through voluntary trade, but is achieved through the initiation of physical force to expropriate all property from individuals and place it in control of the government.

Under capitalism, one firm will not come to own all the productive assets. In a capitalist society, one sees firms "spinning off" (or divesting) unprofitable assets because they cannot run them efficiently. Further, one often sees firms laying off workers because they have grown too large and inefficient. As long as some people think they can do a better job producing a good on their own, one firm will not acquire all the productive assets. Quite often, top executives of one firm will leave their employer, start their own business, and compete with their old employer because they think they can do a better job and earn more money on their own. Only under socialism does one organization acquire all the productive assets. Under socialism, the government has a (political) monopoly in the provision of all goods.

Economic versus Political Power

One major source of the fear of large corporations comes from the equivocation of economic and political power. Therefore, special attention must be given to these types of power. The equivocation between these two types of power is what leads many people to believe there is a legitimate need to control economic power, through the antitrust laws, that large corporations acquire. In fact, it is this equivocation that leads people to believe that one giant firm owning all the assets in the economy is socialism. Nevertheless, these types of power are two very different types of power. Here I will show why economic power is not to be feared and therefore why no laws are necessary to control it. In fact, I will show that the economic power people gain is of benefit to everyone.

Economic power is derived through voluntary means: by producing and trading goods that other people value. Political power is obtained through the threat and use of force: by using compulsion and coercion against others. As stated by Ayn Rand, "economic power is exercised by means of a positive, by offering men a reward, an incentive, a payment, a value; political power is exercised by means of a negative, by the threat of punishment, injury, imprisonment, destruction. The businessman's tool is values; the bureaucrat's tool is fear."[1]

Economic power that a person gains is not a threat to anyone. The example of Bill Gates discussed in chapter 1 can help illustrate this point. For Bill Gates to gain greater economic power (i.e., acquire greater wealth and have more productive assets under his control) he must produce and offer something that others value because he must get others to voluntarily purchase what he has to sell. In a capitalist society, Bill Gates (or any one else) cannot hold a gun to people's heads and force them to buy his product. Therefore, when he gains greater economic power everyone involved in the trade benefits. He earns a larger income and his business expands; his customers obtain better computer software that improves their lives.

In fact, the more economically powerful one's trading partners are the better off one will be because this means one's trading partners have more to offer in trade. If one's trading partners are more economically powerful they will be able to produce more and better goods and will be able to do so more efficiently. Hence, everyone gains from a person's acquisition of economic power.[2]

As I stated in chapter 2, no matter how large a business is, it must produce goods that other people value in order to remain in business. If a large corporation produces worthless products that no one wants to buy, it will run itself out of business.[3] As stated by the philosopher Harry Binswanger, "A business can only make you an offer, thereby expanding the possibilities open to you. The alternative a business presents you with in a free market is: 'Increase your well-being by trading with us, or go your own way.' The alternative a government, or any force-user, presents you with is: 'Do as we order, or forfeit your liberty, property, or life.'"[4]

Based on this discussion, in a fundamental sense, it is impossible for a person to have too much economic power. More economic power simply means a greater supply of wealth and a higher standard of living. To believe a person can have too much economic power is to believe that one's standard of living can be too high. It is to believe that one can be too productive and thus too good at supporting his own life.

The same is not true with political power. Political power can be dangerous if it is allowed to go beyond its appropriate bounds. Political power can be a danger if, as shown in chapter 1, it is used to initiate physical force against individuals. This is why political power must be rigidly controlled. It must be controlled through a proper constitution that strictly limits the government's use of force so that force is used only in retaliation against those who initiate it; i.e., so that force is used only to protect individual rights and not violate them.

One might ask at this point, can't economic power be used to gain political power and, if so, can't economic power therefore become a threat to people? For instance, if a wealthy businessman uses his wealth to obtain special favors from the government, isn't economic power in this case a threat to people? The problem with this question is that, in asking it, the questioner equivocates between economic and political power. In a mixed economy, a man can use his wealth to "buy" favors from a politician or finance his own campaign, win an election, and use his newfound political power to initiate force against others. However, the power that is a threat here is the political power that has been allowed to go beyond its appropriate bounds. It is not the economic power that is a threat.

A government can use its power to seize wealth, provide special favors, restrict competition, send people to concentration camps, or for many other purposes that involve the initiation of force. However, when it does these things it is the government's *political power* that is a threat. It is not economic power—the power of production and trade—that is being used to attack people.

In a capitalist society, no matter how wealthy a person is, he cannot (legally) use his wealth to initiate force against others. Even if he uses his wealth to finance someone's election campaign, any political power gained is limited only to protecting individual rights. No amount of wealth can be used to buy political favors in a capitalist society because the government is not in the favor business. Its only "business" is to protect individual rights, which it does equally for everyone no matter what his economic status.

The solution to the problem created by the mixed economy is not to have the government intervene further to prevent the acquisition of economic power. This will only serve to extend the political power of the government farther beyond its appropriate bounds, which is a threat to everyone. The solution is to ensure that the government's power is limited to its proper function of protecting individual rights. Which means, the solution is to abandon the mixed economy and establish a capitalist society. If this is done, the political power will no longer be a threat to anyone.

If one does not understand the fundamental difference between political and economic power, one will believe that both can be threats to people if someone has too much of either type of power. By understanding the radically different nature of these two types of power one can see that economic power is not a threat to anyone (and, in fact, benefits everyone). One can also understand that there is no need to have laws, such as the antitrust laws, to control this type of power. The controls that are needed are those that protect people from the type of power that can be a threat to people: political power. In other words, the controls that are needed are those that limit the government to its appropriate function of protecting individual rights.

What Are the Antitrust Laws?

There are many specific laws that are subsumed under the antitrust laws and I will not present them all here. Further, I will not go into great detail to describe the ones I do present. I will only present enough for you to understand the nature of the antitrust laws.

The first antitrust law, passed in 1890, was the Sherman Act. This law has two provisions. The first provision says, in part, that "[e]very contract, combination in the form of a trust or otherwise, or conspiracy, in restraint of trade or commerce among the several States, or with foreign nations, is declared to be illegal." The second provision states, in part, that "[e]very person who shall monopolize, or attempt to monopolize, . . . any part of the trade or commerce among the several States, or with foreign nations, shall be deemed guilty of a felony. . . ."[5] In brief, this act says it is illegal to form a trust, to "restrain" trade, and to form a monopoly (based on the economic "concept").

The Clayton Act, passed in 1914, was the next antitrust law. This act outlaws a number of specific business practices that could allegedly lead to monopoly. These include (1) mergers where the effect is to substantially lessen competition or there is a tendency to create a monopoly, (2) the tying of contracts between a supplier and a buyer where the buyer is prevented from using the products of a competing supplier (An example of this would be if a person bought a car at a car dealership and as a part of the purchase contract the car dealership required that the individual get, and pay for separately, all service work performed at that dealership. Here, the service work would be tied to the purchase of the car.), and (3) interlocking directorates, which exist when the same person serves on the board of directors of competing firms (such as GM and Ford).

The Federal Trade Commission Act was also passed in 1914. This declares "unfair" methods of competition in commerce to be illegal. The last antitrust law I will discuss is the Robinson-Patman Act, passed in 1936. This law prohibits, among other things, price discrimination between buyers when it is not justified by cost differences, discounts by suppliers to customers unless they are offered to all customers, and so-called predatory pricing: the practice in which a large or dominant firm in an industry temporarily and arbitrarily reduces its price to damage or eliminate smaller and weaker rivals, so that it can raise its price above its costs at a later time. The activities prohibited by the Robinson-Patman Act can allegedly reduce competition.

The Nature of the Antitrust Laws

The first thing to notice about the antitrust laws is how subjective and arbitrary they are. For instance, the Sherman Act declares activities that "restrain" trade and attempt to "monopolize" trade illegal. The Clayton Act declares mergers that "substantially lessen" competition to be illegal. The FTC Act renders "unfair" methods of competition in commerce illegal. What constitutes an act that "restrains" or "monopolizes" trade? Likewise, when is competition "substantially lessened" and what methods of competition are "unfair"? Is it "unfair" when a company produces a superior product at a lower cost than its rivals? If it drives its rivals out of business as a result, is it guilty of "restraining" or "monopolizing" trade? Maybe it depends on the number of rivals it drives out of business? If so, how many must it drive out? Two? Three? All of them? Which mergers "substantially lessen" competition? Vastly different answers can be given to these questions, all of them seeming to be correct, because the antitrust laws are arbitrary and subjective, and therefore any claims made based on them will be arbitrary and subjective. This is exactly the manner in which the laws have been interpreted and applied throughout their history.[6]

How is a businessman supposed to know whether he is breaking the law with such subjective and vague laws? How is a businessman supposed to know whether he is engaging in an act of "unfair" competition before being accused of doing so or whether a merger will "substantially lessen" competition before he is informed that it has? Good law is objective, not subjective. With good law, one knows exactly what is and is not allowed by the law prior to being accused of violating it. For instance, with laws pertaining to murder, one knows exactly what is and is not allowed by the law and knows, before having violated it, exactly what one would have to do to be in violation of the law. This is not the case with the antitrust laws.[7]

The antitrust laws have helped to paralyze American businesses precisely because of their subjective nature. Businessmen must be (and have been) reluctant to take certain actions in running their businesses for fear of having their actions declared illegal after they have engaged in them. This makes U.S. businesses less productive and less competitive in world markets than they otherwise could be.

Further, notice how the antitrust laws prohibit activities that are a part of actual competition. They prohibit activities that are a part of businesses competing to produce and sell a good or service in the context of voluntary trade. For instance, they prohibit price discrimination even though charging different individuals different prices is a part of attempting to get individuals to voluntarily buy one's product. Also, they prohibit the tying of contracts, interlocking directorates, discounts to customers, and many mergers. All of these activities are a part of voluntary trade and are therefore a part of the continuous process of economic competition. None of these activities involve the use of force and therefore none of them fall outside the scope of economic competition.

Take the case of a company tying contracts. This was one of the accusations made against Microsoft. Microsoft required computer manufacturers, as a condition for receiving a license to install Microsoft Windows on their products, not to remove Microsoft's internet browser and not to allow a more prominent display of a rival browser (Netscape). This was a case of Microsoft tying the display of its browser and the display of Netscape's browser in with the purchase of a license to use Windows. The claim by antitrust supporters was that the antitrust laws had to be used to prevent Microsoft from using its dominance in the market for PC operating systems to gain a dominant position in the internet browser market. If Microsoft were allowed to do so, it would allegedly decrease competition and create a "monopoly" for Microsoft.

What supporters of the antitrust laws fail to recognize is that the actions of Microsoft are fully consistent with voluntary trade and competition among businesses. In order to have voluntary trade *both* sides must agree to the trade. This is required no matter how large and economically powerful one party to the trade is relative to the other. The economically powerful party must voluntarily agree to the trade just as the economically weak party must voluntarily agree. The weak party has no right to get the government to intervene on its behalf and force the powerful party to engage in the trade. The weak party has no right to get the government to force the powerful party to "agree" to terms of the trade that the powerful party considers unacceptable. If the weak party does this, it is guilty of initiating physical force against the powerful party. Here, the weak party is guilty of gaining monopoly power (in the proper sense of that term; i.e., in the political sense).

Microsoft may have a dominant position in PC operating systems, but it is a position it has gained and maintained through voluntary trade; it has not achieved its position with the aid of any government protection. Further, when Microsoft places requirements on computer manufacturers as a part of the conditions of the sale of a Microsoft product, this is also a part of voluntary trade. Potential buyers of Microsoft's products are not forced to buy its products. They can always refuse to do so. This applies no matter how "unfair" buyers feel the terms of sale are for purchasing a Microsoft product.

One must always keep in mind that Windows is Microsoft's property and no one has the right to dictate its terms of sale except Microsoft. Therefore, no matter how dominant Microsoft (or any other company) becomes, in order for voluntary trade to exist—in order for individual rights to be protected—Microsoft must be able to determine the terms of trade of its products. Gaining a dominant position and being able to set favorable terms of trade for one's products are a part of voluntary trade and competition.[8]

Microsoft has been extremely innovative and has earned its dominant position. For instance, it was the first to develop a commercially viable graphical operating system for IBM based PC's. It integrated its products together (such as Windows and Internet Explorer), making computer technology easier to use. It continuously innovated and drove the prices of its products down (even giving away Internet Explorer for free), thus making it necessary for its competitors to do the same.

One must remember that winning is a part of competition and some companies will grow larger than others by successfully competing. Competition does not suddenly disappear after a company gains a dominant position. Such a dominant position is achieved through intense competition and, to emphasize what I stated in the previous chapter, industries with a small number of large firms are among the most intensely competitive. If a firm wants to be competitive in such an industry, it must achieve the low costs of production that existing firms have achieved through economies of scale, and it must also be able to match the existing firms' high quality.[9]

Further, one must remember that in a free market, where the complete freedom of competition exists, a firm can maintain its dominant position only by getting people to repeatedly buy its products. Therefore, such a firm must constantly innovate to maintain its dominant position (i.e., it must compete successfully over and over again). If it does not continuously provide what individuals in the market demand, it will lose its dominant position. This has been shown again and again throughout the history of capitalism in America.[10]

Economically and morally, Microsoft (and every company) is justified in charging whatever price it thinks its customers will pay. Economically, everyone is a winner when individual rights are protected and voluntary trade exists. As firms compete with each other in this context, efficiencies are gained, new products are developed, the supply of wealth is increased, and the standard of living is raised. Morally, the owners of Microsoft have a right to their own lives and property and should use both to pursue their own rational self-interest.

The desire by people to attack Microsoft with the antitrust laws is ultimately based on a desire to cut it down because it has been innovative and successful. It is a motivation based thoroughly on the corrupt altruist code of morality. It is based on a desire to sacrifice those who are successful in production to those who are incompetent and unsuccessful (or less successful).[11]

Microsoft is not the only innovative and successful company to be attacked with the antitrust laws. Throughout their history, the antitrust laws have been used to attack innovative and successful companies—from Standard Oil in 1911 to Alcoa in 1945 to IBM in the 1970s, and many more. The three companies mentioned were major innovators in oil products, aluminum, and computers, respectively. Just to name a few of their achievements, from 1870 to 1897 Standard Oil drove the price of kerosene down from 30 cents to 6 cents. From 1880 to 1890, it helped drive petroleum prices down by 61 percent. It also developed three hundred different byproducts from oil and was far more efficient than its competitors. Alcoa drove the price of aluminum ingots down from $5 per pound to 22 cents per pound between 1887 and 1937. IBM introduced many improvements to its computers. It was probably the most innovative firm in the United States at the time the Department of Justice brought an antitrust suit against it. These companies were attacked because they rose too high, made too much money, and were too good at competing.[12] The economic results of sacrificing the most productive individuals and companies should be obvious. It will lead to a lower productive capability and standard of living.[13]

Economically, the antitrust laws are based on the invalid concept of economic monopoly. They are based on the belief that the fewer the firms in an industry, the more monopoly power the firms possess. This is not true. As was shown in chapter 2, the existence of monopoly means that competition has been restricted in some way. However, firms gaining a dominant position through voluntary trade is a part of the competitive process. The only way for competition to be restricted is when the government (or someone sanctioned by the government) inhibits or prevents it. Only in this way can monopoly power be created.

Far from decreasing the monopoly power that firms possess, *the antitrust laws actually create monopoly power*. They do so because the government initiates force to keep those individuals who have the talent and ability to enter and/or dominate an industry from doing so. The antitrust laws give monopoly power to those firms who are protected from companies that would have entered and/or dominated an industry. The laws make competition less intense by preventing firms who are attacked with them from competing (or by preventing these firms from competing more effectively). Those firms protected by the antitrust laws are able to obtain a larger share of the market in a particular industry than they otherwise would have been able to had they not been protected.

One can see explicitly that the antitrust laws create monopoly power, and thus make competition less intense, in the fact that twenty out of twenty-one antitrust cases are brought forward by private parties.[14] Companies bring these cases forward to restrict the competitive ability of their superior rivals. The Microsoft case provides an excellent example of this. Here, Netscape, Sun Microsystems, and America OnLine (competitors of Microsoft in internet browsers, PC operating systems, and online services, respectively) were among the most vehement in claiming that Microsoft was harming consumers with its "monopoly power" and that the government must use the antitrust laws to do something about it. This is a clear case of companies running to the government for protection from competition in a free market.

The antitrust laws should be abolished because they violate individual rights and are economically destructive. The laws are economically destructive because they reduce competition, economic efficiency, the ability to produce wealth, and the standard of living. Further, even though it is thought by many that the antitrust laws protect people by preventing economic power from becoming too concentrated; ironically, the laws represent an actual threat to people because they are an example of political power going beyond its appropriate bounds. The laws are an example of political power being used to initiate physical force against individuals. Here, one sees, again, the link between violating individual rights and harming the economic system, as well as its obverse. This link, as a general principle, always exists. Violating individual rights, in general, creates economic inefficiency and a lower standard of living.[15] The antitrust laws are no exception.

Predatory Pricing

As stated above, one of the antitrust laws (the Robinson-Patman Act) places special attention on predatory pricing. The claim here is that a larger, dominant firm can temporarily reduce its price below its costs to damage a smaller and weaker competitor or drive it out of business. The larger firm can then raise its price later, when there are no other firms left in the industry, and earn higher profits. The belief is that because of the large firm's size it can sustain a temporary loss in an easier fashion than a small firm, wait for the small firm to go out of business, and then raise its price. The alleged problem with predatory pricing is that large firms are able to obtain monopoly power through the use of such pricing policies. What I will show is that such pricing schemes rarely exist under capitalism and even when they do they do not create monopoly power.

Why Firms Do Not Use Predatory Pricing

The first thing to recognize is that more than one firm in an industry is the norm in cases where it is alleged that large firms engage in predatory pricing. For instance, in the hardware supply business it is claimed that large firms, such as Home Depot, have arbitrarily lowered their prices to drive out small hardware stores. However, there are many firms competing with each other (including both large and small alike) in the hardware business. The same is true of other industries, such as the pet supply business (where it is claimed that large stores, such as Petco, pursue policies of predatory pricing), video rental stores (where Blockbuster is claimed to pursue such a policy), and discount department stores (where Wal-Mart is the alleged culprit). If the claims concerning predatory pricing were true, one would expect to see only one or a few large firms left in each of these industries and in any industry where such a policy was practiced. One does not see this because such pricing strategies are typically not used.

Big chain stores do not *arbitrarily* lower their prices (i.e., lower their prices below their costs of production) to take business away from small, independent rivals. *Big chain stores charge lower prices based on lower costs of production* (and they often provide better service also). The economic history of big chain stores driving small rivals out of business has lead to *permanently* lower prices for customers, not higher prices.[16] This has occurred precisely because the lower prices charged by large businesses were not arbitrarily low, but were based on lower costs of production that they achieved. Low costs allowed them to charge low prices and still earn an acceptable rate of return.

If large firms were driving out small rivals through predatory pricing one would expect to see prices fall only temporarily and in the long run be raised to higher levels. Since this has not yet occurred, if the claims concerning predatory pricing are true, when will it happen? Are large firms keeping their prices "temporarily" low for decades? The fact is prices will not be raised because the claims concerning predatory pricing are false.

It does not pay large firms to temporarily lower their prices below their costs to drive small firms out of business because the large firms stand to lose much more money than they can gain. Even if a large firm incurs losses for only a short period of time, and then can gain the profits of the small firm indefinitely, it still will not pay the large firm to engage in predatory pricing against the small firm.

For example, suppose a small firm earns $500,000 in annual revenue, has $450,000 in costs, and thus $50,000 in annual profits. Further, suppose a large firm that competes with it has $10 million in annual revenue, $9 million in costs, and thus $1 million in annual profits. If the large firm was to lower its price to its costs of production, and thus the small firm was forced to follow suit or lose a substantial amount of business, the large firm would reduce its annual profits by $1 million while the small firm would reduce its profits by only $50,000.

If one makes the further assumption that each firm has costs of 90 cents per unit and initially charges a price of $1 per unit, one can show that if the large firm lowers its price below its costs it will have to take a bigger loss than the small firm because the large firm sells a larger volume of the good. For instance, if the large firm sells at a price of 80 cents and its annual revenue falls to $8 million, it now incurs an annual loss of $1 million.[17] If the small firm matches the large firm's price, it would have annual revenues of $400,000 and losses of only $50,000. What one can see here is that it simply does not pay the large firm to incur large losses to obtain a small gain when it drives the small firm out of business. It does not pay, for instance, to incur a $1 million loss to make the $50,000 in profits that the small firm previously earned. It simply does not pay to spend a lot of money to make a little. This is a sure way to lose money and harm oneself financially.

To continue the example, imagine it only takes a year for the large firm to drive the small firm out of business and therefore the large firm gives up $2 million (the $1 million it was earning in profits plus the $1 million loss it incurs as the result of selling below cost). In this case, it does not pay for the large firm to lower its price below its cost, even if it could earn the small firm's profits into the indefinite future, if the going rate of profit is above 2.5 percent. This is so because, based on present value analysis, the $50,000 annual profits are worth less than $2 million when the desired rate of profit is greater than 2.5 percent.[18] Hence, if the desired (or going) rate of profit was above 2.5 percent, it simply would not pay the large firm to drive the small firm out of business because it would be earning an inadequate rate of return on its investment. If it took longer than a year to drive the small firm out of business the money given up by the large firm would be even greater, and therefore the investment would earn an even lower rate of return.

Based on the above example, one can see that even though the large firm may have a larger amount of funds available to it, the total of these funds is simply not available to sustain the losses it will incur when it tries to drive a small competitor out of business. No matter how large a firm and no matter how large the quantity of funds it has available to sustain losses, it simply does not pay for a firm to spend a lot of money to make a little (even if it receives that small amount in perpetuity). The great bulk of the large firm's money simply is not available to use to drive out small firms. If the large firm uses its funds in this way, it will lose money and become small very fast.

In the above example, if the going rate of profit is 10 percent, anyone with $500,000 to spend could attempt to run the small firm out of business. This is the most anyone who wants to earn a 10 percent rate of return would be willing to spend to get $50,000 per annum in perpetuity. This applies no matter how much wealth one possesses. Any party that has the $500,000 to spend could play the predatory pricing game. If businesses actually played such games, once a business enters the game it opens itself up to similar predatory attacks. This is the case because if a business spends $250,000 in its attempt to drive the small firm out and earn the small firm's profits, now it has only $250,000 left to complete the task. However, new "predators" have the entire $500,000 available to spend to wrest control of the $50,000 in annual profits. If it spends more than $500,000 total to gain the prize, the rate of profit falls below the going or desired rate. If firms actually behaved this way there would be an endless parade of predatory attacks, with each newcomer ready to spend a fresh $500,000 to gain control of the annual prize. We do not see this behavior because it is not rational (i.e., profitable) to engage in policies of predatory pricing.

Even if the large firm had lower costs of production than the small firm in the above example (say 80 cents per unit instead of the 90 cents that was assumed), it would still not pay the large firm to lower its price to drive the small firm out and gain the small firm's business. This is the case because if the large firm lowered its price to 80 cents, as in the example above, even though here it would not be incurring a loss it would still be giving up $2 million in annual profits that it could have made if it kept its price at $1. In this case, the additional profits the large firm could earn on the small firm's volume would be $100,000, instead of $50,000, by virtue of the fact that it has lower costs than the small firm. Nevertheless, if a 10 percent rate of return was the desired rate, it still would not pay to give up $2 million to earn even a $100,000 annual perpetuity because the rate of profit achieved would only be 5 percent.[19]

Even though it would not pay the large firm to lower its price to drive the small firm out of business, the large firm does have an incentive to lower its price to keep out potential entrants and, possibly, earn higher profits. If the large firm lowers its price to, say, 90 cents (with the 80 cents per unit cost), this will provide much less incentive for other firms to enter the industry. Also, if the firm can increase its sales volume by a large enough amount it can make larger profits at the lower price. As a consequence, the small firm may be driven out of business since it will earn no profit at the lower price. However, this is not a case of predatory pricing—it is not a case of lowering one's price below one's cost *temporarily* to drive a small rival out of business—it is a case of achieving *permanently* lower prices based on lower costs of production.

If the large firm tried to raise its price above the $1 original price once the small competitor was out of business, it still would not pay to drive the small firm out of business. If it did this, it would quickly provide an incentive for new competitors to enter the industry. This would be easy for someone to do because of the leftover plant and equipment of the small firm. Even if the large firm acquired these assets, which would be an added expense and would make the venture even less attractive financially, it still would not be able to raise the price of its product above the point where it would be profitable for potential competitors to build new plant and equipment. If one thinks that the large firm could immediately lower its price as soon as there was the threat of a competitor entering the field, and could do so every time there was such a threat, customers of the large firm could take advantage of this behavior by repeatedly threatening to enter the field to get the large firm to keep its price low.[20] More than likely, however, if the large firm behaved in this manner it never would have become large in the first place. Such bizarre behavior is indicative of a lack of rationality that would prevent it from succeeding and becoming a significant competitor.

When firms price below cost they are typically not doing so to drive small firms out of business. Such a pricing strategy is usually a marketing expense and is often engaged in by firms when they are initially entering a market. They do so to induce people to try their product so they can quickly gain market share. Eventually, of course, the firms will have to increase their prices so they do not continuously incur losses. If firms did not spend money to market their products in this way, they would spend money in other ways (such as on advertising or free samples) to market their products.

The actual case of predatory pricing is the exact opposite of what its adherents think. It is the small firms, not the large firms, that have an incentive to engage in predatory pricing. Small firms have the incentive because they stand to make huge gains in market share if they can drive their larger competitors out of business. Even if they cannot do this, if they can take away just a small fraction of their larger competitor's market share it could be a big gain in revenue and profits to the small firm. For example, if a firm that has only a 5 percent market share can take just 5 percent away from its much larger rival that has a 95 percent share, the small firm can double its market share and, potentially, its profits. Hence, it turns out that predatory pricing, far from driving small companies out of business, if it played any role in the economy at all, would work to make small companies larger until they became so large that it would no longer be worth it to them to engage in such a policy. Therefore, if anything, predatory pricing is a tool that would be used *by* small companies, not against them.[21]

Why Predatory Pricing Would Typically Fail Even If Firms Used It

The above shows that it is unprofitable for large firms to drive small rivals out of business using a predatory pricing policy. However, even if large firms were irrational enough to attempt to drive small rivals out of business through a policy of predatory pricing, they would typically fail at the attempt.[22] There are several reasons why this is so.

First, customers could simply refuse to give all their business to the large firm. This would prevent the large firm's predatory pricing policy from being successful and insure that it is not the only firm in the industry. Second, customers could engage in long-term contracts (with the big and/or small firms) to ensure a stable price of the good.[23] Third, customers of the large firm could use a part of their savings from the artificially low price, established by the large firm, to subsidize the small firm that is being attacked by the predatory pricing policy. This would keep the small firm in business and force the large firm to maintain its low (predatory) prices. This would cause the large firm to lose more money while its customers would continue to enjoy lower prices.[24]

Fourth, the large firm might have to be willing to incur losses on a larger volume of goods sold. This is the case because the lower the price it charges, the higher the quantity demanded will be. Hence, in the first example given above in which the large firm lowers its price from $1 to 80 cents, the large firm might incur a loss of more than $1 million. This would occur if the large firm incurred an additional cost of more than 80 cents per unit to produce the additional units sold at the lower price.[25] This would make the predatory pricing venture even more unprofitable than I have shown it to be above.

The large firm's efforts to drive the small firm out of business would be further frustrated if the large firm increased the quantity demanded of its own product so much, due to the predatory pricing policy, that it could not meet the demand from its regular customers. If the regular customers had to go to the small firm to purchase the good, the demand the small firm experienced and the price it received might actually *increase*. To prevent this from happening, the large firm must keep enough excess capacity on hand to be able to meet the increase in the quantity demanded that results from its predatory pricing strategy. This makes the predatory pricing venture even more unprofitable.

Fifth, suppliers to the industry in which prices are artificially low due to the predatory pricing policy, and producers of goods complementary to the good whose price is artificially low, have an incentive to keep the small firm in business. The suppliers to the industry have an incentive to keep the small firm in business because the artificially low price for their customers' products increases the quantity demanded for those products and thus increases the demand for the inputs needed to produce those products. However, the suppliers have not lowered the prices on the goods they sell. Hence, they enjoy a greater sales volume and higher profits as long as the artificially low price is maintained on their customers' products. So the suppliers have an incentive to keep the small firm in business as long as possible and would be in a position to do so by subsidizing the small firm with a portion of the additional profits they earn.

Likewise, producers of complementary goods (goods consumed in conjunction with one another, such as automobiles and gasoline or tea and lemon) have the same incentive because when the price of a good falls, the demand for goods that are complementary to it rises. Hence, producers of complementary goods will also experience greater sales volume at an unchanged price and thus an increase in profits. They, too, could subsidize the small firm with a portion of the additional profits they earn.[26]

Finally, if a large firm wants to drive a small firm out of business quickly, it must charge a price low enough so that the small firm cannot cover its variable (or operating) costs. If the price is high enough that the small firm can cover its variable costs (such as labor, materials, and fuel costs), the small firm has an incentive to stay in business until its plant and equipment (which are fixed costs) are used up.[27] Charging a price low enough so that the small firm cannot cover its variable costs means the large firm will have to sustain greater losses over any given period of time in order to drive the small firm out of business quickly. Otherwise, the large firm will have to sustain losses over a much more protracted period of time until the plant and equipment of the small firm are used up. Charging a price below the small firm's variable costs also exacerbates the problem of excess capacity mentioned above.[28]

If it seems I am belaboring the point that predatory pricing is not profitable to engage in and, in general, could not be used successfully to drive small firms out of business even if one attempted to use it, it should seem that way because that is exactly what I am doing. This is what one must do because supporters of the doctrine come up with a litany of bizarre cases that allegedly show how predatory pricing could be used as a successful competitive strategy. I pretend their arguments are not rationalizations based on their underlying hatred of capitalism, and their jealousy of those who succeed under capitalism, but are made in a honest attempt to understand how competition takes place in a capitalist society.[29] Doing this enables me to thoroughly refute the predatory pricing argument by showing that it agrees neither with the facts of reality nor a logical analysis of the facts. It is not how competition takes place because those who might actually attempt to engage in a policy of predatory pricing would not remain competitive for very long.

Conclusion to Predatory Pricing

Predatory pricing should be legal. It is an activity fully consistent with the protection of individual rights and voluntary trade. It would not create a monopoly for a firm (even if it did work) because it does not involve the use of force to gain access to a portion of a market, and it is a competitive strategy that firms can choose to pursue. However, even though in a free market it would be legal, no rational firms will use a policy of predatory pricing because they would only succeed in driving themselves out of business.

Conclusion to the Chapter

As one can see, neither the antitrust laws nor predatory pricing provides an indictment of the market. The only failure for which they provide evidence is the failure of people who believe in them to comprehend the nature of reality.

People's desire for the antitrust laws is based on an equivocation of economic and political power. Their desire is also based on an acceptance of an erroneous view of monopoly. These views lead people to call for inappropriate responses from the government to correct the problems that people think exist.

As I showed in chapter 2, the acceptance of the invalid economic concept of monopoly is based on the acceptance of an invalid theory of competition (i.e., perfect competition). Going deeper than economics, and as was also shown in chapter 2, people's acceptance of perfect competition and economic monopoly is based on their acceptance of egalitarianism and the altruist code of morality. In the antitrust laws we see the vicious nature of egalitarianism because, through these laws, egalitarians lash out at those who have succeeded and attempt to cut them down to the level of their inferior competitors. The acceptance of altruism leads people to a hatred of anyone that has succeeded and a desire to cut them down because success is incompatible with the altruist code of morality.[30]

With respect to predatory pricing, enemies of the market do not understand that it is unprofitable and irrational, and would be virtually impossible for any firm to practice. As in the case of the antitrust laws, the claims concerning predatory pricing are based on a hatred of anyone who has succeeded in business. These claims, too, are based on a moral disdain for the free market, which comes from one's acceptance of the altruist code of morality.

It would be an intellectual failure for any rational person to accept as valid the antitrust laws, the predatory pricing doctrine, and the destructive ideas on which they are based. In order to succeed (both intellectually and economically), one must reject these laws and ideas. One must embrace the free market, as well as the individualism and egoism on which it is based. These fundamental economic, political, and moral ideas are consistent with the requirements of human life. They help one understand that each individual has a right to his own life and that no one should be sacrificed to the needs or whims of others. They help one understand that competition consists of individuals vying to outdo each other in the production and exchange of wealth and that individual differences are a part of competition. They lead one to admire success, not despise it. They lead one to realize that only the government's use of the initiation of physical force can create monopolies and bring on all the destructive economic consequences that flow from them. They help one understand that a free market leads to the maximum amount of competition that is possible by allowing humans to be free to use their minds to think and produce, and that that is why a free market leads to the greatest rate of economic progress and highest standard of living that are possible. They help one realize that capitalism is the only social system that allows human life to flourish and that that is precisely why it succeeds.

Notes

1. Ayn Rand, *Capitalism: The Unknown Ideal* (New York: Signet, 1967), 48.

2. To better understand why an individual's acquisition of more economic power benefits everyone, see the discussion on why even the "losers" in competition benefit from competition in the section titled "The Morality of Rational Self-Interest and Capitalism" in chapter 1.

3. See the section titled "The Nature of Competition" in chapter 2.

4. Harry Binswanger, "The Dollar and the Gun," in *Why Businessmen Need Philosophy*, ed. Richard E. Ralston (Irvine, Calif.: Ayn Rand Institute Press, 1999), 153-165, especially 156-157. Dr. Binswanger's essay provides a detailed and excellent discussion on the difference between economic and political power.

5. These provisions are quoted from John D. Blackburn, Elliot I. Klayman, and Martin H. Malin, *The Legal Environment of Business*, 4th ed. (Homewood, IL: Irwin, 1991), 716.

6. I refer again to the contradictory rulings made by judges and the contradictory conclusions reached by economists in the Microsoft case as excellent examples of the arbitrary nature of the antitrust laws. See the section in chapter 2 titled "Economic versus Political Monopoly" for more on this.

7. For more on the vague nature of the antitrust laws, see Alan Greenspan, "Antitrust," in *Capitalism*, Rand, 63-71, especially 63.

8. As long as Microsoft, or any company, does not threaten people with physical harm, death, or destruction of their property (or actually commit such acts), it is engaging in voluntary trade and is acting within the sphere of its rights. In other words, as long as it does not initiate physical force in any way it is acting within the sphere of its rights. Imposing terms of trade that others dislike or consider unfair does not constitute an instance of the initiation of force and thus does not violate individual rights.

9. For more on this, see the sections in chapter 2 titled "Perfect Competition" and "Economies of Scale."

10. See the section in chapter 2 titled "The Nature of Competition" for more on this.

11. On the innovativeness of Microsoft, see Stan J. Liebowitz and Stephen E. Margolis, *Winners, Losers, & Microsoft: Competition and Antitrust in High Technology*, (Oakland, CA: The Independent Institute, 1999), 135-200. In addition, I recognize that not all people who believe in the validity of the antitrust laws want to sacrifice the successful to the unsuccessful. Some might genuinely, but mistakenly, believe that these laws actually make competition more intense because they believe in the validity of perfect competition and economic monopoly. Nevertheless, the altruist code of ethics does provide the moral base for the antitrust laws (just as it provides the moral base for perfect competition and economic monopoly). The causal link between altruism and the antitrust laws exists regardless of how many people recognize it because this link is based on the nature of the antitrust laws and the nature of altruism, not on whether people explicitly recognize that this link exists.

12. On the innovativeness of these companies, see David B. Kopel, *Antitrust After Microsoft: The Obsolescence of Antitrust in the Digital Era* (Chicago: The Heartland Institute, 2001), 8, 99, and 114-121.

13. This illustrates, once again, the link between sound moral theory and beneficial economic results on the one hand, and bad moral theory and harmful economic results on

the other. For more on this, see the "Epilogue" and the section titled "Patents, Copyrights, and Trademarks" in chapter 2.

14. James D. Gwartney and Richard L. Stroup, *Microeconomics: Private and Public Choice*, 8th ed. (Orlando, FL: Harcourt Brace & Company, 1997), 297.

15. If not a lower standard of living in absolute terms, then at least a lower standard of living relative to what it would have been had the laws not existed.

16. Of course, when I say lower prices I mean in real terms. That is, in prices adjusted for the general price rise that has occurred in our economy due to the increase in the supply of money and volume of spending. The best way to see that prices have fallen dramatically in real terms is to calculate how much time the average person must work now to buy a specific good and compare it to how much time the average person had to work in the past (say fifty or one-hundred years ago) to buy that same good. The time required has dramatically fallen for virtually all goods.

17. For the sake of simplicity, I assume both firms sell the same amount of the good at the lower price as at the higher price.

18. According to present value analysis, the value of a $50,000 annual perpetuity when the desired rate of profit is 2.5 percent is $50,000/0.025 or $2 million. In other words, $2 million is the most one would be willing to pay now for $50,000 per annum in perpetuity if he wanted to earn at least a 2.5 percent rate of return. If any higher rate of return is desired, one must pay less than $2 million for the annual perpetuity.

19. The profits would by $100,000 instead of $50,000 because the large firm's costs are 80 cents per unit instead of 90 cents per unit. If the small firm sells 500,000 units (calculated by dividing the original $500,000 revenue by the original $1 price per unit), the total costs to the large firm for selling those units is $400,000, instead of $450,000 for the small firm. When the $400,000 cost is subtracted from the $500,000 revenue, the result is $100,000 in profits.

20. Investors could take further advantage of the large firm's behavior if the large firm's stock trades on a stock exchange. Here, investors could sell the stock short and threaten to enter the large firm's industry. This activity would make large sums of money because threatening to enter the industry would cause the large firm to lower its price, which would lower its profits and stock price.

21. Of course, we do not see small companies using it either. This is because the doctrine really has nothing to do with how competition typically takes place under capitalism. Competition occurs in the form of businesses creating new products, improving old ones, providing better service to customers, and driving costs down by creating new methods of production and improving upon old ones. This is exactly how capitalism, throughout its brief history, has lead to a higher quality and wider variety of goods at continuously lower prices (in real terms) and thus a higher standard of living.

22. A firm might be able to get away with it in an isolated case, but failure would be the norm.

23. This would probably occur long before a large firm began to pursue a policy of predatory pricing. Further, long-term contracts would be advantageous not only to buyers, but sellers as well. Stable prices are beneficial to sellers as well as buyers.

24. Some readers might think that customers would not be intelligent enough to see the benefits of keeping the small firm in business. However, it is unlikely that *all* customers would not see the benefits. It only takes a few intelligent individuals to see the opportunity to save some money and take advantage of it. Others can then follow the example set by the intelligent. Further, business customers would be much more likely than individual consumers to see the benefits of keeping the small firm in business because the former are usually more financially astute and they also purchase much

larger amounts of goods than the latter and thus have a much stronger incentive to obtain the lowest price possible. Finally, the "prey" has an incentive to inform its customers of what is occurring. This actually occurred in the case of Southwest Airlines when it entered the airline industry in Texas. At the time it faced stiff competition from Braniff Airlines, a well-established competitor who decreased its prices to drive Southwest out of the industry. Southwest appealed to its customers and told them they would pay higher prices if Braniff was able to drive Southwest out of business. Braniff Airlines eventually went bankrupt.

25. The cost being referred to here is the marginal cost. The marginal cost is the additional cost incurred to produce an additional unit of a good. If the marginal cost is more than the price charged to sell the additional units, the firm loses money on each additional unit sold. For instance, if the marginal cost is 85 cents then the firm will lose 5 cents on each additional unit of the good it sells (at the reduced price of 80 cents). This additional loss would be added to the firm's $1 million loss incurred in the first example with the 80 cents selling price.

26. Suppliers and producers of complementary goods might be in a position to take advantage of the irrationality of the large firm simply by threatening to go into business against it, which would cause it to lower its price.

27. Variable costs are costs that change in the same direction as the amount of output that is produced in any time period (i.e., they increase when more is produced and decrease when less is produced). Fixed costs remain constant over large ranges of output. If a firm is incurring a loss, as long as the revenue it generates covers its variable costs, a firm has the incentive to stay in business until its plant and equipment are used up. This is the case because the losses the firm would incur by shutting down (which would be equal to the firm's fixed costs) would be greater than if it continued to produce. Only when the revenue does not cover the variable costs are the losses incurred from shutting down less than the losses from continuing to produce. For example, if a firm had $1000 in revenue, $900 in variable costs, and $800 in fixed costs, it would lose $700 ($1000-[$900+$800]) if it continued to produce. However, it would lose $800 (the $800 fixed costs) if it produced nothing. With the revenue greater than the variable costs (i.e., $1000 > $900), it pays the firm to continue to produce because it can cover its variable costs and use the revenue in excess of its variable costs to cover a portion of its fixed costs. On the other hand, if a firm had only $600 in revenue and the same costs, it would lose $1100 ($600-[$900+$800]) if it continued to produce, but only $800 (the same fixed costs) if it shutdown. With revenue below its variable costs (i.e., $600 < $900), it pays the firm to shutdown because it cannot even cover all of its variable costs if it produces.

28. One might wonder, by this point, why the large firm would not just buy the small firm instead of trying to drive it out of business through a policy of predatory pricing. It could do this. However, this is a slightly different situation than the case of predatory pricing and I do not address it in this chapter (except in this note) because it is not widely used to attack the free market. The first thing to consider in this type of situation is that an adequate rate of return would still have to be earned on the investment to make the purchase worthwhile. Further, even if the large firm was able to buy the small firm, it would still face the threat of potential competitors and therefore, after it bought the small firm, it could not raise its price above the point where it is profitable for new firms to enter the field without losing substantial amounts of business. Also, if the large firm bought small firms as a policy, just to keep them out of the market, small firms could take advantage of this behavior by entering the market just to be bought out. As one can see, although this case is slightly different than the case of predatory pricing it is not fundamentally different and therefore many of the same issues are relevant to it.

29. I understand that some people probably honestly, but mistakenly, believe that predatory pricing is a tool one can successfully compete with under capitalism. However, I see many people cling to their belief in the predatory pricing doctrine even after they have been shown that the doctrine is thoroughly false. From my experience with these people and my knowledge of philosophy, I believe many of them continue to embrace the doctrine because of an underlying hatred of capitalism and jealousy of those who succeed under capitalism. For the reason why people have this hatred and jealousy, see the conclusion to this chapter and the references given there.

30. For why success is incompatible with altruism, see the section titled "The Ethical Basis of Perfect Competition and Economic Monopoly" in chapter 2 and the sections titled "The Morality of Wealth and Income Inequality" and "The Logical Implications of the Equality of Opportunity" in chapter 7.

Chapter Four

Externalities

What Are Externalities?

The next attack on the market that I will address comes from the so-called externality argument. An "externality" (sometimes called a spillover or third-party effect) is a cost imposed, or benefit bestowed, on people other than those who purchase or sell a good or service. The recipient of the externality is neither compensated for the cost imposed on him, nor does he pay for the benefit bestowed upon him. These costs and benefits are labeled "externalities" because the people who experience them are outside or *external* to the transaction to buy and sell the good or service.

There are two types of "externalities." When a person not involved in the production or consumption of a good receives a benefit for which he does not pay, he is said to be the recipient of a "positive externality." An example of this is immunization. Individuals not involved in the sale or purchase of immunization shots benefit from such shots without paying for them. They benefit because the more people that become immunized, the less likely it is that the individuals not involved with the purchase or sale of the immunizations will be exposed to the dreaded disease, since fewer people will contract the disease. Because the individuals are outside the transaction and because they receive this benefit at no cost to themselves, they are said to be the recipients of a positive externality. A beautiful home with a well-manicured lawn and garden is another example. In this case, passersby who did not help to pay for the home or landscape the grounds still gain from the pleasure of being able to enjoy the view. They, too, receive a benefit without paying. A lighthouse provides another example. Ship owners who have not helped to pay for the construction of the lighthouse still benefit from it when they pass by at night.

The second type of externality is a "negative externality." This exists when a person who has nothing to do with the sale or purchase of a good has a cost imposed on him for which he is not compensated. A leading example of a negative externality is pollution being emitted from, say, a steel mill. In this case, people who neither buy nor sell steel may experience the harmful effects of the pollution (such as sooty curtains or dirty air to breathe) but are not compensated for the negative effects they experience.[1]

Why Markets Allegedly Fail Due to Externalities

The alleged failure of the market occurs because, it is claimed, the market provides too many goods that produce negative externalities and too few goods that create positive externalities. Too many goods that create negative external effects are allegedly produced because the costs imposed on those who experience the negative externalities are not taken into account in the production of the goods creating the negative side effects. Remember, these costs are imposed on people who neither buy nor sell the goods. If these costs were accounted for in the production of such goods the cost of producing them, and therefore the price needed to purchase them, would be higher. Hence, fewer of them would be produced and purchased.

For example, in the case of a good such as steel, if steel manufacturers were required to compensate individuals whose curtains became dirty or who had to breathe in the dirty air, the cost of these negative externalities would be included in the production of steel and would raise the cost of producing it.[2] This, in turn, would cause the profitability of producing steel to decrease and decrease the quantity of steel demanded as the price rose to cover the additional costs. This would decrease the total production and purchases of steel to a level that allegedly takes into account the effects of the pollution.

With respect to goods that create positive externalities, too few are allegedly produced because the recipients of the externalities do not pay for the benefits bestowed upon them. Hence, these benefits provide no extra inducement for the suppliers of such goods to produce more of them. If the recipients had to pay for the benefits, this would provide a greater incentive to produce these goods and increase the quantity supplied.

An example of this is as follows: when passing by a beautiful home and garden, if every person who gained some pleasure from what he saw was required to pay the owner a small fee, the profitability of creating beautiful homes and gardens would increase and cause more to be produced. Hence, the supply of these goods would reflect all the benefits people received from the goods.

In both the case of the positive and negative externality, the market is said to fail to capture all the effects involved in some transactions, and thus market prices of goods allegedly fail to reflect all the costs and benefits associated with the goods. The "solution," in both cases, is government intervention into the market. In the case of negative externalities, it is claimed the government must take some action to restrict the production of these goods by, perhaps, imposing a tax on the producers of such goods so that these producers will experience the effects of all the costs they impose on others. This tax will increase the cost of producing the goods, decrease the profitability of producing them, and thus decrease the supply of the goods. This will cause the supply to allegedly reflect all the costs associated with producing the goods. With the case of goods that create positive externalities, it is claimed the government should take some action to stimulate the production of these goods by, perhaps, providing a subsidy to producers of such goods to compensate them for all the benefits they bestow on others. This will create a greater incentive to produce these goods, increase the supply of the goods, and therefore cause the supply to allegedly reflect all the benefits associated with the goods.

The Politics and Economics of Externalities

The Economic Implications of Externalities

To see why the externality argument does not provide a valid critique of the market, one must first look at the economic implications of this argument.

If all those who created a "negative externality" were required to pay for the cost they imposed on others and those who created a "positive externality" were paid for the benefits they bestowed upon others, it would lead to economic stagnation or regression! This can be seen in the case of positive externalities if one considers the large number of payments that would have to be made to those responsible for innovations that are easy to copy but that are not eligible for patent or copyright protection. This alone would probably lead to economic stagnation.

For instance, people would have to compensate the first fast-food restaurant that used a drive-through window, the first airline that gave out frequent-flyer miles, the first store owner who came up with the idea to allow customers to buy merchandise on layaway, and the first cook to create a great recipe. While such fresh thinking is rewarded by those who purchase the products or services offered by the innovators, these original thinkers are not paid by those who copy them. Therefore, this is a benefit bestowed upon the imitators (and their customers) for which they do not pay.[3] They are provided with an innovative idea free of charge. The number of payments that would be required if one implemented laws consistent with externality theory could be multiplied as many times over as there are innovations that are easy to copy but that are not eligible for protection. This would lead to an enormous number of payments.

Further, based on negative externality theory, inventors and innovators that drive other producers out of business (or cause other businesses to incur losses), due to their innovations, would have to compensate those they drive out of business. For example, the original Henry Ford would have had to compensate horse breeders, buggy makers, and blacksmiths that he drove out of business. According to externality theory, in driving them out of business by producing an affordable, high quality means of transportation, Ford imposed a cost on them for which they were not compensated. To remedy the situation, Ford should have compensated them. One can easily imagine the large number of payments that would have to be made by those who created this type of negative externality.[4] If payments were actually required to be made for positive and negative externalities, the result would be an endless series of payments, very little production, and a much lower standard of living.[5] This result could hardly be deemed "a success."

The Solution to Negative Externalities

If it would lead to stagnation to require everyone to pay for negative externalities they create and be paid for positive externalities they create, how does one answer the question concerning who should pay and be paid? With regard to negative externalities, the only ones for which people should be compensated are those that cause demonstrable physical harm to a person or his property and can be traced back to the actions of an individual or a group of individuals working in concert. In order to do this, one must have well-defined and protected property rights.

For example, a negative externality is said to exist in the case of a downstream landowner's land being contaminated by, say, fertilizer used by a farmer whose land is upstream. This is said to be the case because the cost imposed on the downstream landowner is not accounted for in the costs that the farmer incurs to grow his crops. However, if property rights are well-defined and protected, the downstream landowner could sue in a court of law to be compensated for the farmer's actions and get a court injunction imposed on the farmer requiring him to cease the relevant activities. This is a legitimate case for government action against the farmer because he is violating the property rights of the downstream landowner. The farmer is altering the downstream land-owner's land against his will. Further, the violation can be traced back to a single individual.

The above example is not a case of market failure. It is a situation where the government must step in to preserve the existence of a free market. A free market can only exist when individual rights are protected, including private property rights. This is the case because a free market is based on *voluntary* trade. The "free" in free market refers to the absence of the initiation of physical force, in any of its variations, including physical alteration to one's property against one's will. Hence, the failure in this case is the failure on the part of the farmer to act within the principles on which the free market is based. Thus, it is proper for the government to step in and protect the property rights of the downstream landowner to preserve the free market. However, when the government does this, *it is correcting the farmer's failure, not the failure of the free market.* This is true for all so-called negative externality cases where it is legitimate for the government to take action. It is always the case that the government is correcting the failure of some individual(s) to respect the rights of others.

In this case, one must also take into account any rights that have already been established. For instance, if the farmer began using fertilizer and contaminating the land downstream before anyone owned the land, then the farmer acquires the right to contaminate the land. Someone who then settles on the land must accept the land as it is or pay the farmer to stop contaminating the land.

People who have so-called negative externalities imposed on them that cannot be traced back to an individual or group of individuals working in concert should not be compensated. Examples of this kind of externality include smog in a city created by millions of people independently operating motor vehicles or flooding downstream on a river from development and flood control devices used by millions of people living upstream on the river. These cases are natural byproducts of economic activity and must be considered the same as other natural phenomena that produce harmful effects (such as bad weather). One cannot yoke the individual to the collective and treat people who acted independently as if they acted collectively. Each individual acting independently causes a negligible amount of pollution or flooding (or whatever else it might be), which *does not cause any physical harm.* Therefore, no individual should be held accountable for harmful results for which he is not responsible. Further, because no physical harm has been done by an individual or group of individuals acting in concert, no one's rights have been violated and so it is not proper for the government to take action in this case.[6]

Human beings are not, fundamentally, a collective. They are individual, independent, autonomous beings and should be treated as such. In order for individuals to act collectively, they must choose to do so. Therefore, unless one has some basis to show that individuals have made a concerted effort to act collectively, i.e., to act as a single entity, one has no basis to treat a group of individuals as if they have acted in a collective manner. To do so is to ignore the fact that individuals are acting independently of each other, and thus no *one* individual is responsible for the cumulative effect of the actions of *all* the individuals. Nor is he responsible for only a small portion of the *demonstrable* harmful effects. Each individual, acting alone, is responsible only for what he has contributed, which by the nature of the case is negligible and *does not cause any harm.*

By ignoring the fact that the individuals are acting independently, one makes erroneous conclusions and engages in or advocates harmful actions. That is, one treats people as if they have done something that they have not done (i.e., acted in a collective manner), and one holds them responsible, and would presumably want them punished, for results that they did not, as independently

acting individuals, bring about (i.e., one holds them responsible for demonstrable amounts of pollution, flooding, or whatever it might be). Punishing
the individuals who are allegedly responsible for demonstrable amounts of
pollution or flooding is harmful because it is a violation of individual rights,
since it requires the initiation of physical force (given that the actions of any one
individual, or individuals acting in concert, have not harmed anyone). This is
one of the problems with ignoring facts of reality: it leads one to make false
conclusions and to take inappropriate actions. It is not a good habit to practice
because it makes it harder for one to understand what is occurring in reality and
to act successfully in reality.

A final issue with regard to negative externalities is that one must also
consider the cost of getting rid of them. A good example to illustrate why one
must consider this cost is the creation of pollution in Pittsburgh from the
production of steel during the height of that industry.[7] Because of the production
of steel, many people probably had to breathe polluted air and deal with soot on
their curtains. However, in such a situation, one still has to show that the
pollution has caused physical harm to oneself or one's property for one to have a
legitimate case against the steel manufacturers. Further, if one is able to show
this, and which particular steel mill or steel mills working together created the
pollution that is causing the harm, one must also consider the cost of getting rid
of such pollution. Steel mills should not be required to implement pollution
control devices that are so costly they are forced to shut down. In general, if
rights are violated, one must weigh the magnitude of the harm done against the
cost of getting rid of the harmful action or the compensation to be provided to
those harmed. The cost imposed on the guilty party should not be large
compared to the harm done.[8] In addition, one must take into account any prior
established rights the steel mills acquired by operating in an area before anyone
else moved in.

In this case, one must also consider the advantages of an industrialized
society versus a non-industrialized society. Having to deal with sooty curtains or
breathe air with trace amounts of pollutants is a small price for individuals to
pay to get the enormous benefits of an industrialized society. The standard of
living and the average lifespan have risen dramatically thanks to
industrialization.[9] In the case of the steel mills in Pittsburgh, the people who
lived there owed their incomes—and thus their lives—to the existence of the
steel mills. Destroying the steel industry would have made the standard of living
of people in Pittsburgh—and anyone anywhere else that ever benefited from
goods produced with steel (such as bridges, automobiles, skyscrapers, and so
on)—much lower. Hence, it would not have been in people's self-interest to
destroy the steel industry, whether they lived inside or outside Pittsburgh.

The Solution to Positive Externalities

With respect to positive externalities, individuals should pay others only for benefits they *voluntarily* contract to receive from others. Government force needed to increase the supply of goods that create positive externalities violates individual rights. This is no solution because it leads to the sacrifice of some individuals (such as taxpayers) to others (such as those who benefit from the goods whose production is subsidized by taxpayers). Typically, activities or goods that create external benefits are not lacking in a capitalist society. A good example is charity. Charitable donations are a 100 percent positive externality because the recipient does not pay for the charity he receives, and the donor receives no compensation in return for his charitable contribution.[10] Therefore, according to externality theory, too few charitable activities allegedly exist in a capitalist society and the government should either subsidize these activities, or completely take them over, to increase the supply so it allegedly reflects all the benefits bestowed upon the recipients.[11] This, of course, would violate individual rights and be economically destructive.[12] Nonetheless, a large amount of charitable giving takes place in a free society. Each year, Americans give hundreds of billions of dollars to charities, and they would be able to give much more in real terms if their incomes were not eroded through massive amounts of confiscatory taxation and the inflation of the money supply, both of which are forms of government intervention into the economy (i.e., ways in which the government initiates physical force).[13]

Free and rational individuals are capable of finding ways to provide goods that create positive externalities. For instance, with the case of a lighthouse it is claimed that no one will want to pay to help build it because once it is built, a ship owner can "free ride" off of those who have paid to help build it. Here, the ship owner gets the benefit of the lighthouse even though he does not pay to help build it. Since everyone has the incentive to free ride, it is claimed that few people will want to pay for the construction of lighthouses, and thus an inadequate number of them will be built because the funds will not be forthcoming from those who could benefit from the lighthouses. Hence, it is claimed the government must tax everyone and build the lighthouses itself.

This argument ignores the fact that the majority of lighthouses built in Great Britain, starting in the early-seventeenth century, were built by private individuals. Here, lighthouse fees were collected at ports located near the lighthouses. Lighthouses continued to be owned and operated by private individuals in Britain up through the 1830s, when the British government bought the last remaining privately-owned lighthouse. It is hard to believe that private individuals could operate lighthouses for two-hundred years if it was not a profitable activity.[14]

This argument also assumes ship owners (and businessmen in general) are irrational and short-sighted and want to get something for nothing. Such an argument is based, not on a view of man as the rational animal—the being who possesses reason—but on a view that man, by his nature, is irrational. This is a false view of man's nature and is not an appropriate foundation on which to base one's economic analysis. If such a view was valid, man never would have made all of the advances he has so far.

If necessary, rational ship owners will gladly pay a portion of the cost to build a lighthouse because they know it is in their rational self-interest to do so. They know that lighthouses are necessary so that ships do not run aground and thus so they can run successful shipping businesses. It could be that large shippers in a region get together to pay for the lighthouses in their region. Here it would be to the self-interest of the large shippers to build the lighthouses even though some of their smaller competitors might benefit from the lighthouses. This is true because to the extent that shippers are large, they have much more to lose if their ships run aground. It could be that shippers in a region engage in a contingent contract, which stipulates that they will pay for a stated portion of the construction of a lighthouse if, perhaps, 50 percent or 75 percent of other shippers in the region sign the contract. The cost of building the lighthouse may be divided up based on the amount of shipping each company does in the region in a typical year. Whichever way it is done, such goods could and would be provided in sufficient quantities (and have been provided in the past, as the history of the lighthouse in Great Britain attests) because it is in the self-interest of those involved to provide such goods. Small obstacles like those associated with the lighthouse are not hard for free and rational individuals to overcome.

Finally, if individuals are not willing to pay for more of something voluntarily, then more of it should not be provided (i.e., the good or service is not under provided). Forcing individuals to pay for something they do not want is economically harmful because it decreases satisfaction and well-being in the economy. It forces people to spend more money on things that bring them less satisfaction and less money on things that would bring them greater satisfaction.[15] How could this be considered "a success"?

More fundamentally, forcing individuals to pay for such things is immoral because it violates individual rights (usually the rights of taxpayers). Notice once again the link between individual rights and economics. Violating individual rights harms the economy, in this case by decreasing the overall level of satisfaction and well-being achieved by individuals in the economy. Likewise, when the government protects individual rights, by allowing individual taxpayers to be free to spend their money on what they see as best for them, this benefits the economy by increasing the level of satisfaction and well-being that each individual is able to attain.

Conclusion to the Politics and Economics of Externalities

As one can see, from a political and economic standpoint, if one acted on externality theory in a consistent manner and implemented policies based on it, it would lead to economic stagnation, a much lower standard of living, and thus a much lower level of individual satisfaction in the economy. As the economist George Reisman has stated, "It is in the nature of a division-of-labor, capitalist society to bestow enormous benefits for which people do not have to pay. Indeed, in such a society perhaps 99.9 percent or more of everyone's standard of living comes as an 'external benefit' provided by the thinking of others past and present."[16] It certainly would not be a success to eliminate all externalities. It is beneficial to eliminate only those externalities that violate individual rights. When individual rights are protected consistently, it protects the existence of the free market and leads to the highest productive capability, standard of living, and level of individual satisfaction that are possible.

A Deeper Analysis of the Concept "Externality"

The Invalid Nature of the Concept "Externality"

In the above I focus on the political and economic aspects of externalities and show why it would not be beneficial for the government to implement policies based on the externalities doctrine. Further, I show that if individual rights are protected, the problem associated with externalities disappears. However, there is a more fundamental, philosophical argument that can be made against externality theory. That is, the concept "externality," including its positive and negative variations, is an invalid concept because it classifies fundamentally different things together, as if they were the same. This, as stated in chapter 2, is not appropriate when forming concepts.[17]

Take the case discussed above of the person who owns property downstream and has his land contaminated by a farmer using fertilizer upstream. This is an example of a so-called negative externality and represents a violation of individual rights (the property rights of the downstream landowner). In this case it is proper for the government to take action to protect the property rights of the downstream landowner by requiring the farmer to compensate the landowner, or pay for the cleanup of the chemicals, and ensure that it does not happen again.

In contrast to the above example is the case of Henry Ford driving the horse breeders, buggy makers, and blacksmiths out of business. This is also an example of a negative externality. However, this occurs in the context of voluntary trade and the protection of individual rights. Ford was able to get people to voluntarily switch to his product. If the government had acted in this case and forced Ford to compensate these producers, kept him out of business, or prevented people from buying his product, this would have been a violation of individual rights. Here, it would have been improper for the government to act to correct the negative externality.

Likewise, if a passerby enjoys the view of a beautiful home, according to the externality doctrine, the government should force the passerby to pay for the privilege of viewing the home. Again, however, it would be improper for the government to act to eliminate the externality because it would violate the rights of the passerby. In general, when the government acts to eliminate positive external effects it violates individual rights to expropriate money and subsidize, or completely take over, the activity creating the effect.

Recall from the discussion on concept formation in chapter 2 that a concept should not obliterate, ignore, or even push into the background fundamental distinctions between concretes. In this case, it should not obliterate the distinction between actions that violate individual rights and actions that respect individual rights. But this is what is done when the actions of Ford, the builder of the beautiful home, and the farmer are said to create externalities. By subsuming these actions under the same concept, based on the non-essential characteristic of having some effect on others, these actions are evaluated as being fundamentally the same when, in fact, they are not. If one attempts to consistently apply the concept "externality," one will believe the government should use force in each case. With regard to negative externalities, people will believe the government should use force to prevent the individuals from creating the external costs. In the case of positive externalities, people will believe the government should use force to make the recipients pay for the external benefits.

However, depending on the nature of the case, the effect of the government taking action will be radically different. In the case of Ford and the passerby, the government would be *initiating* force and thus *violating* individual rights. In the case of the farmer, the government would be using force in a *retaliatory* manner and thus *protecting* individual rights. This is a fundamental political distinction that cannot be forgotten when determining whether the government should act or not. It is a distinction that the concept "externality" ignores.

The Absurdities of "Externality"

There are other problems with the "concept" externality. The term is supposed to identify and help one understand some significant phenomenon, as any term that is important to an academic field should. However, upon closer inspection, it turns out the term identifies a phenomenon that is so widely prevalent that it is meaningless and implies many absurdities. For example, when an individual buys any good in limited supply, such as a house, this has a negative external effect because now this good is not available for others to purchase, and this makes it harder for others to obtain the good. In other words, whenever *any* good in limited supply is purchased a cost is imposed on those who consume the good, or who might have consumed the good, because less of it is available for them to purchase and they are not compensated for that cost. If individuals refrained from purchasing a good, more would be available for others and therefore it would be easier for others to obtain the good. The implication is that people who purchase any good in limited supply should be forced to pay all other individuals who consume, or might consume, the good to compensate those individuals for making the good harder to obtain. Clearly, this is absurd.

Based on the logic of externality theory, compensation should be paid to anyone that consumes, or might consume, virtually any good in limited supply, even goods radically different from the good in question. This is true because the production and consumption of any good consumes resources (i.e., capital and labor) that could have been used to produce virtually any other good. Therefore, it can be argued based on externality theory that the supply of many goods has been decreased, and thus the goods have been made harder to obtain, due to a person's consumption of any other good.

This example illustrates, more forcefully, how implementing policies based on externality theory would lead to economic stagnation. Imagine the massive costs imposed on the economic system, and thus the economic stagnation that would result, if individuals who consumed any good had to compensate all others who might have purchased any good in limited supply (whether the good in question or any other good in limited supply). Imagine the cost of trying to figure out who might have purchased which goods and how much they might have purchased. Imagine the cost of keeping track of who owes money to whom and the proliferation of pleas by people that they should be compensated because they have been harmed by a particular individual's purchase.[18]

The absurdity does not stop here. In some cases the buyer of a good can also be said to be imposing a positive externality on suppliers of the good because when the buyer purchases the good this might cause the price at which the good can be sold to increase. Here, one can imagine buyers of the good calling for payments from sellers of the good for the positive externality the buyers have created. At the same time, those buyers of the good who must pay the higher price will be calling for payments from the buyers whose purchases drove up the price. In essence, redistribution from sellers to buyers would take place.

The opposite would occur if individuals refrained from purchasing a good and this caused the price of the good to fall. Here, the individuals who refrained from purchasing the good would call for payments from buyers that had an easier time obtaining the good. Further, sellers would demand payments from the individuals who refrained from making purchases. In essence, redistribution from buyers to sellers would occur.[19]

If the measures necessary to act consistently on the "concept" externality appear ridiculous, they should appear to be so because they are, and they should be taken as a clue to the invalid nature of the concept.

The absurdity continues. What about, for example, when a person dresses nicely for a job interview? This has a negative external effect. When a person is well dressed for an interview he makes it harder for other people to get the job. This is a cost imposed on them for which they are not compensated. The same can be said about being intelligent and articulate. Should those who are well dressed, intelligent, and articulate be forced to pay the sloppy, ignorant, and incoherent? Clearly not. But this is the conclusion one would come to if he attempted to consistently apply the term "externality."[20]

The absurdity can be taken even further. What about the positive external effects created by the cosmetic surgery industry? Should people be forced to subsidize doctors who perform tummy tucks, face-lifts, Botox injections, and breast enlargement operations? What about the external effects of beautiful and ugly people in general? Should others be forced to compensate handsome men and beautiful women for the privilege of being able to look at them? Likewise, should ugly people be forced to pay everyone else as compensation for having to look at them? What about the negative external effect of a person's unpleasant body odor in a crowded elevator? There are many absurd implications one could draw if one took the "concept" externality seriously.[21] Further, as one can see, acting on this "concept" would paralyze the economic system.

The Altruist and Collectivist Nature of "Externality"

Finally, "externality" is a collectivist term used to attempt to justify forcing individuals to live for some group or collective. Whether it is Ford being forced to support horse breeders, buggy makers, and blacksmiths; taxpayers being forced to pay for the production of goods that create "positive externalities"; or those who purchase a product being forced to compensate others, those who criticize the free market using the "concept" externality seek to sacrifice some individuals for the sake of others. As I have stated throughout this book, forcing individuals to live for some collective is destructive to human life and must be rejected. Only by embracing and acting consistently on individualism and egoism will human life be able to flourish. Only then will each individual be able to live his life for his own enjoyment and not be used as a sacrificial animal off of which others feed.

Conclusion

The market neither under- nor over-provides goods, as one would believe based on externality theory. Ultimately, the market provides the right amount of goods because it provides them based on people's own voluntary choices. If some good is temporarily under- or over-provided, prices adjust based on supply and demand and people react correspondingly to correct the situation. Goods provided in an economy guided by the externality doctrine would not be provided optimally because the initiation of physical force would be used on a massive scale to provide more of some goods and less of others, against the voluntary choices of individuals.

The "concept" externality should literally be thrown out. It should not be used in intellectual discourse or debate. It does not provide a critique of the market because it is an invalid and thus harmful concept. Such a concept does not help one gain a better understanding of some aspect of reality; it only leads to greater confusion because of the absurd implications of the concept, the altruist and collectivist nature of it, and because it leads people to ignore (or, at least, not recognize the importance of) fundamental political distinctions, such as the distinction between the government acting to violate individual rights and protect individual rights.[22]

In saying that the term "externality" should be thrown out, I am not denying the existence of what the term attempts to categorize. The actions of people can have effects on others. However, what I am saying is that the use of such a term is cognitively unnecessary and harmful to one's understanding of the world. It leads to the support of all the false conclusions and harmful actions I have been discussing. That is why the term must be thrown out.

After the term "externality" is thrown out, one can still recognize all the effects of a person's actions on others; however, one can do so while giving proper consideration to the facts involved, particularly the requirements of human life. The proper consideration with respect to a person's actions is not whether those actions have a positive or negative effect on others. The proper consideration is whether a person's actions respect or violate individual rights. If a person's actions violate individual rights, it is appropriate for the government to act to protect the individual whose rights have been violated. If no one's rights have been violated, then the government should take no action.

The externality argument does not provide any evidence of market failure. The only evidence of failure this argument provides, as with all the arguments against the market, is the failure of contemporary economists and other intellectuals to embrace sound concepts and ideas. By rejecting the externalities argument and coming to an understanding of the importance of protecting individual rights, a large step will be taken toward establishing the science of economics on a sound base.

Notes

1. For a typical presentation of externality theory, see Roger A. Arnold, *Economics*, 5th ed. (Cincinnati: South-Western College Publishing, 2001), 702-705.

2. For those who are not familiar with the terminology of contemporary economics, this is known as "internalizing" the externality.

3. I will grant that the innovator gains a competitive edge over his rivals and may enjoy a temporary increase in business and/or profits due to his innovation, which are rewards of being an original thinker and a form of compensation for his originality. However, since it is not possible to patent or copyright his innovation, he is not paid by his competitors who copy it, nor is he paid by their customers who benefit from it.

Therefore, these people receive a benefit for which they do not pay (i.e., a positive externality).

4. Some contemporary economists would argue that this type of externality is not a "real" externality but merely a pecuniary externality. Pecuniary externalities are only experienced through changes in prices and income and thus, it is claimed, require no adjustment to the production of the good creating the externality (and thus no payments to or from people due to the externality). Some contemporary economists also claim that pecuniary externalities create no "net external effect." Such a situation would exist if the prices the horse breeders, buggy makers, and blacksmiths were able to charge for their products fell due to the actions of Ford. Here, the horse breeders et al. would experience a negative externality (because of the lower price they would receive for their products), but their customers would experience a directly offsetting positive externality (because of the lower price they would pay for the products). Nonetheless, pecuniary externalities can have a net external effect, as in the case presented in the main text. In that case, the lower income received by the horse breeders et al. (a negative externality) is not offset by another externality. (The additional income received by Ford might offset the income lost by the horse breeders et al.; however, Ford's additional income is not an offsetting *externality* because he created the negative externality experienced by the horse breeders et al.) Regardless of whether pecuniary externalities are offsetting or not, contemporary economists would say such externalities are best left to be worked out in the market. While it is true that these situations should be worked out in the market, the important point to recognize here is that pecuniary externalities are still a type of externality. Hence, my criticisms of externalities in general apply to pecuniary externalities as well.

The attempt, by some economists, to make a distinction between pecuniary and non-pecuniary externalities is arbitrary. It is an attempt by those who subscribe to externality theory, and who recognize that "externalities" exist everywhere, to try to prevent the theory from becoming meaningless and leading to many absurdities. Forcing some people to pay others is consistent with externality theory regardless of the type of externality created. For instance, with regard to the directly offsetting pecuniary externalities Ford might create, payments from Ford to those experiencing the negative externality and to Ford from those experiencing the positive externality could be justified. In essence, redistribution would take place from those who received the positive externality to those who experienced the negative externality. The wide prevalence and absurdities of externalities will be discussed in this chapter in the section titled "The Absurdities of 'Externality.'" For an example of the argument that a distinction must be made between pecuniary and non-pecuniary externalities, see Jack and David Hirshleifer, *Price Theory and Applications*, 6th ed. (Upper Saddle River, N.J.: Prentice Hall, 1998), 485. This reference also provides an indication that those who believe in making the distinction between pecuniary and non-pecuniary externalities also believe pecuniary externalities could provide justification for income redistribution.

5. By far the two dominant lines of work in an economy in which an attempt was made to consistently act on externality theory would be the accountants who kept track of who owed what to whom and the lawyers who exacted payment for their clients.

6. However, in the case of smog, a private road owner might properly be held liable for smog generated by users of his roads if it is great enough to cause demonstrable physical damage.

7. I am indebted to Ayn Rand for this example. She used it in her audio taped lecture titled *The Intellectual Bankruptcy of Our Age* (Gaylordsville, Conn.: Second Renaissance Inc., 1961). Hear especially the question and answer period.

8. In essence, what I am saying is that the punishment must fit the crime. Determining what remedies are proper in different cases is a complex legal matter that falls well outside the scope of this book.

9. Consider that the average lifespan in Great Britain prior to the industrial revolution (i.e., prior to the mid-eighteenth century) was about thirty years. Any reader over the age of thirty (or who plans to live to be older than thirty) probably owes (or will owe) his life to industrialization. Consider also the standard of living prior to the industrial revolution. Many people worked eighty hours-per-week performing back-breaking labor all for a standard of living probably not too far above the level of a modern-day Ethiopian.

10. Some might think a tax deduction is compensation to the donor. However, this is not compensation, but a reduction in the effective cost of the charitable contribution.

11. Unfortunately, to a great extent this is what has been done in the form of government welfare programs.

12. For why "charitable" activities (viz., welfare) provided by the government are destructive, see chapter 7.

13. It is easy to understand how the government initiates force when it confiscates money from people in the form of taxes; however, it is more difficult to understand how the government initiates force when it inflates the money supply. I am not going to explain here how inflation represents an act of the initiation of physical force by the government, but for a thorough explanation, see George Reisman, *Capitalism: A Treatise on Economics* (Ottawa, IL: Jameson Books, 1996), 508-510, 511-517, and 920-927.

14. In fact, R. H. Coase indicates that some of the lighthouse owners made a fortune in the business. See his, "The Lighthouse in Economics," *The Journal of Law and Economics* 17, no. 2 (October 1974): 357-376, especially 360-368, for a detailed investigation of the lighthouse in Great Britain.

15. One does not need to commit the error of making interpersonal utility comparisons to make this statement. One just has to understand that, given the income individual taxpayers earn, they achieve a higher level of satisfaction and well-being when they can spend their income on things they voluntarily choose to spend it on. When the government expropriates, say, 20 percent of each person's income in taxes and spends it on something that each person has shown through his own voluntary action that he would *prefer not* to spend it on, the level of satisfaction in the economy decreases.

16. George Reisman, *Capitalism*, 97.

17. See the section in chapter 2 titled "An Important Epistemological Discussion: The Nature of Concepts" and the references given there. Also, in contrast to my treatment of the economic concept of monopoly discussed in chapter 2, my treatment of "externality" in this section is not a case of treating a valid concept that has been defined incorrectly as if it was an invalid concept. "Externality" *is* an invalid concept. What this difference means will become apparent by the end of this chapter. For more on the relationship between a valid concept that has been defined incorrectly and an invalid concept, see note 4 in the section titled "Economic versus Political Monopoly" in chapter 2 and the references given there.

18. There is no doubt that such pleas would lead to greater income redistribution from the rich to the poor since, it would be claimed, the rich consume more goods than the poor and thus allegedly impose greater costs on the poor than vice versa. For the destructive nature of income redistribution, see chapter 7.

19. Although there is obviously no transaction to buy and sell a good when individuals refrain from purchasing a good, even in this case one could argue for

payments from some people to others, based on externality theory, because of the (external) effects this might have on others.

20. Some economists might argue that this and the example with the buyers that have effects on others are not "real" externalities because they are pecuniary externalities. As with the example of Ford discussed in the section on "The Economic Implications of Externalities," economists would claim that these externalities should be worked out in the market. Nevertheless, as I stated earlier, these externalities are still a type of externality and therefore are still subject to all the criticisms I have been making with regard to the subject. Furthermore, as I also discussed in connection with the example of Ford, if one attempted to consistently apply externality theory these types of externalities could still be used to justify redistributing income from those who experience the positive externality to those who experience the negative externality.

21. Like the example above of the person refraining from buying a good, the examples pertaining to compensating beautiful people and calling for payment from ugly people or those with bad body odor are different from the typical examples of an "externality" given by economists (such as those I gave at the beginning of this chapter) because there are no purchases of goods or services involved. Nonetheless, it is still valid to use these examples to show the absurdity of "externality." They do provide examples of situations where one person has an (external) effect on others. These examples are simply variations on the standard examples of externalities. One could easily turn these examples into more traditional examples of externalities. In the case of the unpleasant body odor, one could use this to claim that subsidies are needed for businesses that help improve people's personal hygiene (such as manufacturers of soap, deodorant, mouthwash, etc.) because these companies create positive externalities. In the case of the beautiful and ugly people, one could use this to claim that subsidies are needed for the beauty industry (such as the cosmetic surgery business that was mentioned in the main text, as well as makeup companies, clothing companies, hair salons, etc.) because companies in this industry also create positive externalities.

22. This paragraph provides a good opportunity to highlight an important difference between invalid concepts and valid concepts that have been defined incorrectly. As I state in the main text, invalid concepts must be discarded. Valid concepts that have been defined incorrectly must be redefined using the proper rules of definition. These latter concepts are cognitively beneficial once they have been properly distinguished from other concepts through the use of a good definition.

Chapter Five

Regulation of Safety and Quality

Introduction

In this chapter I focus on the claim that the market fails to provide adequate levels of safety and quality, and that government regulation is necessary in order to correct these alleged deficiencies. Without regulation it is claimed that many people would be harmed by low quality and unsafe products, as well as poor working conditions. It is believed that the government must step in and fix these alleged market failures.

Regulation, in general, occurs when the government intervenes in the market by initiating physical force to change some outcome that government officials, or those that influence them, do not like. The government may intervene for alleged worker health and safety reasons, environmental concerns, to restrict the types of products that can be sold, and for many other reasons. It does so through a variety of agencies including, but not limited to, the Food and Drug Administration, the Environmental Protection Agency, the Consumer Product Safety Commission, the Securities & Exchange Commission, the Occupational Safety and Health Administration, and the Federal Aviation Administration. In this chapter, I will focus primarily on alleged deficiencies in the market concerning the quality and safety of working conditions, products, and services.

The Economic Effects of Regulation

Regulation of Products and Services

To begin to understand why the regulatory argument against the market is invalid, one must understand that regulation raises costs to businesses and thus prices to consumers. A good way to see how regulation raises costs is to imagine that government regulators suddenly have a desire to increase the quality of the average car on the road, so that it is safer to drive a car. To do this, perhaps the regulators decide to make it illegal to drive any car on the road that is of lower quality than, say, a five-year-old Chevrolet Impala. Further, imagine the regulators also come up with a method for determining whether any other make and model, of any age, is of greater or lesser quality than a five-year-old Chevy Impala.[1] If the government did this, it would, indeed, be able to raise the quality of the average car on the road. Many older cars would cease to be driven for fear of the fines or jail terms the government would impose on people for violating the regulation. However, the government would also make it much more expensive to own a car and thus decrease the ability of people to afford a car.[2] People who could not afford to own a later model car would have to go without a car or pool their funds together with friends or family members to purchase a car and deal with all the inconveniences that this would entail.

The above result applies to any situation where the government forcibly prevents producers from selling products and services that do not meet a minimum level of quality. For instance, it applies to government regulation on services in the form of licensing and certification laws, which are intended to raise the quality of the affected services. Such laws exist for a myriad of professions, including doctors and other medical professionals, lawyers, accountants, carpenters, plumbers, electricians, beauticians, etc. These laws raise the cost of the services by forcibly imposing stricter requirements to enter these fields.

In essence, licensing laws prevent many trades from taking place that otherwise would have taken place without the initiation of physical force or fraud. This is true because any one who can do a competent job in a given field but is unable to meet the minimum requirements set by the government will not be able to legally provide the service. This is true even if the person barely misses achieving the minimum requirements, and even if the person could get people to purchase his services voluntarily, with full knowledge of the skill level involved. Thus, many beneficial trades will not occur that would have otherwise taken place. Restrictions on the quality of products have a similar effect.

The strongest short-term economic incentive that exists for the implementation of regulation on safety and quality, in the form of restrictions on who can enter a given field, comes from those currently working in the field. These people often push for regulation, claiming that it is needed for the public's safety. What these people often want to do, however, is gain a monopoly to increase the prices they charge. Here, the government initiates physical force to reserve the market or a portion of the market for existing producers. Again, such action may raise the level of quality of the goods and services provided in these fields, but it also increases the cost of purchasing the goods and services provided.

By decreasing the supply of goods and services and making them more expensive, regulation decreases the choices consumers have available to them. It does this by limiting the range of choices that are available to consumers with regard to quality. People might be forced to buy a higher level of quality than they want to, or they might be forced to go without the good or service. Regulation ignores whether a person can afford a given level of quality and ignores an individual's judgment concerning what level of quality is best for him.

Workplace Regulation

Arbitrarily high standards set by the government with regard to working conditions have negative effects also. Such standards decrease workers' wages. There are a few reasons why this is so. First, if companies are forced to spend money on improving the working conditions in their facilities (such as, perhaps, if they are forced to provide cafeterias for workers or air conditioning), this means they have less money available to purchase other resources, including labor services. If everything else remains constant, including the supply of workers, this implies that the average wage must fall in order to hire the same number of workers. However, even if the average money wage does not fall, workers' real wages will still fall. This is because if businesses cannot decrease their costs in other ways, they will have to raise their prices to cover the higher costs.[3]

Further, when companies hire workers they take all non-monetary advantages and disadvantages associated with a job into consideration (including health benefits, working environment, work location, etc.) to determine what money wages they must pay in order to attract and retain good workers. For instance, jobs that have many perquisites (such as jobs where workers receive gifts from suppliers or take trips to exotic locations), which are non-monetary advantages, tend to pay less than jobs that require a similar skill level but that do not have the perquisites. This is because, other things being equal, a job with non-monetary advantages is more attractive to workers than jobs without the non-monetary advantages (or with non-monetary disadvantages). Therefore, companies do not need to pay as high a wage to attract workers to the positions that have non-monetary advantages. As a result, to the extent that companies are forced by the government to provide improved working conditions, this non-monetary advantage will be offset by a corresponding monetary disadvantage (i.e., lower wages). Companies will be able to lower the wages they offer because it will be easier to attract and retain good workers with the improved working conditions.

* * *

One can see that regulation of safety and quality leads to higher costs of production, a reduced supply of goods, monopoly power for existing producers, higher prices, fewer trades taking place, and fewer products to choose from. All of these lead to lower wages and a lower standard of living. In addition, below it will be shown that regulation of safety and quality *does not* lead to a higher level of safety and quality in the goods, services, and working conditions that exist in the economy.

What Will Happen Without Regulation?

Without regulation, it will not be the case that anyone will be able to enter and compete in any field he wants to regardless of his skills. Barbers and butchers will not be able to become doctors under capitalism. Without regulation, competition will establish education and performance requirements. Those who provide services will have to get people to buy their services *voluntarily* and thus will have to provide a level of quality that is acceptable to their customers. If they cannot get people to buy their services they will not be able to succeed in the field. However, if regulation did not exist there would be many more people, in probably every field, who could enter and successfully compete by providing acceptable services.

For instance, without licensing laws for doctors, there are many nurses, physicians assistants, and paramedics who could be competent doctors. They may not be the doctors with the greatest skills, but they could easily deal with basic medical cases and make referrals to more talented doctors in difficult cases. The existence of a greater number of doctors would help make healthcare much more affordable, all while maintaining an adequate level of quality—a level of quality that healthcare users would help to determine through their own voluntary choices concerning which doctors to see.

* * *

Some might think that, without regulation, people will be able to easily enter an industry by committing an act of fraud (such as by someone pretending to be a doctor). However, this is not true. Fraud, as I have stated in previous chapters, is an indirect form of the initiation of physical force—a violation of individual rights—and would be illegal under capitalism. Hence, anyone caught committing an act of fraud to sell his product or service under capitalism, just as in a regulated economy, would be punished.[4]

However, there is an important difference to emphasize, that often gets overlooked, between a capitalist economy and a regulated economy. That is, there is much greater potential for acts of fraud, and other criminal acts, to be committed in a regulated economy than in a capitalist economy. One must remember that acts of fraud can emanate not only from private individuals, but from government officials. Further, one must always keep in mind that fraud is a type of the initiation of physical force. The initiation of force, ultimately, is what people want to protect themselves from by making fraud, and other criminal activities such as rape and murder, illegal.

The question one must ask here is, what is the government doing when it regulates? The answer: *it is initiating physical force* to impose the will of government regulators on others. Hence, when one allows the government to regulate, one is giving it the ability to do the very thing that underlies criminal activity, including fraud. Therefore, one is making it easier for government officials to engage in such activities on a much wider scale. In contrast, preventing the government from initiating physical force, as is done in a capitalist society, restricts the government to stopping crime; it does not allow the government to participate in such activities.

It is no accident that politics has become more corrupt over the last century as the government's ability to initiate physical force—its ability to rule over people's lives—has expanded. When such an expansion occurs, because the initiation of force is the essence of criminal activity, it provides an incentive for unscrupulous and criminal types to go into politics and commit corrupt and harmful acts. The better and more honest people tend to stay out of politics because they do not want to take part in committing such acts.[5]

A crucial difference between the free market and a society where the government initiates physical force is that in the latter the initiation of force is legal! This gives criminal mentalities a much greater ability to initiate force against others because the initiation of force has become institutionalized. If one is concerned about preventing fraud, and other criminal acts, the worst thing one could do is provide an incentive for criminal types to rise into positions of political power by making it easier for them to initiate physical force against others. In essence, one is providing an outlet for criminal mentalities to commit their destructive acts on a much wider scale than they could possibly achieve acting on their own, privately. This is precisely why the potential for harmful acts, including acts of fraud, is much greater in a regulated economy than under capitalism, and the potential for harmful acts increases the more regulated an economy becomes. Once the *principle* has been accepted that it is okay for the government to initiate physical force and violate individual rights, it is just a matter of time and degree before the government begins to violate rights on a more massive scale.

As evidence that the potential for destruction and fraud increases as the government's power to initiate physical force increases, witness the atrocities committed by totalitarian governments around the globe during the twentieth century. As many as one-hundred million people (and counting) have been murdered under governments that initiate physical force on this massive scale. Further, witness the massive acts of fraud perpetrated by these governments in the form of the socialist propaganda and lies about the West that they disseminated (and still disseminate). These governments include, but are not limited to, the former USSR, Nazi Germany, Communist Cuba, Communist China, Cambodia under Pol Pot, Iraq under Saddam Hussein, Vietnam, and North Korea. These examples demonstrate the destruction and acts of fraud that are possible when the initiation of force is used by a government on the widest of all possible scales. The potential harm created by any private use of the initiation of physical force under capitalism is insignificant by comparison. Likewise, the harmful acts committed by a government such as that in the present-day United States, a mixed economy (or welfare state), do not violate individual rights on as massive a scale as totalitarian governments because governments like that in the United States do not have as great of an ability to initiate physical force. The U.S. government is still greatly restrained in its ability to initiate force by the Constitution.

* * *

One does not need regulation to get firms to provide safe products and working conditions. Competition would also set standards for these. A company does not make large profits by building unsafe products that kill or harm its customers. It would either lose customers or face lawsuits if it was negligent. Neither of these enable a company to succeed. Likewise, a company cannot hire and retain good workers, and thus cannot remain competitive, if it provides working conditions in which no one wants to work. In a free market, a company must provide a level of quality in its products and working conditions that is acceptable to its customers and workers or face the prospect of placing itself at a competitive disadvantage and thus, possibly, losing money and going out of business.

In addition, without government regulation of safety and quality, certification of products and services could be performed by private organizations. The major difference between regulation and the setting of standards by private organizations is that the latter could not initiate physical force to impose their will on others. In essence, these organizations would provide recommendations, or a rating service, regarding the level of quality, but individuals would still be able to make the decision regarding what level of quality is right for them. Individuals could reject the recommendations or choose someone not approved by a particular rating company, or any rating company at all.

Many organizations already exist that could make recommendations and provide ratings. Organizations like Consumers Union (for consumer products), Underwriters Laboratories Inc. (for product safety), Good Housekeeping (consumer products), Moody's (investments), the American Dental Association (dental products), and many others could serve this function in a much greater capacity than they do now. Universities could also play an expanded role in providing ratings for doctors, lawyers, accountants, and many other professionals. Some government agencies, such as the Food and Drug Administration and the Consumer Product Safety Commission, once completely separated from the government and stripped of all their regulatory power, might be able to provide *recommendations* concerning product safety and quality. In conjunction with the above organizations, brand names and word-of-mouth recommendations would play a role. Again, the key difference between recommendations and regulations is that with recommendations no one would be able to forcibly impose a certain level of quality on anyone.

Private certification organizations would have a strong incentive to provide objective evaluations and set reasonable standards, ones that take quality, safety, *and* cost into account. The reputation of these organizations, and thus their financial viability, would depend on providing accurate and timely evaluations and setting reasonable standards. If a rating agency provided inaccurate evaluations, it would tarnish its good reputation (or prevent it from ever gaining one) and lose business (or never gain it). If a rating agency took an exorbitant amount of time to test a product, it would decrease the likelihood that firms would take the time to gain the certification. Further, if it set standards that were too high or too low, it would decrease the incentive for producers to seek certification by making it prohibitively costly (if the standards were too high) or decrease the value of the certification (if the standards were too low). Competition among rating agencies would help to ensure that the standards established would take all factors into account, including quality, safety, and cost.

Rating agencies that are known to provide accurate evaluations and set widely accepted and sensible standards would be sought out by those who produce and purchase goods and services. Gaining the approval of a well-known and reputable rating organization would encourage producers to improve the safety of their products and increase their ability to attract customers. Further, obtaining information from a good rating organization would help buyers make better decisions about whose products and services to buy.[6]

Finally, a free market does not provide an arbitrarily high or low level of quality and safety. It provides a level of quality and safety that consumers and workers want *and* can afford. Consumers and workers would help determine the level of quality and safety that would be established in a free market by purchasing those products and working at those businesses that provide the desired combination of quality, safety, and other characteristics.

The Harm Caused by Regulation

Do-it-Yourself Disasters and Airbags

Regulation can often cause great harm to people and sometimes even kill them. For instance, regulation in the form of licensing laws increases the number of do-it-yourself disasters because it increases the cost of purchasing the services on which it is imposed. For example, because the services of an electrician are made more expensive by licensing laws, many people who do not know very much about electrical work might choose to do the work on their own, instead of hiring an electrician. The results should be obvious. Disasters, such as electrical fires, become more frequent. The implication is that even an electrician who is not of the highest quality is better than no electrician at all.

Another example is the federal government's regulation of airbags. The government originally stipulated that airbags must be able to protect the average adult male not wearing a seat belt. However, the force from an inflating airbag that cushions an adult male can harm or kill a child or small woman. In addition, the government pushed for the mandatory use of airbags starting in the early 1970s. It did this despite the fact that the threat to children and small women had been known by automotive safety engineers since the late 1960s. The government, for the most part, ignored engineers' warnings.

Then, in 1990, a law went into effect that made it mandatory to install either automatic seatbelts or airbags on all new cars. Shortly after automobile manufacturers began installing automatic seatbelts, the seatbelts became unpopular with consumers. Thus, the manufacturers began installing more airbags. Eventually, the government made airbags mandatory on all new cars. While many more lives saved have been attributed to the use of airbags than lives lost, about 250 deaths have been attributed to airbags. Further, a large number of these deaths have occurred in accidents so minor that everyone else walked away. As a result, some people are beginning to demand the ability to turn off the airbags. However, so far the government has refused to allow this, except in special cases. Given the government's role in pushing for and eventually requiring the use of airbags (and not giving people the option to switch them off), the government is at least partially responsible for these deaths.[7]

The Food and Drug Administration

Yet another example, where the death toll is far higher, is the regulation of prescription drugs and other medical products by the Food and Drug Administration (FDA). Here I focus mainly on the FDA's regulation of drugs. The lengthy, expensive procedure that pharmaceutical companies must go through to get a drug approved—more than ten years on average in the 1970s and eight years now—is well known. Prior to 1962, the time for approval was seven *months*.[8] This dramatic increase occurred because in 1962 laws were passed that significantly enhanced the FDA's powers.[9]

Prior to the 1962 laws, the FDA was charged primarily with the task of making sure that drugs were safe before being brought to the market. However, the 1962 laws allowed the FDA to also require drug companies to prove that their drugs were effective before being brought to the market. The task of proving whether drugs are efficacious is much more difficult than proving safety. To a great extent, efficacy is sensitive to individual conditions, and prior to the 1962 laws it had always been judged on an individual basis, by doctors and their patients. In addition, prior to the 1962 laws drug companies had to submit New Drug Applications for FDA scrutiny; however, the application would automatically be approved if the FDA took no action within sixty days. Hence, the default position was that the drugs were approved. After 1962, however, the FDA had to clear all drugs for safety and effectiveness prior to the drug being approved for the market. Because of these changes, the 1962 laws were responsible for considerably increasing the duration of the approval process.[10]

When the approval of a drug is delayed, it is often at the expense of people who could have benefited from the drug. The approval process is often delayed because the FDA is being overly cautious in attempting to ensure safety, although sometimes it is due simply to the bureaucratic nature of the agency. The FDA has a strong incentive to be overly cautious in its drug approval process because if it approves a drug that turns out to be unsafe, any deaths caused by the drug can be easily traced back to the FDA officials who were responsible for the approval. Therefore, it is very likely that the officials will be blamed and punished for approving the unsafe drugs. However, if the FDA does not approve a drug that is, in fact, safe and has some beneficial uses, it is unlikely that the deaths of patients who were unable to get the unapproved drug will be connected to the actions of the FDA. Thus, FDA officials take no blame for not approving beneficial drugs. The result of these incentives is that there is a bias toward not approving drugs to avoid the harsh penalties meted out should an unsafe drug accidentally be approved.[11]

Even if a drug's approval is being delayed to establish its safety, some people might be willing to take the risk of using the drug if it means potentially prolonging their lives or, perhaps, ridding themselves of a disease. When the FDA forcibly keeps drugs off the market, it abrogates the rational judgment of a doctor and his patient in determining whether a given medication is worth the risk. Further, because the approval process is so expensive, it prevents many drugs from ever being developed because it is too costly to develop them. In addition, it makes it much harder for individuals to afford the potentially life-saving drugs that are developed. Due to its harmful effects, it has been estimated that regulation could be responsible for as many as *twelve-thousand deaths per year* at the hands of the FDA alone.[12] Unlike with airbags, however, any short-run gain from the FDA in the form of lives saved does not outweigh the cost of lives lost. This is seen in the estimate of casualties that have been prevented by the FDA's regulation to keep potentially harmful drugs off the market. This estimate shows that, at most, one-thousand *casualties* per year have been prevented. Therefore, the *net* cost of the FDA could be over one-hundred thousand deaths per decade.[13]

DDT

The virtual ban of DDT, a pesticide that kills disease-carrying insects, makes the FDA look benign by comparison. The EPA virtually banned the production and use of DDT in 1972 because, in part, it said DDT posed an unacceptable risk to human health. It is hard to reconcile this alleged danger with the estimated one-hundred million lives saved by DDT in Africa, Asia, and South America during the two decades before its use was virtually banned, as reported by the American Council on Science and Health. Further, this alleged danger is also hard to reconcile with the thirty to sixty million people, estimated by the World Health Organization, that have died from malaria since then—deaths that the use of DDT might have been able to prevent.[14] This is a regulatory holocaust perpetrated by environmentalists that makes the holocaust of the Nazis look small by comparison.[15]

Conclusion to the Harm Caused by Regulation

The choice between not having regulation and many people dying or being harmed, and having regulation and far fewer people dying or being harmed, is a false alternative. The actual choice is between living under complete freedom, without regulation, and having one's freedom taken away with regulation. The end result of the latter process, if it is allowed to continue to its logical and consistent end, is living under a police state, with no freedom!

If you, the reader, think this is not possible, where do you think the United States will end up in, perhaps, fifty or one-hundred years, if an endless stream of laws are passed to create more government control of the economy? If we continue to add to the laws that have been passed over the last century—such as the laws that have been passed to regulate airline services, the quality of housing, lending and banking, medicine, consumer products, working conditions, the trades (such as plumbing and electrical work), investments, food, etc.—where will it all end? If there is always a reason why we need additional government controls in another area of the economy, what will be the end result? The result will be complete government control of the economy. This is exactly what occurred in Germany when it started in the 1880s with the world's first welfare state (similar to our own today) and ended with the rise of Hitler in the 1930s. We are headed toward a similar fate as nineteenth-century Germany if current trends continue.[16]

However, current trends can be changed. Because human beings have free will, we can choose to reverse the destructive path down which we are headed. We can refuse to create any more regulations and abolish existing ones. We can demand that the only laws that be passed are ones that protect individual rights. If we do that, and are vigilant, our freedom will be preserved.[17]

How to Achieve Higher Levels of Safety and Quality

Ultimately, *the government is unable to provide an acceptable level of quality and safety to consumers and workers.* It is unable to do so because it cannot determine what level of quality and safety consumers and workers want in products, services, and working conditions. It cannot do this because it does not act on the profit motive, so it has little or no incentive to determine what consumers and workers want. Because of this, it usually calls for a level of quality and safety, not based on what consumers and workers want, but based on the whims of politicians, government bureaucrats, and the pressure groups that influence them.

The profit motive, far from being an impediment to high quality and safety (as people often think), is the primary motive driving firms to provide higher levels of quality and safety in a free market. However, the profit motive also creates an incentive for businesses to provide the level of quality and safety that people want and can afford. Firms do these things to gain a competitive edge over their rivals. Those businesses that provide a level of quality and safety that people consider to be optimal gain more business or are able to hire and retain better workers (which leads to a competitive advantage and higher profits). Those businesses that do not provide an optimum level of quality and safety place themselves at a competitive disadvantage and thus lose business, workers, and profits. Businesses must take all factors that individuals consider important into account if they are to get individuals to purchase their products and work in their facilities.

One does not need to project the existence of a totalitarian state, as I have done in the previous section, to see the harmful effects of regulation. We are experiencing the harmful effects right now because *the free market provides a higher level of quality and safety than a market hampered by government regulation.* This is the case because a free market leads to the highest rate of economic progress that is possible and thus to the greatest productive capability that is possible. An economic system with a higher productive capability is able to produce more goods and is also able to produce safer and higher quality goods.

For instance, not only can an economy with a higher productive capability produce more automobiles than an economy with a lower productive capability, it can also produce higher quality automobiles. For example, the more productive economy can produce cars with greater safety features, such as antilock braking systems and puncture resistant tires, than the less productive economy. It takes greater knowledge, more capital, and more advanced technology to produce the higher quality car. All of these lead to a greater productive capability.

Another way to think about this issue is to consider that a greater productive capability raises the average level of real income in an economy. This higher income provides people with a greater ability to afford improvements in quality and safety. It is the high and rising standard of living, which the higher real income represents, that has made possible all the improvements in the industrialized nations. These include improvements in working conditions, the quality of products, a decrease in the number of hours that people must work to sustain their lives, the virtual disappearance of the need for children to work to help support their families, and many other improvements.[18] The high and rising standard of living has been created, in turn, by the elements of capitalism that have existed in the Western world during the last two-hundred-and-fifty years of mankind's history. This progress has been made possible by the knowledge acquired under capitalism, and the capital accumulation and technological advancement achieved under capitalism, all of which have raised the productive capability.[19] Capitalism is the cause of all of these: a greater productive capability, a greater rate of economic progress, a higher standard of living, higher real income, and improvements in safety and quality.

By raising the costs of production and restricting competition and the incentive of the profit motive, *regulation has actually reduced the level of quality and safety that exist today*, if not in absolute terms, then at least relative to the level of quality and safety that could have been achieved by now based on the much more rapid rate of economic progress that would have existed in a free market. The rate of economic progress will be lower in a regulated economy because raising the costs of production decreases the ability to produce wealth with any given amount of resources (viz., capital and labor). This is true because higher costs imply that it will take more resources to produce a given amount of wealth. Hence, given a certain supply of resources available at the beginning of any particular year, the wealth produced by those resources will be less if costs are higher; therefore, the rate at which the supply of wealth will increase from year-to-year (i.e., the rate of economic progress) will be lower.

A simple example will illustrate the effect of different rates of economic progress on the productive capability. If the wealth produced each year in a free market increases at a 5 percent annual rate, denoting the wealth produced in a base year with a "1," the wealth produced in subsequent years will rise to 1.05 in year 1, 1.1025 (=1.05 x 1.05) in year 2, and so forth. However, if the costs of production are higher due to regulation, the initial supply of resources (i.e., the same supply of capital and labor initially available in the free market) will not be able to initiate as large of an increase in the wealth produced each year because the same supply of resources now produce less wealth due to the higher costs.

Therefore, the wealth produced may increase at only a 3 percent annual rate. So the wealth produced in year 1 would now be 1.03, in year 2 it would be 1.0609 (=1.03 x 1.03), and so on.

Differences in the rate of economic progress can have dramatic effects on the wealth produced in economic systems over long periods of time due to the compounding nature of economic progress. For instance, if the two economies in the example above continue their respective rates of economic progress, in forty years the free market will more than double its ability to produce wealth relative to the regulated economy. In other words, the wealth produced in the free market economy in year forty would be 7.04 (=1.05^{40}), while the wealth produced in the regulated economy in year forty would be 3.26 (=1.03^{40}). Hence, in forty years the standard of living in the more rapidly progressing economy would be more than twice as great as in the less rapidly progressing economy. Therefore, the ability to afford safer and higher quality products, services, and working conditions would also be correspondingly greater in the more rapidly progressing economy.

With regard to competition and the profit motive, regulation restricts competition by creating political monopolies (such as through licensing laws) and prevents businesses from being able to act fully on the incentive of the profit motive by, for instance, banning the production of some goods (such as DDT) and making it harder to produce other goods (such as prescription drugs). This decreases the incentive and ability to produce more efficiently, slows the rate of economic progress, reduces the economy's capacity to produce safer and higher quality products, and thus decreases the ability of people to afford higher levels of safety and quality. So, as paradoxical as it may seem to some readers, *regulation to improve safety and quality actually reduces the level of safety and quality* that can be achieved in an economy.

Let me emphasize this another way: our ability to produce safer and higher quality products *does not* rest on the existence of regulations calling for more safety and quality. If this was the case, one would be able to, for example, impose America's building code regulations on, say, the Ethiopian economy and by doing so achieve a higher level of quality in the houses built in Ethiopia. Of course, this would not happen because the Ethiopian economy has an extremely low productive capability (because it is not and never has been a capitalist society), and thus Ethiopians are unable to produce and afford better housing, regardless of whether or not they have regulations telling them to do so. All one would do if one required Ethiopians to live in houses built based on American standards is force them out of the primitive dwellings they now live in and force them to live with no protection from the elements. Clearly, the Ethiopians would be worse off. The result is no different in principle when regulations are imposed on Americans.

To one who understands the nature of economic progress, the greater quality and safety achieved without regulation is not paradoxical. This is the case because if one understands the nature of economic progress then one understands that such progress occurs over the long run and, as was shown above, due to the compounding effect, small changes in the annual rate of economic progress can have very large effects on the productive capability over a significant period of time. We are living in the long run right now, and our present standard of living has been affected by all the improvements in production in the past and all the government policies—good and bad alike—that have been implemented in the past.[20] Likewise, the policies we implement today will affect the standard of living, and thus the level of safety and quality, that can be achieved in the future.

A Philosophical Analysis of Regulation

The belief that regulation is needed to improve safety and quality is a logical implication of the morality of sacrifice. This morality says that the only way one person can gain is by sacrificing others. Hence, producers must build shoddy and unsafe products and provide miserable working conditions in order to make a profit. The idea that both parties to a trade can gain is incompatible with the morality of sacrifice.

Furthermore, based on the morality of sacrifice, the "rich" producers have a duty to sacrifice themselves to "poor" consumers. Therefore, according to this morality, the former have a duty to provide greater safety and quality (among other things) to the latter, even if it damages the company providing the safety and quality. If companies are not willing to sacrifice themselves voluntarily, it is perfectly consistent with the morality of sacrifice that producers be forced to sacrifice themselves to consumers through the use of regulations.

Also, as I said at the beginning of this chapter, regulation occurs when the government initiates physical force to change some outcome in the market that it does not like. By doing so, regulation violates individual rights and thus stands in opposition to the requirements of human life. As I have emphasized throughout this book, freedom from the initiation of physical force is a fundamental requirement of human life. People must be free from the initiation of force to perform the tasks their lives require. By initiating physical force, regulation stifles the ultimate source of the creation of wealth: the individual human mind. If wealth is to be created individuals must be free to use their minds to gain and use all the crucial knowledge necessary to produce it. Because regulation stifles the mind—because it stifles the creative thinking necessary to produce the wealth that makes economic progress possible—it leads to a lower standard of living and a decreased ability to improve the safety and quality of the products and working conditions that exist.

There is another way that advocates of regulation reject the role and significance of the mind in human existence. Implicit in the desire for government regulation is the belief that people are too ignorant to make competent decisions to run their own lives. The desire for regulation is based on a belief that people are unable to make rational decisions concerning what is best for them or seek out the right experts who can help them make sound decisions.

Besides rejecting the role and significance of the mind, this belief also contains a contradiction. If individuals are so ignorant that they cannot even run their own lives, how could ignorant individuals, when they become politicians and government regulators, somehow become so intelligent that they are not only capable of running their own lives but are capable of running everyone else's life also? If individuals in general are too ignorant to make competent decisions, then individuals acting as politicians and government regulators will be too ignorant to make competent decisions as well.

Often, in response to the above argument, the claim is made that most people are capable of running their own lives but some people are not capable of doing so. Hence, allegedly government regulation is needed to protect those people who are incapable of running their own lives. However, this does not justify government regulation. One should not attempt to protect the foolish few at the expense of the competent many. One should not sacrifice those who are capable of running their own lives to those who are not capable of doing so by forcibly imposing the standards of the most incompetent citizens on those who are capable of making rational decisions. Everyone would be better off if the competent individuals were left free to make decisions that were in their rational self-interest, instead of cutting the competent individuals down to the level of the incompetent. Here, the competent individuals could provide guidance to the incompetent by serving as role models to the latter.

Conclusion

The argument for the regulation of safety and quality does not provide a critique of the market. It simply shows, again, that some people are capable of accepting false, and therefore destructive, ideas. A free market is superior in every way to a market hampered by government regulation. The free market achieves the highest level of safety and quality that are possible in products and working conditions by virtue of the greater productive capability and rate of economic progress it achieves relative to any other type of economic system. The free market is also consistent with the requirements of human life because it allows people to be free to use their minds to do the necessary thinking and acting to achieve greater safety and quality in products and working conditions, and to choose the level of safety and quality that is right for them.

Finally, this chapter illustrates, once again, a principle that appears through-out this book. This principle says that protecting individual rights increases eco-nomic efficiency, the rate of economic progress, the standard of living, and the ability of individuals to further their lives and happiness. It also illustrates its obverse, which says that violating individual rights decreases economic effi-ciency, progress, the standard of living, and the ability of individuals to further their lives and happiness. This causal link, as a general principle, always exists. Regulation is no exception.

Notes

1. Perhaps a blue-ribbon panel is commissioned to determine that, for example, an eight-year-old Toyota Camry is equivalent in quality to a five-year-old Chevy Impala.

2. Such a law would, of course, affect poor people the most, since they would be the ones least likely to be able to afford the newer, higher quality cars required by the law. I make this comment not because I think any special attention should be given to the poor when creating laws, but because those people who want government intervention to improve quality and safety are usually the same people who want higher incomes for the poor. This is a contradiction because regulation actually reduces the real income of the poor by making goods more expensive.

3. Real wages are measured in terms of what a worker can buy with the money wages he receives. If the prices of goods workers buy rise while their money wages remain constant, workers cannot afford to buy as many goods and thus real wages have fallen. In addition, improvements in working conditions do not always lead to lower wages. However, such improvements do not need to be forced on businesses and workers; they will be adopted voluntarily. These improvements are beneficial to both workers and employers. These types of improvements are discussed in chapter 5, appendix (a).

4. A discussion on how to establish standards and definitions by which allegations of fraud can be adjudicated, while extremely important, is outside the scope of this book. This is a task for those in the field of law.

5. Of course, the rise in the government's power to initiate force is not causeless. It comes from the general abandonment of reason, egoism, and individualism; and the corresponding embracement of mysticism, altruism, and collectivism; that has been occurring in America and around the world. The beginning of this process preceded the start of the government's rise in power by about a century. For why the embracement of mysticism, altruism, and collectivism lead to the use of force, see Ayn Rand, *Philosophy: Who Needs It* (New York: Signet, 1982), 62-63 and 70; *For the New Intellectual* (New York: Signet, 1961), 53-54; *Capitalism: The Unknown Ideal* (New York: Signet, 1967), 136-137, 180-181, 195, and 269; and *The Virtue of Selfishness* (New York: Signet, 1964), 112 and 149-151. Also, see Leonard Peikoff, ed., *The Voice of Reason: Essays in Objectivist Thought* (New York: Meridian, 1989), 89 and Harry Binswanger, ed., *The Ayn Rand Lexicon: Objectivism from A to Z* (New York: Meridian, 1986), 8-9 and 74-75.

6. This latter would be particularly important for buyers such as retailers and wholesalers because their reputation, and thus their survival, depend on the quality of the goods and services they sell to customers.

7. On airbags, see James R. Healey and Jayne O'Donnell, "Deadly Air Bags: How a Government Prescription for Safety Became a Threat to Children," *USA Today*, 8 July 1996, B1 and Bruce Mohl, "U.S. Advises Car Makers on Dangers of Rear Air Bags," *Boston Globe*, 15 October 1999, A12. Although the use of air bags has been a net benefit in terms of the lives saved versus the lives lost, the point I am trying to make here is that regulation can harm or kill some people, which it has in this case.

8. On the duration of the approval process, see Daniel B. Klein and Alexander Tabarrok, "Theory, Evidence and Examples of FDA Harm," 2003, <http://www .fdareview.org/harm.shtml> (30 Aug. 2004) and "The Drug Development and Approval Process," 2003, <http://www.fdareview.org/approval_process.shtml> (30 Aug. 2004). These websites are published by The Independent Institute of Oakland, California.

9. These laws are known as the Kefauver-Harris Amendments to the Food, Drug, and Cosmetic Act of 1938.

10. On the history and effect of drug regulation in America, and specifically on the 1962 laws, see Daniel B. Klein and Alexander Tabarrok, "History of Federal Regulation: 1902-Present," 2003, <http://www.fdareview.org/history.shtml> (30 Aug. 2004). Some might think the Thalidomide tragedy in West Germany in the early 1960s proved that the 1962 laws were necessary. However, this reference and Dale H. Gieringer, "The Safety and Efficacy of New Drug Approval," *Cato Journal* 5, no. 1 (1985): 177-201, especially 193-194, refute this claim.

11. For more on the incentives for the FDA to be overly cautious, see Daniel B. Klein and Alexander Tabarrok, "Why the FDA Has an Incentive to Delay the Introduction of New Drugs," 2003, <http://www.fdareview.org/incentives.shtml> (30 Aug. 2004).

12. This estimate comes from Gieringer, "The Safety and Efficacy of New Drug Approval," 184-196.

13. For the estimate of casualties prevented, see Gieringer, "The Safety and Efficacy of New Drug Approval," 184-196. This number and the estimate for the number of deaths caused by the FDA are both maximum estimates. The maximum estimate was used for both because, in the study referenced, the maximum estimates are the only two values for these parameters that can be properly compared. However, even if one takes the most conservative approach in estimating the harm caused by the FDA (and uses the estimates for the maximum casualties prevented and minimum deaths caused by the FDA), one will find that the FDA is still responsible for about eleven-thousand deaths per decade on net. Furthermore, for a number of reasons, the net cost of the FDA given here far underestimates the harm done by the FDA. First, the cost due to FDA regulation includes only *deaths*; it does not include the number of *morbidity* cases. The estimate for morbidity cases would almost certainly dwarf the estimate for deaths. Second, these deaths are due only to the *delay* of new drugs and do not include death or morbidity estimates attributed to the new drugs whose development has been *prevented* because of the additional costs imposed on drug manufacturers by FDA regulation. Third, the short-run benefit of FDA regulation includes the number of *casualties* prevented, which includes the number of deaths *and* morbidity cases. Since the net harm caused by the FDA is determined by subtracting the number of casualties prevented from the number of deaths caused by the FDA, this dramatically reduces the estimate of harm caused by FDA regulation. In addition, the estimate of net FDA harm given here pertains only to its regulation of drugs. It does not include the net harm due to regulation in other areas, such as medical devices. The FDA's effect in the area of medical devices is similar to its effect in the prescription drug industry. For a discussion on the FDA's regulation of medical devices, see Noel D. Campbell, "Exploring Free Market Certification of Medical Devices," in *American Health Care: Government, Market Processes, and the Public Interest*, ed. Roger D. Feldman (Oakland: The Independent Institute, 2000), 313-344. Finally, note that the net cost of the FDA includes the effect of the Thalidomide tragedy. Even so, the net cost is still massive.

14. Editorial, "The Life and Deaths of DDT," *Wall Street Journal*, 14 June 2002, A12.

15. Just why it is accurate to describe this as a "holocaust" will become clear in chapter 6 when the nature of environmentalism is revealed.

16. For more on the parallels between nineteenth-century Germany and the United States, see Leonard Peikoff, *Ominous Parallels: The End of Freedom in America* (New York: Stein and Day, 1982).

17. At a more fundamental, philosophical level, preserving freedom in a country requires the widespread acceptance of reason and egoism. For more on the link between egoism and freedom, see my discussion on egoism and capitalism in chapter 1 and passim. Also, see Rand, *For the New Intellectual*, 81-82. On the link between reason and freedom, see Ayn Rand, *The New Left: The Anti-Industrial Revolution*, Revised edition (New York: Signet, 1975), 227-229 and *Philosophy*, 62-63; Peikoff, *The Voice of Reason*, 89; and Binswanger, *The Ayn Rand Lexicon*, 410.

18. For more on the improvement of working conditions and the elimination of child labor, see chapter 5, appendix (a).

19. For more on how capitalism achieves the highest standard of living that is possible, see the section titled "Capitalism" in chapter 1.

20. It must be recognized here that John Maynard Keynes was wrong when he said, "In the long run we are all dead." We are living in the long run right now because economies exist in the long run.

Appendix A: Some Notes on Working Conditions and Wages

Working Conditions and Wages in Late-Nineteenth and Early-Twentieth Century America

What were the quality of working conditions during the late-nineteenth and early-twentieth century under capitalism? Were conditions getting better, worse, or remaining stagnant? Although the answers to these questions can be inferred from the discussion in chapter 5, special attention must be given to them because they are so important. The actual history of capitalism has been distorted to such a great extent by the enemies of capitalism that it is widely believed that working conditions became worse in the early days of the industrial revolution compared to what they were prior to the industrial revolution. It is believed that working conditions eventually improved only because of government imposed regulations. This could not be farther from the truth.

Working conditions began to improve immediately under capitalism and, thanks to the remaining elements of capitalism that exist today, working conditions continue to improve.[1] As stated in the chapter, our ability to have better working conditions is based on the productive capability of the economic system. The greater the productive capability, the easier it is to produce the things that make better working conditions possible (such as indoor plumbing, heating, air conditioning, ventilation systems, and so on), and thus the more we are able to afford better working conditions.

Compared to today's standards, working conditions were miserably poor in late-nineteenth and early-twentieth century factories. This is true because the productivity of labor (i.e., how much each worker was able to produce) was extremely low. The methods of production used during this time period were primitive compared to today's methods; hence, very little of anything could be produced compared to today. In addition, it was not the case that the wealthy capitalists of the day were hoarding all the indoor plumbing, air conditioning, electric heating, and ventilation systems that could have been used to improve working conditions. These things simply did not exist. Working conditions were poor, not because the rich were hoarding all the wealth, but because very little wealth was produced compared to today. Relative to today, little economic progress had taken place up until that point in time; therefore, the economy was simply unable to produce the goods that make better working conditions possible.

It is only because of capitalism, the incentive to produce provided by the profit motive under capitalism, and the acquisition of knowledge, capital accumulation, and technological advancement that occurred based on this incentive that the productive capability increased and working conditions improved. As this happened, and workers began to prefer improved working conditions over even more rapid increases in pay, businesses began to offer better working conditions as a way to hire and retain workers. However, right from the start of the industrial revolution, working in a factory was a better option for many than the alternative (which was probably working on a farm or in one's home manufacturing some primitive product). Evidence for this is seen in the fact that people *voluntarily* chose to work in the factories rather than elsewhere. Why would they have made such a choice if they did not consider it a better option? Why would they have made such a choice if the factories did not offer better pay and working conditions (or some preferred combination of the two)?

People also had to work long hours and women and children had to work in the factories because of the miserably low productive capability, and thus the low wages, that existed. It was not because greedy capitalists forced people to work. For children whose parents did not have the skills to earn enough income to support their entire family, the option was to work to help support the family or face the prospect of starving in the streets. The same was true for why people had to work such long hours and why women had to work. Only as the productive capability improved, and thus wages rose sufficiently, could people afford to work fewer hours and could women and children afford to stay home. Moreover, in response to the desire to work less, businesses had to offer a shorter work week as a way to attract and retain workers.

The poor working conditions during the early days of capitalism were not caused by capitalism; they were inherited by it. The poor working conditions were caused by the non-capitalist, feudal societies that existed prior to the rise of capitalism. These societies did not respect individual rights and thus had very low and stagnant productive capabilities. If capitalist societies had been established sooner, the standard of living would have started to rise sooner and working conditions would have improved sooner.

The ultimate evidence for the beneficial effect capitalism had on people during the early days of its history lies in the facts of that time period. As one historian, Robert Hessen, writes about the rise of the factory in eighteenth-century England (the essence of which applies to late-nineteenth and early-twentieth century America), "the factory system offered a livelihood, a means of survival, to tens of thousands of children who would not have lived to be youths in the pre-capitalistic eras." As Hessen further states,

> The factory system led to a rise in the general standard of living, to rapidly falling urban death rates and decreasing infant mortality—and produced an unprecedented population explosion. . . . Both the rising population and the rising life expectancy give the lie to the claims of socialist and fascist critics of capitalism that the conditions of the laboring classes were progressively deteriorating during the Industrial Revolution.[2]

This last sentence states it most succinctly. If things were becoming worse for workers during the industrial revolution, why were more people able to live—and able to live longer? Indeed, things were getting better for workers *because* of the industrial revolution. That is why more people were living—and were living longer.

Regulations do not make it possible for women and children to stay at home, working conditions to improve, and the hours of work to be reduced. If they did and America had the same workplace regulations during the late-nineteenth and early-twentieth century that it has now, families would have been magically able to afford to allow wives and children to stay at home, working conditions would have been magically brought up to today's standards, and people would have been magically able to afford to work only forty hours-per-week. Of course, none of this would have happened. In a similar fashion to America's building codes being imposed on Ethiopia (as discussed in the chapter), the only thing that would have resulted from imposing today's workplace regulations on late-nineteenth and early-twentieth century America is that all the factories would have been forced to close down due to violations of the regulations. This would have decreased the productive capability even further and forced people to live in even greater poverty.

Regulations to improve working conditions during the late-nineteenth and early-twentieth century were either redundant, in that the improvements had already been adopted by businesses as the standard, or they imposed standards that people could not afford. To the extent regulations forced working conditions on people that they could not afford, it harmed workers. As I said in the chapter, there is a trade-off between the level of wages and the quality of working conditions. The better the working conditions, other things being equal, the lower wages will be. Forcing improved working conditions on workers prevents them from making choices about what working conditions they want *and* can afford. By forcibly imposing better working conditions, the government forces workers to accept lower wages without regard to whether the workers are willing to give up some of their wages to have the better working conditions. The market, as I have said, provides the working conditions that people want and can afford because workers choose to work at those businesses that provide the desired conditions.

Some might think that money could have been expropriated from wealthy business owners, during the late-nineteenth and early-twentieth century, to improve working conditions and raise wages. However, this is a mistaken belief. First, one must recognize that the *average* person was poor relative to today, so there just was not much money to take to make improvements and raise wages. Second, expropriating funds from wealthy individuals decreases the amount of funds they have available to invest in businesses. This, in conjunction with taking away the incentive for wealthy individuals to invest, by taking away money they earn from their investments, dramatically decreases the amount of money the wealthy are willing and able to invest, and thus it decreases the amount of money available to businesses. This means spending by businesses for capital goods and labor will decrease. Further, businesses will produce less (because they will have less money available to invest in the production of wealth) and thus there will be a lower productive capability and standard of living in the economic system.

Both of these effects—less spending by businesses and less production—decrease the average wage and the quality of working conditions. This is the case because less spending means less money will be spent to hire workers. Therefore, as stated in the chapter, if the supply of workers remains constant, the average wage must fall. Furthermore, less spending means less money will be spent on maintaining adequate working conditions, which will lead to a deterioration of those conditions. In addition, since the productive capability will be lower, fewer goods will be available to improve working conditions and for workers to buy with the money they earn. Hence, *working conditions will actually become worse and wages will fall if one attempts to expropriate money from business owners to improve working conditions and raise wages.* This illustrates, yet again, the link between violating/respecting individual rights and harming/benefiting the economy.

Some might think that forcibly requiring businesses to provide better working conditions would improve the productivity of their workers enough to make both the businesses and the workers better off. If this was the case, businesses would adopt the improvements voluntarily because it would be in their self-interest to do so. If the rise in productivity was enough to offset the cost of the improvements, businesses could obtain a competitive advantage in attracting good workers by offering the better conditions. If the rise in productivity more than offset the cost of the improvements, businesses could earn higher profits by making the improvements. Hence, the government would not have to force businesses to make the improvements.

Improvements that do not pay for themselves through increases in productivity are in the interests of businesses and workers only if the workers value the improvements enough to be willing to accept lower wages in exchange for the improvements. Here, workers obtain what they value the most and the profitability of businesses is maintained. If workers do not value the improvements more than the foregone wages, then the improvements are not in the interests of workers. Even if businesses completely absorb the added cost of the improvements (and thus workers' monetary wages are not lowered), the improvements are still not necessarily in the interests of workers (and obviously not in the interests of businesses). In this case, even though workers' monetary wages would not fall, their real wages would still fall due to the higher costs of production and the higher prices that the increased costs would bring about. Hence, workers would still have to value the improvements more than the reduction in their wages in order for the improvements to be in the workers' interests. If one thinks that workers could gain if businesses are forcibly prevented from raising prices (and paying lower wages) to cover the cost of the improvements, one should recall the effects of expropriating money from businesses discussed above. There it was shown that forcibly reducing business profitability actually reduces wages and the quality of working conditions because it decreases the willingness and ability of business owners to invest in their businesses.[3]

"Sweat Shops"

"Sweat Shops" Inside America

Related to the topic of working conditions and wages in late-nineteenth and early-twentieth century America is the issue of so-called sweat shops. To the extent that factories with poor working conditions still exist in America today, they do so largely because of government intervention in the economy (i.e., because of *violations* of the free market). Working conditions in factories in which illegal immigrants are recruited to work are typically not as good relative to working conditions in other factories. It is laws restricting free immigration into America that are responsible for the working conditions in the factories that recruit illegal immigrants. Laws against free immigration represent government intervention because they initiate physical force against U.S. employers who want to hire foreign workers and against foreigners who want to come to the United States to seek a better life. Neither of these groups' actions represent the use of force; both groups' actions are based on voluntary trade. Therefore, when the government uses force against them it is initiating force and thus violating individual rights. As a result of laws restricting immigration, workers who are brought here to work illegally are unable to quit their jobs and seek employment elsewhere (for fear of being deported). Hence, the laws force them to work in factories under conditions they might not otherwise tolerate. Further, because the employers know the workers cannot switch jobs (or because they will not let the workers switch jobs), the employers can get away with providing poorer working conditions than they would have to provide in a free market. Therefore, working conditions in these types of factories would improve if laws restricting immigration were abolished.[4]

Even if there were no laws against immigration into the United States and no regulations pertaining to the workplace, factories might still exist in America that have working conditions that are not acceptable to all Americans. The work might be laborious and repetitive, there might be unpleasant smells, it might be hot, and workers might have to work long hours. However, as long as the employer does not initiate physical force against its workers and informs the workers of all the hazards of the job, this is perfectly acceptable because no one's rights are violated. The workers choose to work in a particular location voluntarily and they can always choose to work in another location.

Conditions in some factories might not be acceptable to many people; however, these conditions might be the best that unskilled workers can afford and would represent an enormous improvement over the conditions in which immigrants from poor, undeveloped countries would have to work in their native land. (This is one major reason why people leave their native land for jobs in the United States.) If the employers were forced to provide better conditions, the businesses would very likely be taken overseas to places where costs of production are lower. This would lead to greater unemployment and lower wages for unskilled workers in the United States. Therefore, in order for the businesses to remain competitive with foreign firms, and for workers to keep their source of livelihood, the workers might have to work in a place with poor working conditions until they can gain more skills and move into a better position or simply find a better job somewhere else (both of which the skills gained in their current position will help them do).[5]

One must remember that forcing employers to provide better working conditions does not make workers better off. It raises costs, lowers the productive capability, lowers wages, and prevents workers from choosing what conditions are best for them. Furthermore, even conditions in the most unpleasant jobs, along with their wages, constantly improve over time under capitalism. This is true because the productive capability, and thus the ability to pay higher wages and provide better working conditions, continuously rises. Such progress is undermined by forced improvements in working conditions.

"Sweat Shops" Outside America

So-called sweat shops are much more prevalent in countries other than the United States. This is true for two main reasons: first, in some countries dictators force people to work in such conditions. This is not the result of capitalism, but of its exact opposite. Replacing the dictatorships with capitalism would make it possible for working conditions to begin to improve in these countries. Second, other countries may not have dictatorships, and may even have some significant elements of capitalism, however, they may have only just begun to develop and, as a result, have a low productive capability. Therefore, in terms of working conditions, these countries are in the same position as nineteenth-century America, or worse. More consistently implementing capitalism in these countries would make it possible to improve working conditions at a more rapid rate. Either way, capitalism is not the cause of poor working conditions, but the way to achieve better working conditions.

Here, it is important to remember the benevolent role of foreign investment into free (or, at least, semi-free), but temporarily poor, countries. Companies such as Nike, which are typically denounced for paying wages and/or requiring workers to work in conditions that some consider unacceptable, are actually the greatest benefactors to the workers in these countries. Companies such as Nike provide citizens of poor countries with economic opportunities they would otherwise not have and thus help to lift these individuals out of poverty. Companies like Nike build modern factories in these countries, raise the productivity of the average worker, and pay them much higher wages than they could otherwise earn. By means of foreign investment, poor countries have the ability to progress much more rapidly, and thus improve working conditions and wages in a much quicker fashion, than they otherwise could. This is the case because these countries can gain access to the latest technology and far more capital through foreign investment than they themselves possess. (If one is thinking Nike could be forced to pay higher wages and improve working conditions, the discussion on forcing capitalists of the late-nineteenth and early-twentieth century to improve working conditions is relevant here. The negative effect this would have on wages and working conditions would be the same in foreign countries because the incentive for Nike to invest in the foreign countries would be significantly reduced.)

It is crucial to understand that the moral justification for companies investing in undeveloped countries is not that these companies help to raise the standard of living of the people in the poor countries. That is an altruistic justification, and it has been shown throughout this book that it is immoral to act altruistically. Companies should invest in poor countries only when it is in their rational self-interest to do so. That is, only egoism provides a proper moral justification for firms investing in undeveloped countries because, as I have also shown throughout this book, egoism is the only code of morality that is consistent with the requirements of human life.

Nike, and every other company, has a moral right to offer whatever wages and working conditions it thinks are sufficient to voluntarily attract and retain good workers, no matter how low or poor others might consider the wages or working conditions to be. The company owners have a right to their own lives and property and therefore have a right to determine how their property will be used. If one recalls the discussion on rights in chapter 1, one will remember that no one has a right to a certain level of wage or quality of working conditions. This is the case because forcing employers to pay a higher wage or provide better working conditions violates individual rights, since force must be initiated against the employer to make him pay the wage or provide the working conditions. Of course, such action is immoral. In addition, it has all the negative economic effects one would expect from a violation of individual rights.

Getting workers to voluntarily choose to work for a "low" wage or in "poor" working conditions is fair and just. It is fair because it is based on voluntary trade and neither party to the trade is forced to enter into it. It is just because each party gets what it deserves. Each party to the trade chooses to deal with the other based on the other party's merits.[6] Of course, such activities will lead to the highest productive capability and standard of living that are possible for all involved, employers and workers alike.

Some might disagree with my statement in the above paragraph that says neither party is forced to make the trade. They might think that workers are "forced" to accept a certain level of wage or quality of working conditions because it is necessary for workers to earn a living to survive. However, this is an invalid conclusion. First, even though workers must earn a living to survive, they are not forced to accept any particular offer. They could choose to work for another employer, or they could choose to work for themselves. Second, this is an equivocation on the use of the term "force." The fact that reality "forces" people to work to support themselves, or starve, is not the same as some people forcing others to work for them. The requirements of human life imposed by the facts of reality and an individual working under conditions of slave labor are two very different things and must not be equated with each other. The former is a metaphysical fact that no one can escape—everyone depends on production for his survival. The latter is a relationship in which one person is a master and another person is his slave. This is the exact opposite of the relationship between an employer and employee under capitalism because the employer/employee relationship is one that exists in a context of freedom (i.e., the absence of the initiation of physical force), while the master/slave relationship exists only when freedom is absent (i.e., it requires the initiation of physical force). Remember from the discussion on freedom in chapter 1 that freedom does not mean freedom from the facts of reality, such as freedom from having to work to support oneself; it means freedom from the initiation of physical force and nothing more.

The Invalid Nature of the Concept "Sweat Shop"

There is one final point to make on this subject. The term "sweat shop" lumps together fundamentally different things and therefore should be thrown out. In other words, "sweat shop" is an invalid concept. It lumps together low wages and poor working conditions that exist within the context of voluntary trade (such as in poor countries that have only recently embraced capitalism) with low wages and poor working conditions that exist within the context of slave labor (such as in statist countries). That is, the term lumps together situations in which individual rights are protected with situations in which individual rights are violated. As I have stated throughout this book, these types of situations cannot be lumped together because protecting individual rights furthers human life and well-being, while violating rights destroys human life. This is a fundamental distinction that cannot be ignored or evaded.

In fact, "sweat shop" is an anti-concept. As defined by Ayn Rand, an anti-concept is "an artificial, unnecessary, and (rationally) unusable term, designed to replace and obliterate some legitimate concepts—a term which sounds like a concept, but stands for a 'package-deal' of disparate, incongruous, contradictory elements. . . ."[7] The term "sweat shop" attempts to obliterate the perfectly legitimate and moral act of getting people to voluntarily work for wages and in working conditions that some might consider unacceptable. "Sweat shop" does this by equating this legitimate act with slave labor.

Notes

1. For historical accounts of the improvements achieved during the early days of the industrial revolution (in all aspects of people's lives), see Robert Hessen's essay "The Effects of the Industrial Revolution on Women and Children," in *Capitalism: The Unknown Ideal*, Ayn Rand (New York: Signet, 1967), 110-117 and T. S. Ashton's essays "The Treatment of Capitalism by Historians" and "The Standard of Life of the Workers in England, 1790-1830," in *Capitalism and the Historians*, ed. F. A. Hayek (Chicago: The University of Chicago Press, 1963), 31-61 and 123-155.

2. See Hessen, "The Effects of the Industrial Revolution on Women and Children," 110-111 for this and the previous quote.

3. Fortunately, workers can have both increasing wages and improved working conditions in a capitalist society thanks to the rising productive capability made possible under capitalism. A rising productivity of labor is necessary for both higher wages and better working conditions for all the reasons discussed in this appendix and the chapter.

4. One must keep in mind that the number of factories like this in the United States is probably extremely small. Furthermore, even though immigrants would enter the United States at a greater rate if laws against immigration were abolished, which would initially cause a slight general decline in working conditions for low skill, low wage workers (the type of workers being referred to in this example), the working conditions in the relatively small number of factories that previously recruited illegal immigrants would still improve. This is the case because the number of workers that would leave the factories that previously recruited illegal immigrants would, more than likely, be far greater than the number of new immigrants that would want to work at those factories. Hence, the companies that formerly recruited illegal immigrants would face a large net decrease in the number of workers willing to work in their factories. This would occur because the former illegal immigrants and the additional immigrants who are coming to the United States due to the abolition of the laws would have a much larger number of opportunities open to them beyond the companies that previously recruited illegal immigrants. Therefore, these companies, to the extent that they want to remain in business, would have to offer better working conditions (and higher pay) to attract and retain workers. In fact, these companies would be in a position to offer better pay and

working conditions since the cost of transporting and hiding illegal immigrants would be eliminated.

5. One should not think based on what I have said here that foreign competition is harmful to American businesses and workers. Allowing foreign competition is a part of protecting the freedom of competition discussed in chapter 2 and helps to improve efficiency and the overall productive capability of the world economy. This raises the standard of living of everyone, including businesses and workers in America. For more on this issue, see the discussion, provided in chapter 1 under the section titled "The Morality of Rational Self-Interest and Capitalism," on how economic competition benefits everyone (even the "losers"). Also, see George Reisman, *Capitalism: A Treatise on Economics* (Ottawa, IL: Jameson Books, 1996), 350-362.

6. Barring any fraudulent activities by either party. Of course, such activities would be punished under capitalism.

7. For this definition and a more detailed discussion of "anti-concept," see Ayn Rand, *Capitalism*, 173-182.

Appendix B: How Does One Protect Individual Rights?

I often get the objection, when discussing the regulation of safety and quality, that it is too difficult to determine how to protect individual rights in many cases, so it is better to have regulations to prevent people from being harmed. Students usually present a litany of "what if" scenarios that are supposed to show the difficulty of protecting individual rights, including the difficulty of determining whether someone's rights have been violated and the difficulty of determining how to compensate those whose rights have been violated. The objections are usually in the following form: "What if a product that has the potential to harm people is produced?" "What if all the negative side effects of a product are not discovered before people start using it and people are harmed as a result?" "What if a person uses a product inappropriately and harms himself or others?" What these students usually want to do is to have the government establish regulations to determine how products should be produced and used and, in fact, if people should be allowed to manufacture and use certain products at all.

These objections raise some legitimate and very important issues. However, the solution to these issues in no way involves the use of government regulation. As I stated in the chapter, one does not protect people from harm by having regulation. One might prevent the occasional accident or prevent an individual from being exposed to a poorly built product, but as I have shown with respect to do-it-yourself disasters, the forced use of airbags, the FDA, and the ban on DDT, people are harmed—and often killed—*because* of regulation. Further, as I have also discussed, regulation decreases quality and safety in the long run because it raises costs, lowers the productive capability, the rate of economic progress, and the standard of living. This says that, other things being equal, more harm will be caused by regulation in the long run (and often in the short run) than without it.

In addition, by imposing regulation on people, one replaces a *potential* violation of individual rights with an *actual* violation of rights by the regulators. Without regulation, it is true there is the potential for the rights of individuals to be violated. For instance, it is possible for a person to be harmed by a defective product about which the manufacturer knew but did not inform consumers. For example, it might be discovered in laboratory testing that a drug has harmful side effects, but the drug manufacturer might ignore and attempt to conceal the test results. However, unless a cover-up has been discovered, when the government uses force against manufacturers (in the case of drugs, perhaps by requiring all manufacturers to follow certain testing procedures) it is *initiating* physical force against them to make them obey the regulation and is therefore violating their rights.

It is extremely dangerous, as well as immoral, to allow the government to use force against individuals merely because they have the potential to commit harmful acts. Such a position denies the *principle* of individual rights and thus endorses the use of the initiation of force. If taken to its logical and consistent end, it would lead to a proliferation of the use of force by the government and massive violations of individual rights. For instance, virtually everyone has the physical capability, and thus the potential, to commit murder. If the government's use of force must be based simply on the potential that someone could commit murder, the government could justify throwing anyone in jail by claiming it is preventing a particular person from committing murder. This is a case of assuming a person is guilty before he has committed a crime and thus of *initiating* force against an innocent man and violating his rights.[1] The same is true of regulation of safety and quality. Here the initiation of physical force is required to get businesses to follow the arbitrary dictates of the government. In order to restrain the use of force—in order to prevent the government from using force in an arbitrary and capricious manner—the use of force must be restricted to situations where rights have actually been violated, or when it is imminent that rights will be violated. This is the only way to make the government a protector of the people, instead of the greatest threat to the people.

Given that regulation does not protect people, what happens in the case where some new product is created (maybe an extremely powerful new pesticide is developed) and someone is harmed by the product? How does one determine who is at fault? How does one determine whether a person should be compensated and, if so, how much they should receive? More importantly, how does one prevent rights from being violated in the first place?

Determining how to protect individual rights is an extremely important question. It involves trying to determine what concrete actions are consistent with the principle of rights. It is a much more difficult question to answer than the question concerning whether individual rights should be protected. However, *the question concerning how to protect individual rights is less fundamental than the question concerning whether rights should be protected*. Whether or not individual rights should be protected is a fundamental political question. This is true because the answer that one provides to this question determines whether one is a friend or an enemy of human life. If one answers no to this question, then one is an enemy. If one answers yes, then one is a friend. One's answer to this question establishes whether one is a friend or enemy of human life because, as I have stated throughout this book, freedom from the initiation of physical force is a fundamental requirement of human life. People need freedom so they can use their minds to think, act on their own rational judgment, and pursue the values their lives require. Given that one is rational and answers this question in the affirmative, now it is possible for one to deal with the question of how to protect individual rights. However, only after one understands the appropriate response to the more fundamental question can one begin to think about answers to the less fundamental question.

Answering the less fundamental question is more difficult than answering the more fundamental question because there are a myriad of cases to consider, each with a specific set of circumstances, when answering the less fundamental question. Because of this, each case might require a different application of the principle of individual rights. For example, protecting individual rights in one case might involve the government using force against the manufacturer of a product who has concealed the results of product testing to prevent important information about potential harmful characteristics of a product from becoming known (such as the case of the drug with harmful side effects mentioned above). In another case, it might involve the use of force against an individual who is using a product in such a way that it is violating the rights of others (such as if an individual fires a gun into the air from his backyard when he has neighbors close by). In addition, new cases are always arising with the creation of new inventions. However, the fundamental guiding principle always remains the same: that individual rights be protected. As long as one understands this principle and is guided by it, answers can be found in every case that arises.

One must also keep in mind that there are many options that can be used to protect individual rights. For instance, jail time might be appropriate in one case, monetary compensation in another case, replacing property that was destroyed in another, or simply requiring the violator to cease the relevant activities in others. In many cases, different options might be equally good alternatives or a combination of the options might be the best alternative. One must consider the particular circumstances of each case to determine how to protect individual rights. For example, if an individual represents a physical threat to others (such as a murderer), jail time would be appropriate. However, if an individual unknowingly pollutes another person's land (such as in the case of the farmer polluting the downstream landowner's land discussed in chapter 4), requiring the perpetrator to compensate the victim might be appropriate.

Further, one must recognize that it is often appropriate (within certain limits) to compromise on the issue of *how* to protect individual rights, such as compromising on how much money a violator must pay a victim. In such a compromise, the principle that an individual deserves to be punished for violating someone's rights is still recognized. The question here is how much punishment he deserves. However, no compromise can take place on the issue of *whether* individual rights should be protected. In any compromise between protecting individual rights and allowing them to be violated, it is always the latter that wins out. This is true because if a violation of individual rights is allowed to go unpunished in any given situation then rights are not protected. In order for one to protect individual rights *on principle*, one must protect rights fully and consistently. In the case above of deciding how much a violator of rights should pay, if it is decided that the violator should not pay at all, he gets away with the violation. He is treated in the same manner as someone who has committed no violation. The principle being discussed here says that one can properly compromise *within a (valid) principle*, but one cannot compromise *on the principle* itself because once this is done, the (valid) principle is completely thrown out and its opposite (the invalid principle) is accepted.[2] In this case, it is accepted that violations of individual rights should be tolerated. The only details that may need to be worked out here are what types of violations should be allowed. However, the fact remains that if *any* rights are allowed to be violated, one is not going by the principle of protecting individual rights. One is acting on another principle or without principles at all.

The issue of how to protect individual rights is a technical, legal issue and it is the function of those in the field of law to answer this question in all cases. The fact that this question may sometimes be difficult to answer does not mean one throws up one's arms and says, in essence, "to hell with individual rights, this case is too difficult to apply the principle, so let's violate individual rights by imposing regulation on people." The difficulty of applying the principle in a particular case does not deny the validity of the principle that individual rights should be protected.

Let's consider some of the specific issues concerning the case of the newly developed, extremely powerful pesticide mentioned above to see what needs to be done to protect individual rights. If someone other than the producer or user of the pesticide is harmed by it, one needs to use the best known standards of the day to determine if adequate safety precautions were followed by the user, and one must also determine whether the best known standards are adequate for this pesticide and therefore whether different standards should be applied to it. One must also determine whether the manufacturer has provided adequate information to users of the pesticide and has tested the chemical sufficiently. Further, one must determine if the person who was harmed by the pesticide was at fault.

If the person harmed was at fault, no rights were violated. However, if the person using the pesticide used it inappropriately or the manufacturer knowingly withheld important information regarding the proper use or dangers of the chemical (or was negligent in its testing of the chemical), then the rights of the person harmed have been violated.[3] Further, it might be that blame for the harm done falls on some combination of the parties (whether two of them or all of them). Here, some procedure would have to be devised to determine what portion of the blame each guilty party bears.

Even if the person who used the pesticide took all known safety precautions and the manufacturer provided adequate information and tested the product thoroughly, if the person harmed is harmed through no fault of his own, his rights have still been violated. In this case, it might be that the safety standards used (whether existing safety standards developed for other, less powerful pesticides or new standards developed for this pesticide) are not adequate. It is proper for the manufacturers and users of new products to bear the responsibility for the unknown risks of those products. Unsuspecting victims should not have to take on risks they have not chosen to bear.

In connection with the above discussion, and as discussed in the chapter, standards for the production, testing, and use of products should not be set through government regulation. Standards should be set by private individuals and organizations, such as manufacturers, industry groups, and certification organizations, in conjunction with court cases that arise due to the production and use of products. Courts would typically not set standards (and it is preferable that they do not). However, standards, such as those for product safety, might be influenced by court decisions. For example, by ruling in favor of an individual who was harmed by a particular product, a court might influence manufacturers to establish more stringent safety standards with regard to the use of that product. In fact, if the harm is great enough, or occurs repeatedly enough, a court might actually require manufacturers to establish stricter safety standards. In the case of the new, more powerful pesticide under discussion, by ruling in favor of an individual who has been harmed, a court might influence manufacturers to abandon standards that had originally been adopted for existing, less powerful pesticides and create new standards for the new pesticide.

One must also keep in mind that standards should not be set, and legal decisions should not be made, with "perfect" safety—i.e., the belief that products can be made so no one will ever be harmed—as the standard. Risk-free life is impossible. As stated in the chapter, the cost of safety standards must also be taken into account. Imposing exorbitant costs on manufacturers in an attempt to achieve unreasonable levels of safety in products and services would violate individual rights and lower the productive capability and thus actually reduce the level of safety that can be achieved.

If someone's rights have been violated, one must determine how the victim can be compensated (if at all), how much compensation the person deserves, and what must be done to prevent the violation from occurring again. If the person has been significantly harmed, such as if he has been killed, it may be impossible to compensate him or his family fully. No amount of money is going to bring a person back from the dead. However, this is neither a problem of protecting individual rights nor a justification of regulation to prevent potential harm from occurring. Again, the analogy to one's potential to commit murder is apropos. If a person is murdered, his family cannot be fully compensated. However, this does not justify throwing people in jail based on their potential to commit murder. This would be a violation of individual rights and does not correct the situation. Again, the same is true for regulation of safety and quality. One does not justify *actual* violations of individual rights by the government, through regulation, because of the *potential* for people to be harmed (even if there is the potential for great harm).

If someone's rights have been violated, but it is determined that the person harmed is partly to blame, this would decrease the guilt of the violator and decrease the compensation to the victim (and/or the penalty imposed on the perpetrator). Further, if multiple parties are to blame (not including the victim), the penalty on each of them would be less than if one was solely to blame. Also, if there was negligence on the part of the perpetrator(s), the penalty and/or compensation would be greater.

The only way to protect individual rights is to use force only when they have actually been violated or when it is imminent that someone's rights will be violated. If rights have been violated, to achieve justice, one punishes the perpetrator and/or compensates the victim. As long as one acts on the principle of protecting individual rights, justice can be achieved. The principle serves as a beacon guiding one through the complexities that can sometimes exist in the details of a particular situation.

I am not pretending to have exhausted all the relevant considerations with regard to how to protect individual rights. There are often a large number of factors to take into account in any one particular case and there are many I have not considered in the one hypothetical case I used as an illustration. This is why legal proceedings often use previous cases to determine how to protect individual rights in a specific case. Here, one uses previous applications of the principle of protecting individual rights as a guide to determine how best to apply the principle in a current case.

It is neither the task of an economist nor the task of this book to provide a comprehensive treatment on how to protect individual rights. However, a major task of this book is to provide an answer to the more fundamental question of whether individual rights should be protected. I, of course, show why they should be protected. Nevertheless, hopefully one has begun to gain an understanding of the basic procedure that one must follow to determine how to protect individual rights.

Notes

1. I am not referring to a case where the police have evidence, say, that someone paid a hit man to kill a person and they therefore arrest the individuals involved before the murder is actually committed. This is a case where it is proper for the government to act because it has actual evidence that, given the progression of events, a murder *will be* committed. I am referring to a case where the police have no evidence but arrest someone

simply because he has the physical ability to pull the trigger of a gun and thus has the potential to commit murder.

2. On this issue, see Ayn Rand, *The Virtue of Selfishness*, (New York: Signet, 1964), 79-81.

3. Determining what represents negligent behavior and what information manufacturers should provide to consumers (if any) is outside the scope of this book. This is a task for (private) certification organizations, companies in the industry, and individuals in the field of law. For leads on how to answer these questions, see the relevant discussion in this appendix, below, and the relevant discussion in the section titled "What Will Happen Without Regulation?" in the chapter.

Chapter Six

Environmentalism

Introduction

The critique of the market emanating from the environmentalist movement is the claim that when people are left free to act in their own rational self-interest, the activities they engage in allegedly damage the environment by causing pollution, the extinction of species, the depletion of natural resources, plus many other things. Because of this, it is claimed, the government must intervene in the market with some type of environmental regulation to prevent the environment from allegedly being damaged. Going even further, it must restrict people's activities and make them repair some of the alleged damage they have done. Let's see where this claim goes wrong.

A Political and Economic Analysis of Environmentalism

Economic Progress and the Environment

Economic progress under capitalism always tends to improve the environment; that is, it tends to improve the environment in which people live. This can be seen in many different ways. For example, when it is cold outside, people can be in a nice warm environment inside thanks to the modern heating systems made possible by economic progress under capitalism. Likewise, when it is hot and humid outside, people can be in a cool, comfortable environment thanks to the modern air conditioning systems created under capitalism. Further, the invention and widespread use of the automobile has reduced the amount of pollution people live in by eliminating the equine waste which used to line city streets. In addition, the development of modern pipe, plumbing, sewage systems, and pumping stations has made it so human waste must no longer line city streets.[1] Also, improvements thanks to capitalism bring clean, hot and cold running water in reach of everyone, everywhere, at virtually every moment of the day. Furthermore, industrialized societies have progressed from the use of coal to oil to nuclear energy and natural gas to produce electricity, all the while becoming cleaner and cleaner. Similarly, they have moved from the use of wood to coal to oil to natural gas for heating, becoming cleaner and cleaner every step of the way. All of these advances have been achieved through economic progress under capitalism. All of them represent a dramatic improvement in our environment. The environment, properly understood (and to which I refer here), is the surroundings of man.

Environmentalists have something else in mind when they use the term "environment." When they use the term they are referring to nature as such, regardless of its relationship to and influence on man. However, the concept "environment" is a relational concept. As stated by the writer, Peter Schwartz, "there can be no concept of an 'environment' that is not the environment *of* someone (or something)—any more than there can be 'property' that exists independently of the owner of the property."[2] (Emphasis in original.) Although when one refers to an "environment" one might be referring to the environment of any living organism, later in the chapter I will show the importance and significance of man's environment and why this is the environment with which we should be concerned. I will also discuss some of the errors in the environmentalists' definition of "environment." In this part of the chapter, as the title explicitly states, I want to focus on an economic and political analysis of environmentalism. However, some clarification of the concept "environment" was necessary at this point in order to help one better understand the crucial issues being discussed here.

The Effects of Environmental Regulation

The basic economic effects of environmental regulation are no different than the effects from the types of regulation discussed in chapter 5. It raises costs to businesses, prices to consumers, and thus lowers the standard of living. Environmental legislation does this, for example, by preventing some resources from being used in production (such as coastal areas, so-called wetlands [i.e., swamps], the continental shelf [which could be used for oil drilling], and national and state parks). This decreases the amount of resources that can be used in production, thereby decreasing the ability to produce wealth and lowering the standard of living. Further, environmental legislation often requires a large number of arbitrary rules to be followed, many studies to be performed, and much paperwork to be filled out before production can be undertaken (as is the case with the need to perform "environmental impact studies"). This ties up resources in tasks that would not otherwise need to be performed. This, in turn, decreases the resources that can be used to engage in the production of wealth and thus lowers the standard of living. In some cases, the prospect of having to perform "environmental impact studies" and face lawsuits from environmental groups or challenges by the government prevents productive projects that could have enormous benefits to man from ever being undertaken. This occurs because the detailed studies and lengthy legal battles make the cost of undertaking some of the projects prohibitively high.

Preservation of the Natural Surroundings

In a free market, if environmentalists want to keep land in its natural state to preserve the natural surroundings, they could pool their funds together in a voluntary manner to buy land and leave it in its natural state.[3] Of course, if environmentalists want to be able do this, they will need to have their property rights protected. Otherwise, there is the potential that they could have their property forcibly taken from them and used for purposes of which they do not approve.

Environmentalists, however, should not dare force other property owners to maintain their land in its natural state. But this is exactly what environmentalists do, for instance, when they support legislation restricting or outlawing the use of land, when they destroy property owned by others, or when they interfere with the activities of businesses. When environmentalists engage in these activities they initiate physical force, either through the government or privately, to impose their desires on others.[4] The use of these methods violates individual rights and is immoral because it stands in opposition to human life. Further, such actions lead to a lower standard of living because people are not able to use their property for profitable pursuits (i.e., for the production of wealth). The lower standard of living, for now, may only be relative to what it otherwise could be. However, if environmentalists are able to prevent productive activities on a much wider scale in the future, the standard of living will actually fall in absolute terms.

Pollution

Environmentalists say restrictions on economic activity are needed to prevent people from creating unsafe levels of pollution in the air, ground, and water. The existence of harmful levels of pollution, of course, is a legitimate concern. However, the way to solve any genuine problems concerning pollution is to establish and protect private property rights. For instance, if an individual pollutes another person's property against that person's will, the affected person must be able to seek redress in a court of law for this violation of his property rights. By taking legal action, the property owner can get a court order to require the polluter to clean up the property and cease the relevant activities. In a similar manner, any property that would be beneficial to keep clean for man's use can be protected by extending private property rights to *all* areas of the earth, including all areas on the surface, below the surface, and to all bodies of water (such as rivers, lakes, and oceans).[5] No area of the earth should be off limits to ownership by private individuals (including the areas currently designated as national and state parks and so-called conservation areas).

In addition, as was stated in the chapter on externalities, if pollution is created that causes demonstrable physical harm to someone and can be traced back to one source or a number of sources acting together, then the people harmed have a legitimate case to seek compensation in court and get an injunction against the polluter(s). Further, one must take into consideration rights that have already been established, such as those of a steel mill that begins operations before others have moved into an area.

As was also stated in the chapter on externalities, pollution that is the cumulative effect of sources acting independently of each other must be considered a natural byproduct of economic activity. Here, no compensation should be allowed because one would have to treat individuals in a collectivist manner by assuming they acted together when, in fact, they did not. One must remember that if the pollution created by a single individual (or group of individuals acting in concert) is negligible and therefore not harmful to anyone, one cannot properly hold the individual (or group) responsible for any harm done. These cases must be treated in the same manner as the negative consequences of natural phenomena (such as bad weather).[6] In those cases in which legal action would not be possible, one must convince others to voluntarily reduce or eliminate activities that cause pollution.

One issue with regard to pollution that is typically forgotten, ignored, or evaded by environmentalists, but that must also be recognized, is that not all pollution comes from man. Some pollution exists in nature (such as air pollution created by a volcanic eruption or the contamination of a stream caused by decaying organic matter). Pollution is not properly defined as any chemical created by man and emitted into the air, ground, or water. Pollution represents the contamination of these things to such a degree that they are no longer beneficial to human life.[7] This can also occur due to natural phenomena.

Furthermore, one must remember that it is beneficial to "pollute" some areas of the earth. For instance, it is beneficial to use some land for garbage dumps and to use some areas of the earth to dispose of human waste. It is a fact that *all* life (not just human life) produces various forms of waste. The key with respect to waste is to be able to remove it from where we live and, if necessary, chemically alter it to make it less harmful. Through the development of such things as modern sewage systems and transportation systems under capitalism, we are able to remove the waste from where we live, chemically alter it, and therefore live in a much less polluted environment.

One might raise the objection here that all life produces waste, but human life is the only form of life that produces massive amounts of garbage that is not biodegradable, such as plastic bottles and aluminum cans. This may be true, but it is irrelevant. Iron ore is a naturally occurring mineral that exists in abundance and is not biodegradable, and all matter can ultimately be reduced to chemical elements, which themselves cannot be broken down chemically any further. The important and life supporting activity in which man engages is that he takes certain chemicals from one part of the earth, transforms them into such things as plastic bottles and aluminum cans, uses them, and then disposes of them in another part of the earth. The fact that we now have chemicals in the ground in the form of plastic bottles and aluminum cans, instead of the original forms of the chemicals that constitute the plastic bottles and aluminum cans, is irrelevant. There is nothing magical or mystical, as environmentalists believe, about the naturally existing chemical compounds in the earth. Again, the key with respect to waste is to be able to remove it from where we live, and chemically alter it if necessary, after such products are no longer useful to man.[8]

I must highlight here, in connection with the topic of pollution, what was said at the beginning of this chapter. That is, economic progress in an industrialized society always tends to improve the environment. This includes reducing the level of pollution in which humans must live. Environmentalists would like people to think that life before industrialization was much more pollution free and idyllic than life in an industrialized society. The claim by environmentalists is that, due to things such as smog created by automobiles, smoke emitted from factories, garbage created by the production and consumption of large quantities of goods, and many other things, we must live in a much more polluted environment than we would otherwise have to live in if we did not have to deal with these things. However, this claim is contradicted by evidence that shows that air pollution in London, the city for which the best data are available for long periods of time, peaked around 1890. The air in that city is believed to be cleaner today than it was long before industrialization began to take place.[9] Further, this claim is also made as if pollution—as if dirt and filth—was not an all-pervasive problem in pre-industrialized societies (and in non-industrialized societies today). In pre-industrialized societies, food was easily contaminated (there were no plastic or Styrofoam containers to keep it clean and no refrigeration to keep it from spoiling), drinking water was often contaminated (there were no modern purification methods available), sanitation was extremely poor, and infectious disease was common and often killed large numbers of people in periodic plagues.[10] Thanks to industrialization we have far fewer, and relatively minor, pollution problems compared to pre-industrialized societies. Smog, for instance, is a relatively isolated problem (limited to some of the major cities) and can be dealt with easily, simply by choosing not to live in the cities that have such a problem. Further, with improvements in technology and the rising productive capability achieved through economic progress under capitalism, the level of smog can be continuously reduced.

There are more facts that one can present in the case for an industrialized society. For example, in pre-industrialized Great Britain, approximately *75 percent* of all children in London died by the age of *five*. The average lifespan in pre-industrialized societies was about thirty years, compared to over seventy-five years in industrialized societies today. In pre-industrialized societies, people worked from dawn-to-dusk performing back-breaking labor to produce barely enough food to keep themselves alive.[11]

The conclusions to be drawn from these facts are obvious. Most people living today would be dead if not for industrialization. Of those young adults who would not be dead, many of them would be entering the latter phases of their relatively short lives, instead of the early years of their adult lives as they are today. We all owe our standard of living—and thus our very lives—to the industrialized society in which we live. An attack on economic progress and industrialization is an attack on one's own ability to survive. Instead of attacking and denouncing industrialization, people should be supporting and praising it. To paraphrase a statement from one great philosopher, Ayn Rand, and put it as bluntly as possible, those of you reading these words who are over the age of thirty, or who plan to live to be over thirty, should turn to the nearest, smokiest, dirtiest, smelliest smokestack you can find and say a silent, "Thank you."[12] You should do this because you owe your life to that smokestack! You owe your life to the productive capability that that smokestack represents! Economic progress in an industrialized—capitalist—society is of enormous benefit to human life. To any rational individual there is no doubt about this fact.

The Intellectual Bankruptcy of the Environmentalist Movement

In light of chapter 5, it is easy to see the economically destructive effects of environmental legislation because it is similar to the regulation of the safety and quality of products, services, and working conditions, and therefore has the same destructive consequences. However, as is the case with the other arguments against the free market, there are more fundamental criticisms to make against environmentalism. By making these criticisms, the environmentalist movement will be revealed for the thoroughly destructive ideological movement it is.[13]

To understand the intellectually corrupt nature of the environmentalist movement, one must understand the fundamental ideas at the base of the movement. Understanding the ideas at the root of a movement is important to understanding any ideological movement because the fundamental ideas are the ones that determine what actions and less important ideas are consistent with the movement. Hence, one must turn to these fundamental ideas to understand the essence of a movement and to determine, for good or for evil, what a movement is capable of achieving.

Environmentalism is not, fundamentally, concerned with having clean air, rivers, and beaches; "saving the planet" for future generations; or creating "wildlife areas." These do not explain everything one sees coming from the movement. In order to see the essence of the movement, one must search deeper.

There are two fundamental ideas that underlie the environmentalist movement. Based on these ideas, one can explain everything one sees coming from the movement. These ideas are (1) that nature has intrinsic value, value in and of itself, apart from the value that nature represents to mankind and (2) the belief that man should be sacrificed to nature.

If one recalls the discussion on socialism in chapter 1, one will recognize that this latter idea is similar to the moral theory on which socialism is based. Socialism is based on the morality of altruism (the belief that it is virtuous for individuals to sacrifice themselves to others) and it has succeeded tremendously in sacrificing people. The greens of the environmentalist movement are really a step below the reds of socialism. This is true because the socialists at least have the superficial appearance of being for man, in that they want to sacrifice some men to *other men*. The environmentalists are not happy with this arrangement. They want to get man out of the picture altogether. They want to sacrifice man to snail darters, snowy plover birds, spotted owls, and inanimate matter such as rock formations. They want to sacrifice man to everything in nature that is *nonman*. This is why I consider the environmentalist movement to be one of the most dangerous ideological movements in existence today. Hence, it is extremely important to have a proper understanding of the movement.

In my analysis of the environmentalist movement, I will show the nature of the movement and the logical implications of the ideas on which the movement is based. When one sees these, one will have a clear understanding of why the movement is so potentially destructive. The first thing to do in this endeavor is to analyze the first idea named above, at the root of environmentalism: that nature has intrinsic value.

The belief that nature has intrinsic value is often openly expressed by environmentalists. For example, David M. Graber, a research biologist with the National Park Service, states that he "value[s] wildness for its own sake, not for what value it confers upon mankind." He goes on to say, "We are not interested in the utility of a particular species, or free-flowing river, or ecosystem, to mankind. They have *intrinsic value*, more value—to me—than another human body, or a billion of them."[14] (Emphasis added.)

The first thing to understand about the idea that nature has intrinsic value is that it is false. *Nature has no intrinsic value*. Nature derives its value from man's ability to benefit from it.

To have intrinsic value means that something has value by the mere fact of its existence. For example, if nature has intrinsic value then things that exist in nature, such as a wolf, a rat, a tree, and a rock, have value simply because they exist. The problem with this theory is that value does not exist in a vacuum, apart from the person doing the valuing. A value is something that one acts to gain and/or keep.[15] The concept of value therefore implies a relationship between the valuer (the person doing the gaining and/or keeping) and the thing that has value (i.e., the object one is attempting to gain and/or keep).

Nothing, in fact, has intrinsic value. With respect to nature, some things in nature have value because they can be used by man to further his life and happiness. For example, a cow has value to man because he can eat the cow and use it to meet his nutritional needs. Iron ore has value to man because he can use it to build bridges and buildings that help him further his life. However, some things in nature are of disvalue to man because they stand in opposition to his life and happiness. For example, a rattlesnake is of disvalue because it can harm man and his source of food (such as his cows). Trees can also be of disvalue to man because they can stand in his way and make it harder for him to travel. In this case, it would be to man's benefit to cut the trees down, take some chemicals from another part of the earth, and lay them down to form a road where the trees once stood so that it is easier for him to travel.

Whether a thing has value or not is determined by the relationship between man and the thing that exists. It depends on whether man can use the thing to further his own life or whether it has the potential to harm him. The example above with the trees can be used to illustrate this point. When they inhibit man's ability to travel, they harm his ability to survive and thus are of disvalue. However, in a different relationship to man, the trees are of benefit to him. That is, as a source of lumber to build homes, the trees are of value.

As stated in chapter 1, each man's life is his ultimate value and the standard by which one determines whether something is of value or not because each man's life is the source of his values. Without a man's life, nothing is of value to him because he does not exist. So anything that is of actual value must support his highest value: his life. In other words, that which furthers a man's life is of value, that which harms it is of disvalue. To "value" something that is destructive to one's life is an attempt to practice a deadly contradiction. It is to say, in essence, "I value that which destroys my highest value, the source of everything I value, and thus my ability to value. I value that which destroys me. Hence, I value that which is not of value to me."

Even the esthetic beauty of nature does not have intrinsic value. The esthetic beauty of nature has value *only* because it is of benefit to man (i.e., he is capable of enjoying it). However, before man is able to take the time to enjoy the esthetic beauty of nature, he must first use some of the resources in nature to sustain his life. The esthetic beauty of nature is of no value to a man who is starving and freezing to death. At a minimum, he must find something to eat and protect himself from the elements. Only then is he able to take the time to enjoy the esthetic beauty of nature. Of course, in an industrialized society, where man has learned an enormous amount about how to use nature to his advantage, he has much greater time available to enjoy the esthetic beauty of nature. Nonetheless, the esthetic beauty of nature has value only because of its beneficial relationship to man—only because it is of value *to man*.

Even a man's own life has no intrinsic value. A man's life has value to him because it is a source of values *to him*. However, if a man's life becomes unbearable, such as if he contracts a disease that will lead to a painful and protracted death or if he is imprisoned in a concentration camp where torture and death are imminent, his life is no longer of value to him because it is no longer a source of values, and it may be proper for him to end his life in either of these situations. Hence, a man's life does not possess value by the mere fact of its existence; it does not possess intrinsic value.

Based on the false belief that nature has intrinsic value, environmentalists consider any chemical produced by man and discharged into the air, water, or land to be pollution. According to this view, man is altering the alleged source of value (i.e., raw nature) by creating and disposing of something that did not come from that source. Therefore, that which has alleged value is being contaminated by that which is allegedly of disvalue. However, as stated earlier in the chapter, this is an invalid understanding of pollution.

Likewise, the environmentalists' view of "the environment" is based on the theory of the intrinsic value of nature and the non-value of man. They consider only wild nature—nature apart from man—to be the environment. This view ignores the significance of man in the world. It ignores the fact that man is the being who possesses reason (i.e., a conceptual faculty, or a tool his mind possesses that allows him to think in terms of principles and ideas). This is the tool that distinguishes man from the lower animals. It is what makes it possible for man to gain vast sums of knowledge that the lower animals cannot acquire. It enables man to further his life and well-being better than any other living being and gives him the right to actually do so.[16] Any valid view of the environment must take into account these facts. It must take into account the nature of man. If it does not, crucial facts of reality are being ignored. That is why I defined the environment as the surroundings of man earlier in the chapter. This definition takes all the relevant facts into account; it highlights the importance and significance of man.

Furthermore, based on the belief that nature has intrinsic value environmentalists call for the preservation of nature even when it comes at a great cost to man. Based on this idea, environmentalists believe man should allow rivers to be free flowing and therefore not build dams to provide himself with electricity, water, and recreation areas.[17] Based on this idea, environmentalists believe man should not build houses to provide himself with shelter or roads to make it easier for him to travel, but should leave land untouched for wild animals to use. Further, it is believed that man should not drill for oil or mine in many areas of the world so that these "pristine environments" are not disturbed. In other words, based on the idea that nature has intrinsic value environmentalists believe that man should sacrifice himself to nature—sacrifice his own needs and desires so that nature may remain untouched or, at least, touched only "minimally" by his existence. This brings me to the second of the two ideas that lie at the root of the environmental movement.

I showed in chapter 1 the destructive nature of the altruist code of morality in connection with socialism. The situation is no different with respect to altruism and environmentalism. No matter where the belief in self-sacrifice emanates from, it is destructive to human life. If an individual sacrifices himself, whether to other people or to snail darters and spotted owls, the individual still loses. His life is destroyed or he is less able to further his life.

Environmentalists want to sacrifice man to nature so that nature can remain wild. This would have grave consequences for the survival of man. Not very many men could survive in the wild and the ones that could would not have a very happy, or a very long, existence. What man needs to do is *tame* nature—make it more amenable to his survival. Man needs to turn the earth into his garden; he needs to use nature to serve his ends. To do this, he must expand his knowledge of and command over nature through the use of his mind (through the use of reason) and use natural resources to produce the wealth upon which his survival depends. This will help to maintain and expand the industrialized society that is so crucial to his existence.

Invalid Claims Made by Environmentalists

There are further problems with environmentalism. Environmentalists lie and make many invalid claims to further their cause. This is not an arbitrary assertion—an assertion without evidence—that I am making. This is openly admitted by leading environmental "intellectuals." One such "intellectual," Stephen Schneider, of the National Center for Atmospheric Research, states, "we need to get some broad-based support. . . . So we have to offer up scary scenarios . . . and make little mention of any doubts we might have. This 'double ethical bind' we frequently find ourselves in cannot be solved by any formula. Each of us has to decide what the right balance is between being effective and being honest."[18] In essence, he is saying that environmentalists must choose between being honest and offering up scary stories to get people to join the movement and support its causes.

Further, a recent book titled *The Skeptical Environmentalist: Measuring the Real State of the World* documents in detail the fallacies, distortions, and outright lies put forward by environmental "scientists" on a large number of issues.[19] As an example, there is the evidence environmentalists put forward to show that worldwide food production per capita is declining and that, because of this, a worldwide food crisis is allegedly imminent. To substantiate their claim, environmentalists present *only worldwide* data on grain production per capita (including data from both industrialized and non-industrialized, "developing" countries). When one considers only the aggregate worldwide data, food production per capita does, indeed, show a decline since 1984. However, what environmentalists do not show is that when one separates data from industrialized and non-industrialized countries, one sees a leveling off of food production in industrialized countries, but a rising trend in non-industrialized countries at a much lower level of food production per capita than in the industrialized countries. As the author of the book, Dr. Bjorn Lomborg, observes, "In the industrialized countries production of grain steadily increased from the 1950s to the 1980s, stabilizing around 650 kg per inhabitant, essentially because we just cannot eat any more." But the growth trend in food production per capita has continued in the non-industrialized countries and was at about 211 kg in 2000. If one puts these two trends together with the constant population that exists in the industrialized countries and the growing population that exists in non-industrialized countries, one will, indeed, see that the worldwide trend is downward because worldwide food production per capita is an average of food production in industrialized and non-industrialized countries weighted by the respective populations in each.[20] Since the relatively small amount of per capita food production in non-industrialized countries has a growing population weight, the worldwide average is declining. Nevertheless, this declining average does not imply that a food crisis is imminent. Food is becoming more plentiful in the world. By showing only the worldwide trend and making generalizations based on it, environmentalists give a false impression of what is occurring with regard to food production.

Even more revealing are the evasions and dishonesty of environmentalists in their reviews of *The Skeptical Environmentalist*. In a review of Dr. Lomborg's discussion of worldwide food production, instead of acknowledging and apologizing for the error that he and other environmentalists have made, and that Dr. Lomborg has exposed, the reviewer commits the very same error![21] That is, the reviewer uses *only worldwide* data to argue that worldwide food production is declining. He uses the exact same data Dr. Lomborg used to show that environmentalists are engaging in a selective use of data, and the reviewer does not even attempt to address Dr. Lomborg's claim! It is as if the reviewer did not even read the portion of the book he was reviewing! This is not the only review of this type.[22] For alleged scientists to show such a blatant disregard for facts on such a large scale is not an innocent error. It reveals a fundamental disdain for facts and truth.[23] It reveals a desire to cling to one's beliefs even when they are contradicted by the facts.

This is why it is no accident that one after another of the claims made by environmentalists have been shown to be invalid. From the production of food discussed above, to acid rain and global warming, to the extinction of species by man and the depletion of natural resources, to the danger of Alar and the depletion of the ozone layer, to the danger of nuclear power and pesticides, to the danger of genetically modified foods. The list could go on and on. Claims made by environmentalists with regard to these and many other topics have been shown to be either completely untrue or gross distortions of the facts. At best, environmentalists put forward misleading half-truths.

As I have said, they put forward invalid statements to dupe people into believing the environmentalists' claims and joining their cause. I am not going to use the space in this book to analyze every environmentalist claim because it is not necessary to do that to show that their claims, in general, are invalid. If one wants to read a rational response to environmentalists' claims on a myriad of issues one can read the references given in this chapter for further discussion, especially the book titled *Rational Readings on Environmental Concerns*. Here, I will look at only a few of the claims made by environmentalists to give the reader an indication of the invalid nature of the claims made by them in general.

Further, I will also show why environmentalists' claims can properly be dismissed *without consideration.*

Global Warming

Global warming is a favorite of environmentalists. They are using it to try to force the world's Western nations to decrease their consumption of fossil fuels. If they succeed, it will be to the enormous detriment of people because it will cause the standard of living to plummet. Sources I have used for the scientific arguments made against the environmentalists' claims on global warming include papers, by various authors, on the subject of global warming contained in the book *Rational Readings on Environmental Concerns* and all of the book *The Global Warming Debate*, which is a compilation of papers from many different authors.[24] If one has a dispute with the science concerning the claims made here, one should look at the original source and challenge the arguments there, since one's dispute really lies with the arguments made by the scientists there.[25]

The basic claim with respect to global warming is that the temperature of the earth's atmosphere at the surface is increasing due to the burning of fossil fuels by man and the resulting emission of greenhouse gases, such as carbon dioxide (CO_2), into the atmosphere. These gases trap heat from the sun in the earth's atmosphere, cause the temperature at the surface to rise, and thus act like a greenhouse. If one listened only to environmentalists, one would think the activities of man are certain to bring on a warming of the atmosphere (or have already brought it on) and that this warming has grave consequences for life on earth. For instance, the polar ice caps are supposed to melt, cause the oceans to rise, and cause enormous amounts of coastal flooding. Some claim that the weather is supposed to become more severe and erratic, with bigger temperature swings between hot and cold seasons and more severe thunderstorms, tornadoes, hurricanes, and snowstorms. No doubts are mentioned by environmentalists concerning the existence of global warming, and no mention is made of the potential benefits of global warming and the rise in concentration of greenhouse gases that is supposed to cause it. Let's take a look at the facts concerning global warming.

First, according to Dr. S. Fred Singer, a world renowned expert on global climate change and the greenhouse effect, without the *naturally occurring* greenhouse gases, the earth would be a cold and lifeless planet.[26] The average temperature at the earth's surface, according to chemist Dr. Jack Barrett, would be around 0 °F, instead of the 59 °F it is today.[27] Also, according to Dr. Singer, water vapor (which, of course, is not man-made) is the most effective greenhouse gas.[28] This says that large quantities of greenhouse gases exist naturally and are of enormous benefit to human life—and all life—because without them there would be no life on earth.

Next, there are the facts concerning the general circulation models (GCMs). These are the mathematical computer simulations of the earth's atmosphere used to predict the significant global warming that will allegedly come with the increase in man-made greenhouse gases. According to Dr. Singer, there are significant differences in what the models predict. In 1992, models predicted warming of between 2.5 and 8 °F by the year 2050 based on a doubling of atmospheric CO_2. Subsequent predictions, in 1995, forecasted warming of between 2 °F and 6 °F by the year 2100, a smaller prediction over a much longer period of time.[29] Further, according to Dr. Singer, climatologist Dr. Patrick Michaels, and Paul Knappenberger of New Hope Environmental Services, Inc., there is serious disagreement between model results and actual experience from the climate record.[30]

Moreover, physicist Dr. Sherwood Idso states that by allowing for a realistic increase in the number of water-droplet clouds and a decrease in the number of ice-crystal clouds (a likely occurrence with a warming of the earth's atmosphere) the predictions of the models are cut in half. Also, Dr. Idso states, by allowing greater water content in clouds, due to greater land and oceanic evaporation rates, the warming predictions were cut to a third of their original values. In addition, Dr. Idso states that an increase in the temperature of the earth's oceans (which must occur if the atmospheric temperature is to increase) will cause an increase in the amount of algae and phytoplankton. When these organisms die and decay they give off gases that create additional cloud cover. A similar process, according to Dr. Idso, occurs with organisms that live on land. The additional cloud cover from these processes has a net cooling effect and the effect is estimated to be equivalent in magnitude to the CO_2 greenhouse effect.[31]

According to Drs. Singer and Idso, and physicist Dr. Hugh W. Ellsaesser, there are additional problems with the models as well.[32] The most definitive statement on the GCMs, made by Dr. Singer, says that "[t]he mathematical models used for predicting such effects are evidently not complete enough to encompass all the relevant physical processes in the atmosphere, thus throwing grave doubt on the drastic warming hypothesized for the next century."[33] Based on this discussion, one cannot take the predictions of drastic global warming very seriously because such predictions are made using mathematical models that do not simulate the physical processes of the earth's atmosphere very well.

What do historical data show concerning global warming? Data show that warming in the past century has been about 0.5 to 1 °F, much less than environmentalists predict should have occurred based on the increase in greenhouse gases, according to Dr. Michaels and Mr. Knappenberger. Further, Dr. Michaels and Mr. Knappenberger, as well as Dr. Singer, note that most of the warming occurred prior to 1945, but most of the man-made enhancement of greenhouse gases (about 70 percent) has occurred since that time.[34] This is an inconsistency with the environmentalists' predictions concerning global warming. Based on these predictions, more warming should have occurred after 1945 since greater enhancement of greenhouse gases has occurred during that time period.

Additionally, according to Dr. Barrett, satellite data show that atmospheric temperatures can vary widely over short periods of time. For instance, changes of up to 1 °F can occur in as little as *two weeks*. Therefore, as Dr. Barrett states, "It would seem inadvisable to attribute variations of the same magnitude over the course of a century to an enhancement of the greenhouse effect."[35]

Finally, the temperature of the earth's atmosphere has increased in the last century, but according to Drs. Singer and Ellsaesser, the earth was warmer about 800 to 900 years ago, when vineyards flourished in England.[36] This was long before the industrial revolution and the emission of any significant greenhouse gases by humans. Further, there were no catastrophic consequences due to this warming.[37] Hence, the historical data do not show much warming and they show that most—if not all—of the warming comes from nature itself.[38]

I have shown that the data do not substantiate environmentalists' claims that the earth's atmosphere is warming due to the activities of man. However, another topic environmentalists ignore is the benefits to man that global warming and a rise in atmospheric CO_2 might bring. For instance, a rise in the atmospheric CO_2 level would be a tremendous benefit to agriculture. CO_2 is necessary for the survival of plants. Dr. Singer states that more CO_2 in the earth's atmosphere makes it possible for plants to use water more efficiently and to grow faster.[39] This has been proven in hundreds of laboratory and field experiments, according to Dr. Idso.[40] This means that plants can grow at higher altitudes and in more arid climates. This also means the cost of growing food would dramatically decrease if the CO_2 level in the earth's atmosphere actually did increase (whether naturally or due to the activities of man). This would dramatically improve our ability to produce the food people need to survive.

Surprisingly enough, improvements in our ability to grow food might be a relatively minor benefit associated with global warming. This is the case because the rise in the CO_2 level also has the potential to save the human race— and all life—from extinction. Dr. Idso states that estimates of CO_2 levels in the earth's atmosphere show that it has decreased by over 99 percent from levels that existed early in the earth's history. It is believed that the maximum concentration of CO_2 in the earth's atmosphere, toward the beginning of its history, was around 70,000 parts per million (ppm). This is in contrast to a level of around 270 ppm today. If the level of CO_2 continues to drop, plants may disappear (most plants currently inhabiting the earth cannot survive below a level of 50 to 100 ppm). If there is no plant life, then there will be no animal life (including human life).[41] So increased CO_2, due to the burning of fossil fuels by man, could save the human race.

Likewise, the warming itself could help to save the human race. It could do this by postponing or eliminating the next ice age. Past ice ages have had harmful effects on many species, including humans, and scientists know we are overdue for another one. According to Dr. Singer, "actual climate cooling, experienced during the Little Ice Age or in the famous 1816 New England 'year without a summer,' caused large agricultural losses and even famine."[42] The history of the earth has been filled with approximately 100,000 year cycles alternating between glacial periods that are about 90,000 years in duration and warming periods that are about 10,000 years in duration. The current warming period is almost 11,000 years.[43] Hence, we are overdue for another glacial period. We may owe the survival of the human race to global warming.

I have shown the potential benefits of global warming and that the warming that is allegedly occurring is not necessarily being caused by man. However, what would be a rational response to global warming if it was to occur, whether due to man or nature itself? The environmentalists want us to radically reduce our use of fossil fuels (i.e., our consumption of man-made energy). A treaty organized by the United Nations and signed by many countries even calls for the United States and other industrialized nations to reduce their use of energy by 35 percent. This would have extremely detrimental effects because our standard of living is directly tied to our consumption of energy. The industrial revolution has tremendously raised the standard of living for the average person by replacing human and animal muscle power with machine power (i.e., power produced from the consumption of man-made energy products, such as coal, oil, and natural gas). Because of this link between energy consumption and the standard of living, it is no accident that the United States is the world's largest per capita energy consumer and has the world's highest standard of living. The standard of living would fall dramatically if we had to revert back to using human and animal muscle power. In other words, the more we reduce our use of man-made energy, the more our standard of living will fall.

If global warming does come (whether from nature or man) it would be best to expand our productive capability so we can produce the wealth necessary to cope with it. For instance, it would be best to be able to produce more and better housing and more and better air conditioning systems so that we can deal with the warmer weather global warming would bring. Whether or not global warming does come, nature itself will bring us many obstacles to overcome (such as earthquakes, hurricanes, snowstorms, etc.). It would be better to increase our productive capability to deal with these things, through economic progress under capitalism, than to destroy or radically reduce our productive capability through a reduction in energy consumption.

* * *

On the issue of global warming alone, one can see how little the environmentalists are concerned with truth. The data do not substantiate their claims, they make no mention of the potential benefits of global warming, and their suggested response to global warming is destructive because it would greatly harm the ability of man to further his life and well-being. One could multiply the number of invalid claims made by environmentalists by the number of issues addressed by them.

Natural Resources

The next invalid claim made by environmentalists concerns natural resources. The claim with regard to this issue is that we are running out of natural resources. However, this is not true. It is impossible to run out of natural resources, in a fundamental sense, due to the law of conservation of mass. This principle of physics says matter can neither be created *nor destroyed* in any kind of ordinary physical or chemical process. Hence, it is impossible to run out of the basic chemical elements that make up all matter, including natural resources. If man uses certain chemical compounds and disposes of them, the matter does not disappear from the earth. It is simply moved from one part of the earth, where it originally laid, to another part of the earth, where man has disposed of it. If man requires the use of this matter again, he could easily retrieve it from where he discarded it.

Further, although the quantity of natural resources in the earth is finite, for all practical purposes, the quantity is infinite because the earth is a solid ball of natural resources. From the tip of its gaseous atmosphere to its molten core, which is over 4,000 miles below the surface, the earth is nothing but a solidly packed ball of chemicals. Moreover, we have only begun to scratch the surface in terms of gaining access to these natural resources. This is seen in the fact that the deepest mines go, perhaps, *one or two miles* down and the deepest oil wells go nearly *seven miles* down. Remember, however, it is *4,000 miles* to the earth's core.

The key with respect to natural resources is knowing what to do with them and gaining access to them. The quantity of economically useable natural resources has increased throughout the industrial revolution and continues to increase to this day. Prior to the industrial revolution, we could only gain access to resources at the surface of the earth, with a pick and a shovel. Today, with the use of explosives, sonar, earth movers, and other sophisticated technology, we can gain access to resources almost seven miles below the surface. Through the use of man's mind—through the use of reason—man has been able to acquire and learn how to use greater amounts of natural resources. This analysis does not even consider the resources that man will be able to gain access to on other planets and moons if he continues to apply his reason to the task of learning how to use and acquire natural resources.

What about the supply of energy products? Maybe the total supply of matter in the earth is fixed, but certain vital chemicals, such as oil, might be becoming more scarce. This is not true. In general, the natural resources that can be *accessed and used* to produce man-made energy are increasing in abundance. For instance, one measure of abundance is the ratio of the known oil reserves relative to the annual consumption of oil. This gives an estimate of how long current reserves will last if we continue consuming oil at the same pace and no new reserves are discovered. Despite increases in annual consumption over the last eighty years, the number of years-of-reserves for oil has risen from ten to about forty.[44]

Using the same method, one can determine the number of years-of-reserves for other energy products. For instance, in 1973 there were forty-seven years-of-reserves for natural gas. In 1999, there were sixty years-of-reserves. In 1975, there were 218 years-of-reserves for coal. In 1999, there were 230 years-of-reserves. Nuclear power is estimated to have at least 100 years-of-reserves.

Shale oil is believed to have an astronomical 5,000 years-of-reserves.[45] None of these estimates, of course, include the endless amounts of energy that can be produced from hydroelectric power.

The point is that there is no need to be concerned with how we will produce the energy we need to continuously raise our standard of living. There is no need to be concerned as long as we create and maintain the capitalist society on which our prosperity depends. In such a society, people have the freedom and incentive of the profit motive to discover new sources of energy, new types of energy, and new methods of turning fuel into the energy we need. All this is done in a cleaner fashion under capitalism because a greater abundance of wealth exists in a capitalist society, which makes it possible for people to afford to focus on discovering cleaner burning fuels and using currently existing fuels in a cleaner fashion.[46]

In a capitalist society, if one type of fuel does become relatively more scarce, incentives exist to conserve on that fuel and discover new sources and substitutes for that fuel. This is a part of the coordinating features of the price system I discussed in chapter 1. When the price of a good rises (which is what happens when a good becomes relatively more scarce), these are exactly the kinds of incentives that exist. So, based on this knowledge also, if we establish and maintain a capitalist society, there is no need to be concerned with where the fuel will come from to meet our energy needs. One should only be concerned with whether a capitalist society will be created and maintained. If it is not, this will be destructive to the production of energy and the production of everything else. This will be destructive to human life. Yet this is what environmentalists seek to do. They seek to destroy capitalism—the very political/economic system on which our lives depend—by imposing a myriad of government controls to force others to obey their dictates.

What about other commodities, such as aluminum, copper, iron, etc. Evidence shows that these types of commodities are becoming relatively more abundant also. Price indices of commodities show that in real terms the prices of these types of commodities have been falling for over 150 years.[47] Further, the years-of-reserves of key minerals, such as aluminum and iron, have increased over the last half-century despite the fact that consumption rates have increased.[48] As long as people use reason, and have the freedom to act on the incentive of the profit motive, they will be able to discover new sources and substitutes for minerals if particular ones should become relatively more scarce.

What about "renewable" resources, such as trees, agricultural commodities, and livestock? Again, these commodities will exist in sufficient quantities as long as people are free to produce them. In the more capitalistic countries that exist today, there is no lack of cows, pigs, chickens, and other livestock that are needed to supply people with food and other products. There is also no lack of grains and other agricultural commodities people need to survive. Further, we are able to produce an abundance of timber products despite the existence of government restrictions pushed by environmentalists, such as laws prohibiting logging on some land, that inhibit our ability to produce such products.

As long as people are able to act on the profit motive greater supplies of resources, in general, will be forthcoming.[49] If particular resources should become
relatively more scarce, we could mine for them in garbage dumps to increase the
supply available. For instance, if aluminum became more scarce and the price
rose sufficiently it would be profitable to mine for aluminum cans in garbage
dumps. This brings me to the last topic I want to discuss concerning natural resources.

Where will we dispose of all the garbage that is generated from the cornu-
copia of wealth produced in a capitalist society? This is another boogeyman of
the environmentalists. They believe we are running out of space to dispose of
the garbage we generate. As with the belief that we are running out of natural
resources, the belief that we are running out of the space to dispose of matter
also contradicts the law of conservation of mass. Recall that this law says that
matter can neither be *created* nor destroyed. When we dispose of matter in garbage dumps, we are not creating matter. We are simply disposing of matter that
has been taken from one part of the earth and transformed into some product
from which we benefited but that is now no longer useful to us. Our use and
disposal of goods represents, in essence, a transfer of resources from one part of
the earth to another. In this sense, it is impossible to run out of space on the
earth to dispose of the garbage we generate because the garbage is simply matter
that came from the earth in the first place. The key with respect to garbage is to
be able to remove it from where we live and chemically alter it if necessary.

Will we have sufficient space to properly dispose of the garbage? The answer is: "Yes." We will easily be able to dispose of the garbage we generate. It
has been estimated that all the garbage that Americans will generate in the
twenty-first century could be disposed of within a square that is eighteen miles
per side. This is an area that is about 0.009 percent of the total U.S. land area
and is probably much smaller than virtually every county in the United States.[50]

Based on the discussion in this section one should understand that recycling
is a waste of resources. It is a waste of the only resource that is becoming relatively more scarce: human labor. Labor is the only resource whose price (i.e.,
the average wage level), measured in real terms, has steadily increased throughout the history of the industrial revolution. Since prices are measures of the relative scarcity of a good or service, this shows that labor is becoming more scarce
relative to other goods and services. In most cases, it is less expensive to acquire
a fresh supply of natural resources from the ground to make aluminum cans and
other goods than it is to recycle the old materials. This is seen in the fact that it
is often unprofitable to recycle old materials.[51] The losses are incurred because
the resources expended in the recycling process are more valuable than the new
resources created (the new supply of aluminum or whatever). When it is profitable to recycle (as it is in many cases, such as with much of the metal in cars),
an incentive exists for individuals to recycle. Here, there is no waste of resources, since the supply of new resources created is greater in value than the
ones used up in producing the new supply.

Once again we have seen that, upon scrutiny, the environmentalists' claims do not hold up. However, there is one more point I want to make before leaving this issue. Contained within the environmentalists' claims of simultaneously running out of natural resources and running out of landfill space is an inconsistency and another instance of dishonesty on the part of environmentalists. They are simultaneously saying that we are running out of natural resources, as if the resources are magically disappearing from the face of the earth, and that we are running out of space to dispose of the garbage, as if the same resources that are allegedly disappearing are magically multiplying in garbage dumps. Which is it? Is matter being created or destroyed? Of course, the answer is neither. These claims, in addition to contradicting the law of conservation of mass, more significantly, stand in blatant contradiction to each other. However, such contradictions do not phase environmentalists because they are not concerned with consistency or any other requirement of knowledge. Why they are not will be discussed below.

Acid Rain, the Extinction of Species, Ozone Depletion, and DDT

As further indication of the proliferation of invalid claims by environmentalists, here is what the truth actually is in a few more cases. With respect to acid rain, environmentalists claim that due to the activities of man such rain is damaging lakes in certain regions of the world. However, what one does not hear from environmentalists is that *rain is naturally acidic*. Natural rainfall has a pH that averages about 5 (anything under a pH of 7 is an acid).[52] Also, the lakes that are supposed to have been made more acidic by acid rain, such as those in the Northeastern United States and Southeastern Canada, are naturally acidic. These lakes became less acidic for several decades in the late-nineteenth and early-twentieth century due to the slash-and-burn logging method used in these regions during that time. This logging method is characterized by the massive cutting of trees and burning of what remains on the forest floor. It made the runoff regions of these lakes more alkaline, and made the lakes inhabitable by fish. They are now returning to their naturally acidic levels, and thus becoming uninhabitable, due to the cessation of this logging method.[53] So the situation is the exact opposite of what the environmentalists claim with respect to these lakes. It turns out that a man-made activity such as logging, which is hated by environmentalists, was a life-giving activity for these lakes, and a return to the "natural environment" is killing the marine life in these lakes.

* * *

Environmentalists also claim that the activities of man are causing the mass extinction of species. They allege that anywhere from ten to one-hundred percent of all the species on the earth will be extinct in the next fifty years.[54] However, according to the economist Dr. Julian Simon, evidence for mass extinction by man does not exist. He shows that the projections of mass extinction by environmentalists are based on mere guesses and suppositions.[55] In addition, Dr. Bjorn Lomborg presents evidence to show that a more realistic estimated extinction rate is 0.7 percent over the next fifty years.[56]

Furthermore, a point that is related to this issue that environmentalists never mention is that extinction is a natural part of life and occurred on a massive scale long before the existence of man. This is seen in the fact that at least *90 percent* of all species that have ever existed on earth are now extinct and that virtually all of these have disappeared due to natural processes.[57]

In addition, if it was not for extinction, man himself may not exist because if it was not for the extinction of the dinosaurs, man may have never developed. When the dinosaurs roamed the earth, the mammals that existed remained quite small.[58] Only after the extinction of the dinosaurs did mammals become larger and begin to diversify extensively in the kinds that existed.[59] Therefore, the extinction of the dinosaurs may have been necessary for the development of human life.

And as for the extinction of one or two species here or there, which is supposed to have drastic consequences on the allegedly fragile "ecosystem": this fragility is contradicted by the mass extinctions that appear in the fossil record and that are believed to have occurred periodically throughout the earth's history. During one of these episodes over *95 percent* of all species that existed at the time are believed to have become extinct. Further, one of the current hypotheses of how the dinosaurs became extinct is a mass extinction hypothesis. It is believed that around 65 percent of all species that existed at that time became extinct.[60] Yet somehow, after these episodes, the remaining species survived and new species eventually developed. If this is true, one does not have to be concerned with the extinction of one or two—or even one-thousand or two-thousand (or more)—species caused by man.

Moreover, the claims by environmentalists with respect to extinction do not take into account the various species whose numbers have been dramatically increased by the activities of man. They do not take into account the large numbers of dogs, cats, cows, pigs, chickens, etc. whose existence is dependent on man. Nevertheless, man has no duty to protect all currently existing species of animals. That is an altruist belief and it would be destructive (and immoral) for men to act upon it. It would be best (and moral) for man to ensure that the animals on which his survival and happiness depend exist in sufficient numbers and, if necessary, eliminate those that are harmful to him.

* * *

Next is the case of alleged atmospheric ozone depletion and the hole in the ozone layer over Antarctica, for which man is supposed to be responsible due to his use of chlorofluorocarbons (CFCs). CFCs are used in refrigerants and aerosol sprays, among other things. The claim is that CFCs produced by man rise up into the atmosphere and, through a chemical process, destroy ozone. Since the ozone layer blocks significant amounts of ultraviolet radiation, as the ozone layer depletes, more radiation will be able to penetrate to the surface of the earth and allegedly cause an increase in skin cancer rates.

The problem with the claims concerning ozone depletion is that evidence shows that most CFCs do not rise high enough into the atmosphere to be able to destroy ozone. Further, the amount of CFCs released into the atmosphere by man is *insignificant* compared to the release of ozone-depleting chemicals through natural processes, such as seawater evaporation and volcanic eruptions. CFCs account for about *0.1 percent* of the ozone-depleting chemicals released into the atmosphere annually, when compared to those created by natural processes. In addition, environmentalists ignore the one factor that probably has the largest effect on atmospheric ozone: the sun. Scientists generally believe that the sun has the greatest effect on the thickness of the ozone layer. Finally, with regard to the ozone hole over the Antarctic, it turns out that the hole was first discovered in the 1950s, before any significant amount of CFCs was released into the atmosphere, and is probably a naturally occurring phenomenon due to the effects of the sun and volcanic activity on the Antarctic continent.[61] Again, upon examination, the claims of environmentalists do not hold up.

* * *

Lastly, one should recall the ban on DDT mentioned in chapter 5. DDT was essentially banned in the United States in 1972 due to its alleged danger to animals and humans. As an example of its alleged danger to animals, DDT was said to be toxic to birds and to cause thin egg shells, the latter of which can result in the deaths of the chicks. However, many birds that were alleged to be negatively affected by DDT actually increased in number when DDT use was at its heaviest. Further, experiments showed no toxic effects of DDT on birds despite the fact the birds were fed doses *6,000 to 20,000 times more* than they would normally experience in their natural habitat. In addition, experiments designed to show the effects of DDT on egg shells showed no thinning despite the fact that during the reproduction cycle the birds were fed doses *over 650 times* what they would normally experience. Also, the hatch rate was no lower for these birds than for birds in a control group.[62]

With regard to humans, DDT is supposed to be carcinogenic. However, this claim is based on experiments in which doses *100,000 times greater* than the amount of DDT residue found in food were injected into mice. *Human* experiments with DDT, where subjects were *fed* over 500 times what they would normally ingest from residues in food, resulted in no negative effects at the time of the experiments or thirty years afterwards.[63] Furthermore, DDT has actually saved over one-hundred million lives by killing disease-carrying insects and could have saved tens-of-millions more if it had not been banned.[64] In addition, DDT improved the health and nutrition of hundreds-of-millions of people by protecting crops from insects.[65]

Conclusion to the Invalid Claims Made by Environmentalists

With respect to global warming and the rest of the claims discussed, environmentalists raise concerns about many *alleged* dangers to man. They refer to alleged calamities and suffering that man will face if drastic measures are not taken to reduce his influence on nature. However, environmentalists show no concern about the *actual* suffering inflicted upon man because of their actions. For instance, thanks to environmentalists, tens-of-millions of people have died as a result of DDT being banned. Why aren't environmentalists concerned about these deaths? How can they show such a blatant disregard for human life? The answer to this question lies in the altruist code of morality. The opposition to DDT provides a stark example of the sacrifice of man to nature by environmentalists. It shows they are willing to sacrifice man to nature even if tens-of-millions of people must die in order to do so. Environmentalists' opposition to production and technology, in general, as the alleged solution to all the other "problems" they say we face will lead to (and probably has lead to already) an even greater number of deaths and amount of suffering. Such are the results of the altruist code of morality in practice and the concerns of those who advocate it.

Environmentalism and the Abandonment of Reason

One after another of the environmentalists' claims fall victim to a scrutiny of the facts. Why is this so? As I stated previously, their claims are so often in contradiction to the facts because environmentalists are not concerned with facts or truth. Based on their history of lies and distortions, *one should completely dismiss claims made by environmentalists, without consideration*, unless the claims have been substantiated by reputable sources. One should do this because the environmentalists' claims are arbitrary assertions—assertions made without any attempt to understand anything in reality.[66] The reason environmentalists make such claims is to, as I have stated earlier in this chapter, scare people into joining their cause.

One might ask here, why do environmentalists lie and espouse so many invalid claims? How can such a large movement be so blatantly dishonest? To answer these questions, a brief digression is required. The answer to these questions lies in the fundamental ideas influencing our culture and thus the ideas influencing environmentalists. One of the most fundamental influences on our culture over the last two centuries has been the general abandonment of reason. As I have said, reason is the tool that allows humans to think in terms of concepts and principles. The use of reason requires that people base their conclusions on the facts of reality and/or a logical analysis of the facts. Therefore, as a culture abandons the use of reason, it abandons the ability to draw conclusions based on the facts of reality. In other words, it abandons a reality-oriented focus. This is why environmentalist "intellectuals" are not concerned with facts or truth. This is why it is so easy for them to make claims that are in such blatant contradiction to the facts. They are not concerned with such things because they have abandoned the one tool whose use would make facts and logic (i.e., reality) their concern: reason.

As evidence of the rejection of facts and truth by environmentalists, besides the evidence already given in the sections on global warming et al., there is the statement made by a prominent conservationist concerning the claims of mass extinction by environmentalists. He said, "the lack of data does worry me." He made this statement in *Science* magazine and demanded that he remain anonymous because, he said, "they'll [i.e., environmentalists will] kill me for saying this." Presumably this individual is speaking metaphorically; however, if one must fear retribution from one's colleagues to such an extent that one must anonymously point out the lack of data available to support their claim, then one's colleagues have given up any claim to the title "scientist." More significantly, the well-known environmentalist Paul Ehrlich of Stanford University stated, "biologists don't need to know how many species there are, how they are related to one another, or how many disappear annually to recognize that Earth's biota is entering a gigantic spasm of extinction."[67] Here an environmentalist baldly and shamelessly states that "scientists" do not need to be concerned with the facts related to species extinction to "know" that mass extinctions of species are occurring.

The general abandonment of reason has also made it possible for these same "intellectuals" to ignore or evade the destructive consequences of the ideas that lie at the root of environmentalism (these ideas being that nature has intrinsic value and that man must be sacrificed to nature). To see the destructive nature of such ideas, and recognize the significance of this so that one may take the appropriate corrective action, requires that one have a respect for logic and facts. It requires that one understand the logical implications of the ideas one puts forward and that one then act on what one understands. However, seeing logical implications and acting consistently on one's beliefs are not a concern for those who abandon reason because, again, for those who abandon reason, logic and facts are not a concern.

If people in a culture begin to abandon reason, in its place will come some form of emotionalism. Ultimately, the only choice one has in any attempt to understand the world is between reason and emotions. With emotionalism, conclusions are based, not on the facts of reality and/or a logical analysis of the facts, but on one's feelings. Based on this, if an idea makes one feel good, then the idea must be good (or "true"), even if the idea *is not* consistent with the facts of reality. Likewise, if an idea makes one feel bad, then the idea must be bad (or "false"), even if the idea *is* consistent with the facts of reality. Further, if a fact makes one feel bad, then, based on this method of processing information, there is nothing wrong with ignoring or evading that fact. Likewise, based on this method, there is nothing wrong with creating a "fact" if it makes one feel good.[68]

The quote from Paul Ehrlich and the earlier quote from Stephen Schneider are blatant examples of emotionalism. They show utter contempt for reason, which means: for facts, logic, evidence, truth, and science. In fact, all the claims made by environmentalists, from the ones I refuted above to their claims on a myriad of other subjects, are based on emotionalism. The claims are made with complete disregard for science and all its requirements. This is not a characteristic that is isolated to only a few environmentalists. This is a mentality that pervades the movement. This fact is witnessed by the many statements leaders of the movement make that show their disregard for facts and truth (Schneider's and Ehrlich's statements being only two examples of these types of statements).[69] It is witnessed by the fact that other leaders of the movement do not even so much as chide their colleagues for making such statements (let alone condemn their colleagues as they deserve). It is witnessed by the fact that an environmentalist must, for fear of being reproached, anonymously point out the lack of data his colleagues possess to support their claims. It is witnessed by environmentalists' reactions, in general, to refutations of their claims (such as the refutations in *The Skeptical Environmentalist*). And finally, it is witnessed by the myriad of claims made by environmentalists that stand in blatant contradiction to the evidence.

Given the evidence against the environmentalists, the only rational thing to do is dismiss their claims. One does not need to refute any of their claims once one has discovered the corrupt nature of their underlying methodology. Further, if one was to refute the environmentalists' claims without condemning their methodology, one would make it appear that their method is legitimate (i.e., that it is a rational method that can be used to gain knowledge). Their statements are not worthy of the attention of science. Their statements are not attempts to gain knowledge but are emotionalist statements that use science as a veneer to cover up the environmentalists' real motives: to sacrifice man to nature and get people to join them in this cause. Once the veneer is lifted one can easily see the corrupt and destructive nature of their beliefs and motives.

The use of science as a veneer to cover up one's real motives is not original to environmentalists. "Scientific" Creationists have been doing the same thing for much longer. Creationists put forward "scientific evidence" to obscure the actual source of their beliefs: the Bible. Creationists do not want to discover the facts concerning the origin of species any more than environmentalists want to discover the facts about acid rain and global warming. Creationists use science as a veneer to make their views appear rational. Creationists, like environmentalists, cover up their real motives with a scientific veneer in an attempt to use the respectability of science to spread their views. If the Creationists openly professed their views, they could be easily dismissed as having no basis in fact. Creationists and environmentalists attempt to feed, like parasites, off the rationality and respectability of science. As with environmentalists, once the underlying method of Creationists is discovered one should not answer any more of their specific claims. Doing so only makes it appear that their method is legitimate. One should not give their views any attention whatsoever because they are arbitrary assertions.[70]

The general abandonment of reason in our culture, and the corresponding rise of emotionalism, is what makes large numbers of people easy prey for environmentalist "intellectuals" and is thus why environmentalism has been able to spread. The majority of people who claim to be environmentalists probably honestly believe that what they are being told, by the intellectual leaders of the movement, is true. However, they are unable to make a rational assessment of what they are being told because they have not been provided with the mental tools in their education that makes such an assessment possible. For instance, they have not been taught how to use a tool such as logic. This is the case because logic is a tool of reason and, again, due to the general abandonment of reason, logic is largely ignored, and even defiantly opposed, today.[71]

This book is not a book on epistemology or the history of philosophy, so I am not going to discuss at length what reason is, why it is being abandoned, when the abandonment started, and all the specific forms in which the abandonment of reason manifests itself. I will only say here that confidence and respect for reason rose in the Renaissance and peaked in the eighteenth-century Enlightenment. Its decline started in the nineteenth century and was ultimately made possible by one man: the German philosopher Immanuel Kant. Kant put a stop to the Enlightenment. He wanted to supplant reason to make room for faith (which is one form of emotionalism).[72] The history of philosophy and the general spread of ideas since Kant has been a process of inculcating and drawing out the implications of the ideas put forward by Kant. If environmentalism is to be overthrown, and the rational alternative of capitalism put in its place, a return to the ideas of the Renaissance and the Enlightenment—a return to reason—must occur.[73]

The Dead-End of Environmentalism

If environmentalism is not concerned with facts and truth, just what is it concerned with? That is the topic of this subsection.

As stated earlier in this chapter, environmentalism is not fundamentally concerned with cleaning up beaches, lakes, and rivers; "saving the planet" for future generations; or creating "wildlife areas." These do not explain everything one sees coming from the movement. *The environmentalist movement is based on a hatred for man and a desire to wipe him off the face of the earth; it is based on pure nihilism.* This is a strong statement to make. Is it just propaganda on my part, or do I have some basis on which to make such a claim? Let's take a look at the evidence.

One can understand the truth of the above claim if one considers the ideas on which environmentalism is based: namely, the ideas that nature has intrinsic value and that man must be sacrificed to nature. First, let's focus on the former idea. If nature has intrinsic value, value in and of itself, apart from the value that nature represents to mankind, then when man uses nature to achieve his purposes, he is destroying the good (i.e., that which has intrinsic value) and therefore he must be evil. For instance, if nature has intrinsic value then trees have value simply because they exist. Hence, when man cuts down trees to build homes, he is destroying that which is good, and so he must be evil. The larger the scale on which man acts and uses nature to achieve his ends, the more evil he is, according to the theory of the intrinsic value of nature.

Animals survive by adapting themselves to their natural surroundings. Man cannot live like an animal. Man must reshape nature to serve his ends if he is to survive. He must grow, process, and refrigerate food, manufacture computers, produce medicines, build transportation systems, etc. The things man needs to survive do not exist in nature. Man must bring them into existence through his thought and effort. However, this is what the theory of the intrinsic value of nature forbids him to do. With each action he takes to further his own life, man is condemned as evil by environmentalism. In other words, man is condemned as evil for doing what he must do to survive, i.e., for acting as his nature requires.[74]

The belief that nature has intrinsic value implies deadly consequences for man at the hands of environmentalism: it implies that man should be sacrificed to nature. *A desire for the wholesale destruction of man is a logical implication of the ideas on which environmentalism is based.* If one takes the ideas at the core of environmentalism seriously, and acts on them in a logically consistent manner (i.e., if one attempts to act on them on principle), one will be led to the view that man is evil and must be destroyed, and therefore one will lash out at man and attack his efforts to further his life and happiness.

The above is not just a logical theory (although that, in and of itself, would be enough to condemn environmentalism). Many environmentalists have put this theory into practice. The more consistent environmentalists actively attempt to sacrifice man to nature by preventing him from using that which allegedly has intrinsic value to serve his own ends. This can be seen in the actions of such individuals as the Unabomber. Ted Kazinski sent bombs through the mail to businessmen and other individuals because he opposed industrialization and technology. If one reads Kazinski's manifesto, one can easily see his acceptance of the fundamental principles and values of environmentalism. For example, he states, "Only with the Industrial Revolution did the effect of human society on nature become really devastating. To relieve the pressure on nature . . . it is only necessary to get rid of industrial society."[75] Environmentalist "intellectuals" generally agree with the basic ideas in his manifesto. They merely disagree with the methods he used to implement his ideas.[76]

Other environmentalists have acted in a manner similar to the Unabomber. There was the deadly practice by members of Earth First! of spiking trees in the Pacific Northwest in an attempt to stop logging in that region. Ski resorts, businesses, residential construction projects, and other types of property have been burned or vandalized by the Earth Liberation Front (ELF) to prevent man from furthering his life and happiness. The Animal Liberation Front (ALF) has vandalized and destroyed property at laboratories that do research on animals and places where meat, fur, and other animal products are produced or sold. The People for the Ethical Treatment of Animals (PETA) has vandalized property and attacked individuals in attempts to prevent them from using animals to further their lives and happiness. The rhetoric and actions of environmentalists have grown more violent and destructive over time. One environmentalist group has even begun to make death threats against people.[77]

Of course, many will object that I am focusing only on the "extreme" members of the environmentalist movement. Environmentalists are quick to claim that only, perhaps, 1 percent of all environmentalists believe in using violent means against others or their property in the name of environmentalism. The other 99 percent do not believe in using violence to achieve their ends. Nevertheless, while it might be true that most environmentalists do not believe in using violence (i.e., the swift use of force) to achieve their ends, most, if not all, environmentalists do believe in using force to achieve their ends. Virtually all environmentalists believe in initiating physical force through the government to pass laws that impose arbitrary restrictions on people (such as laws restricting the drilling for oil on the continental shelf and in Alaska, and laws requiring emission control devices and gas mileage requirements on motor vehicles).

More fundamentally, however, it is irrelevant whether most people in the environmentalist movement believe in using force or violence. One does not, properly, judge an ideological movement by the John Doe's that make up the movement. One does not judge a movement, whether environmentalism, socialism, capitalism, or any other ideological movement, by the average member of that movement. One judges an ideological movement by the ideas on which that movement is based. One judges a movement by the logical and consistent implications of the ideas that lie at the base of the movement. One must look at what is logically consistent with a movement to determine, for good or for evil, what it is capable of achieving. If one looks at what is logically consistent with environmentalism, one will see that this movement is one of the most potentially destructive ideological movements that exists today or that has ever existed.

Another way of thinking of this issue is to recognize that there are two groups in the environmentalist movement: the violent and the non-violent members. Both groups believe in the same ideas, they just disagree on the methods necessary to implement their ideas (as was explicitly witnessed in the case of the Unabomber). One of these groups is inconsistent. Either violence is consistent with environmentalism or it is not. Based on a logical analysis of the ideas that underlie environmentalism, *it is the violent members of the movement who are acting consistently on environmentalist ideology.* They are the ones taking environmentalism to its logical and consistent end. The rest of the members of the movement simply do not understand the nature of the ideas in which they profess to believe. They do not understand (or care) what is logically consistent with environmentalism. They do not take the ideas they claim to believe in seriously, or they ignore or evade the logical implications of environmentalism.

There is an historical example that will help make clear the position in which the inconsistent members of the environmentalist movement have placed themselves. In Germany prior to the rise of Hitler, many people believed that socialism was good for Germany. They believed socialism would make Germany a strong nation again. They believed, among other things, that it would lead Germany to economic prosperity. However, many, and probably most, socialists in Germany did not believe in committing mass slaughter against millions of individuals. Nonetheless, this was irrelevant to what socialism actually achieved in that country because, as was shown in chapter 1, mass murder is a logical implication of socialism. Socialism (in its Nazi variety) achieved mass murder in Germany (and everywhere else it has been implemented) because mass murder is logically implied by the ideas that underlie socialism. The only thing those socialists in Nazi Germany who did not believe in mass slaughter ended up achieving was to help a vicious monster rise to power and achieve the destruction that he had a desire to achieve and that socialism made possible for him to achieve. These unwitting socialists became, in essence, accomplices in the crimes committed by him. Environmentalism, like socialism, is a thoroughly destructive ideology that provides an outlet for the most vicious and destructive types of individuals to gain power and wreak havoc upon humanity. By supporting environmentalism, whether inconsistently or not, one supports the kinds of monsters that will rise to power based on such an ideology.

This brings me to the last point to be made against environmentalism. The more consistent environmentalists even call for the wholesale destruction of man. David Graber, the research biologist I quoted in my initial discussion on intrinsic value earlier in the chapter, openly wishes for the death of a billion people because he thinks human beings are destroying "the wildness" of nature.[78] He wishes for the death of more people than achieved by Hitler, Stalin, Lenin, Mao Tse-tung, and Pol Pot combined. These socialist dictators were responsible for murdering as many as one-hundred million people. This environmentalist wants *a billion* people dead. The kinds of dictators that will arise under environmentalism will make the socialists look like friends of humanity. If environmentalism is fully integrated into our culture, the world will see the destruction of man on a scale far greater than that seen in the bloody record of socialism.[79]

An environmentalist might respond by saying that what I write about in the above paragraph is the belief of only one person and that it is not proper to judge the entire movement based on what this one person said. However, what is significant about the statement is not how many people have said it or how many people believe in it, but that environmentalism can be used, *at all*, as the basis to justify such destruction. That such a statement is logically consistent with environmentalism, at all, is what is significant. As I have previously stated, one does not judge an ideological movement based on what the average person in the movement believes or even what the majority of people in the movement believe. An ideological movement, because at root it is a movement based on *ideas* (not people), must be judged by the ideas it embraces and what is logically consistent with those ideas, if it is to be judged properly. People can, and often do, act inconsistently on ideas in which they profess to believe. So if one judges a movement by the people in that movement (whether their actions or the ideas in which they profess to believe), one can be led astray in attempting to determine the potential of the movement. If one properly applies logic in assessing a movement, however, this will not be the case.

An environmentalist might also respond by saying that this is a case of good (environmentalist) ideas being distorted by a bad person to justify acts of destruction. However, this is not true. When people use environmentalism to justify destructive acts, it is not a case of good ideas being distorted to justify those acts. Environmentalist ideas are bad—i.e., destructive—ideas. That is why they can be used to justify acts of destruction. Environmentalism, at its most fundamental level, is based on ideas that are thoroughly opposed to human life and to the facts of reality. That is, the morality of sacrifice and the intrinsic value of nature are inconsistent with the facts of reality, including the requirements of human life. These ideas represent a war against reality. In any such war, the end result can only be destruction.

Conclusion

Environmentalism does not provide a critique of the market. It simply shows, once again, that some people have embraced false ideas and that these ideas lead people to make wrong conclusions about the free market. Environmentalism does not have a legitimate claim to science and morality. Environmentalism is thoroughly opposed to science and morality; it is a form of emotionalism, and its ideas are destructive to human life and therefore immoral.

If you value your life, you should reject environmentalism and never associate yourself with the movement. It is not too late to reverse the growing tide of irrationalism that comes in the form of environmentalism. Human beings have free will and do not have to continue down the destructive road on which they are headed. However, in order to reverse the course 180 degrees, they must discover the home they have been looking for but, so far, have been unable to find. They have never been able to find it because their ability to see it has been obscured by the cold, murky fog of such ideas as the altruist code of morality and the intrinsic value of nature. If people reject these ideas, and embrace egoism and recognize the value of nature *to man*, the fog will clear and they will be able to come home for the first time to a political/economic system based on a full and complete form of laissez-faire capitalism.[80] If people do this, human life will flourish.

Notes

1. One can imagine the smell, and thus pollution, emanating from the human and equine waste that used to line city streets on a hot summer's day.

2. See Peter Schwartz, "The Philosophy of Privation," in *Return of the Primitive: The Anti-Industrial Revolution*, Ayn Rand, edited and with an introduction and additional articles by Peter Schwartz (New York: Meridian, 1999), 219-244, especially 228.

3. One environmentalist organization, The Nature Conservancy, already does this.

4. For more examples of how environmentalists initiate force privately, see the section titled "The Dead-End of Environmentalism," in this chapter.

5. Some property rights do already exist with regard to all of these categories.

6. For more on this topic, see the section titled "The Solution to Negative Externalities" in chapter 4.

7. I do not include other forms of life here because many things that may be of benefit to other forms of life can be harmful to human life, and a proper definition of pollution must have human beings as its focus. The reason why humans must be the focus will become apparent as the chapter progresses.

8. For more on this subject, see the section titled "Natural Resources" in this chapter.

9. See Bjorn Lomborg, *The Skeptical Environmentalist: Measuring the Real State of the World* (Cambridge: Cambridge University Press, 2001), 164-165 and 170. This book also provides evidence that environmental regulation, at most, has done very little to reduce air pollution.

10. The Black Death of the mid-fourteenth century (believed to be mainly bubonic plague) is estimated to have killed at least *25 percent* of Europe's population in *two years*.

11. Since famines were relatively common, it was often the case that many people could not even produce enough food to do this.

12. See Ayn Rand, *The New Left: The Anti-Industrial Revolution*, Revised edition (New York: Signet, 1975), 138.

13. Because of the importance of fully understanding the nature of the environmentalist movement, here are some good sources for information and ideas concerning the movement: Jay H. Lehr, ed., *Rational Readings on Environmental Concerns* (New York: Van Nostrand Reinhold, 1992); Ayn Rand, *Return of the Primitive: The Anti-Industrial Revolution*; and George Reisman, *Capitalism: A Treatise on Economics* (Ottawa, IL: Jameson Books, 1996), 63-120. This should by no means be regarded as an exhaustive list.

14. David M. Graber, "Mother Nature as a Hothouse Flower," *Los Angeles Times Book Review*, 22 October 1989, 1.

15. Ayn Rand, *The Virtue of Selfishness* (New York: Signet, 1964), 16.

16. For more on this see the discussion on rights in chapter 1 in the section titled "Capitalism." In addition, rights do not apply to the lower animals because they do not possess reason; therefore, they are incapable of understanding principles, including moral principles, and thus are unable to understand, let alone act on, the concept "rights." In essence, animals fall outside the realm of morality (i.e., they are neither moral nor immoral beings; they are amoral) and therefore rights are inapplicable to them. As further evidence that rights do not apply to animals think of the contradictions it would lead to if "rights" were given to animals. For instance, you would have to respect the alleged right

to life of a grizzly bear; however, he would be unable to respect your right to life. For more on this subject, one should listen to Edwin Locke's presentation on his audio taped debate, with Stephen Sapontzis, titled *Do Animals Have Rights?* (Gaylordsville, Conn.: Second Renaissance Inc., 1990).

17. In fact, some dams have actually been dismantled due to the influence of the environmentalist movement. See Peter Schwartz, "Man vs. Nature," in *Earth Day vs. Man: In Defense of Industry and Technology* (Marina del Rey, Calif.: Ayn Rand Institute, 2000), 1-3.

18. See Stephen Schneider's quote in Jonathan Schell, "Our Fragile Earth," *Discover* 10, no. 10 (October 1989): 44-50. The quote is on p. 47.

19. Lomborg, *The Skeptical Environmentalist*.

20. Lomborg, *The Skeptical Environmentalist*, 93-94. Here is a mathematical example of the phenomenon being discussed: if the population of non-industrialized countries grows from 4 billion to 5 billion people and per capita grain production in these countries grows from 190 to 200 kg during the same period of time, if the population in industrialized countries is 1 billion people (with the 650 kg per capita grain production in industrialized countries) worldwide per capita grain production will decline from 282 to 275 kg despite the fact that per capita grain production in the non-industrialized countries grew. The weighted average grain production per capita in the first year is [4 billion (190) + 1 billion (650)] / (4 billion + 1 billion) = 282 kg. In the second year it is [5 billion (200) + 1 billion (650)] / (5 billion + 1 billion) = 275 kg.

21. David Pimental, "Skeptical of the Skeptical Environmentalist," *Skeptic* 9, no. 2 (2002): 90-94.

22. I owe the point about the nature of the reviews of *The Skeptical Environmentalist*, and this review in particular, to Keith H. Lockitch. See his, "Fighting the Hydra: The Futile Battle of the Skeptical Environmentalist," *The Intellectual Activist* 16, no. 12 (December 2002): 6-18. This article also contains more reviews of this type.

23. Just why environmentalists have little concern for facts and truth is discussed in the section titled "Environmentalism and the Abandonment of Reason," in this chapter.

24. John Emsley, ed., *The Global Warming Debate* (London: The European Science and Environment Forum, 1996). The reference for *Rational Readings on Environmental Concerns* has already been given in this chapter.

25. This is also true of the science presented in my discussions on natural resources, acid rain, the extinction of species, ozone depletion, and DDT.

26. See Lehr, *Rational Readings*, 395.

27. See Emsley, *The Global Warming Debate*, 64.

28. Lehr, *Rational Readings*, 395.

29. Lehr, *Rational Readings*, 147.

30. Lehr, *Rational Readings*, 400 and Emsley, *The Global Warming Debate*, 163.

31. Lehr, *Rational Readings*, 417-419.

32. Lehr, *Rational Readings*, 399-400, 412-413, and 415-417.

33. Lehr, *Rational Readings*, 393.

34. Emsley, *The Global Warming Debate*, 147 and 167-168.

35. Emsley, *The Global Warming Debate*, 69.

36. Lehr, *Rational Readings*, 398 and 406.

37. I owe this observation to Robert W. Tracinski, "Global Warming vs. Science: Global Warming Campaign Subordinates Science to Politics," in *Earth Day vs. Man*, 9-11.

38. The scientists in this section are not the only ones to question the claims about global warming. Over *17,000* scientists have signed a petition circulated by the Oregon

Institute of Science and Medicine that states, in part: "There is no convincing scientific evidence that human release of carbon dioxide, methane, or other greenhouse gasses is causing or will, in the foreseeable future, cause catastrophic heating of the earth's atmosphere and disruption of the earth's climate." See their website at www.oism.org.

39. Lehr, *Rational Readings*, 400.

40. Lehr, *Rational Readings*, 422.

41. Lehr, *Rational Readings*, 424-425.

42. Lehr, *Rational Readings*, 400.

43. Lehr, *Rational Readings*, 407.

44. See Lomborg, *The Skeptical Environmentalist*, 124.

45. Lomborg, *The Skeptical Environmentalist*, 126-129.

46. This occurs in the same manner as the improvements in safety and quality that result from a greater productive capability. After people satisfy more urgent needs and wants (such as producing enough food, clothing, and shelter), they can afford to focus on satisfying less immediate needs and wants (such as developing higher quality and safer goods, as well as cleaner methods of producing energy). For more on this subject, see chapter 5.

47. Lomborg, *The Skeptical Environmentalist*, 138. Real terms means in terms of how much labor must be expended to obtain the commodities.

48. Lomborg, *The Skeptical Environmentalist*, 141.

49. Some environmentalists have recently recognized that we are not running out of natural resources and that we are able to produce an abundance of the products we need to further our lives. Hence, they have switched their story. Now they are arguing that natural resources are *too abundant*. Such a switch is not hard for environmentalists. To understand why, see the section titled "Environmentalism and the Abandonment of Reason," in this chapter. For an example of this switch, see David M. Nemtzow, "More Power to You: On Bjorn Lomborg and Energy," *Grist Magazine*, 12 December 2001.

50. Lomborg, *The Skeptical Environmentalist*, 208.

51. The fact that the government must tax people to try to get them to recycle, such as in the form of deposit taxes on cans and bottles, is proof that it is unprofitable. Otherwise, people would do it on their own and the tax would not be needed to get people to recycle.

52. See John J. McKetta, "Acid Rain—The Whole Story to Date," in *Rational Readings*, ed. Lehr, 46-49.

53. See Edward C. Krug, "The Great Acid Rain Flimflam," in *Rational Readings*, 36 and 39-40.

54. Lomborg, *The Skeptical Environmentalist*, 249.

55. Lehr, *Rational Readings*, 742-744.

56. Lomborg, *The Skeptical Environmentalist*, 255-256.

57. Simon in *Rational Readings*, 742.

58. University of California, Berkeley, Museum of Paleontology, "What Killed the Dinosaurs? The Invalid Hypotheses," *DinoBuzz: Current Topics Concerning Dinosaurs*, 2004, <http://www.ucmp.berkeley.edu/diapsids/extincthypo.html> (31 Aug. 2004).

59. Peter J. Bryant, "The Age of Mammals: Evolution of Mammals," *Biodiversity and Conservation*, 2002, <http://darwin.bio.uci.edu/~sustain/bio65/lec02/b65lec02.htm# MAMMALS> (31 Aug. 2004).

60. For more on mass extinctions, including why they occur, see Donald Goldsmith, *Nemesis: The Death-Star and Other Theories of Mass Extinction* (New York: Walker & Company, 1985). See pages 7-9, 47-49, and 57 for references to the claims made in this

paragraph. Goldsmith provides evidence for the hypothesis that mass extinctions are caused by periodic collisions between the earth and asteroids or comet fragments.

61. The statements in this paragraph are based on Rogelio A. Maduro and Ralf Schauerhammer, *The Holes in the Ozone Scare: The Scientific Evidence That the Sky Isn't Falling* (Washington, D.C.: 21st Century Science Associates, 1992). See pages 11-16, 98-102, 120, 125-127, and 140-143 for references to the specific claims made in this paragraph.

62. For the statements in this paragraph, see Dixy Lee Ray, with Lou Guzzo, *Trashing the Planet: How Science Can Help Us Deal with Acid Rain, Depletion of the Ozone, and Nuclear Waste (Among Other Things)* (Washington, D.C.: Regnery Gateway, 1990), 71 and 72.

63. Ray, *Trashing the Planet*, 72 and 73.

64. "The Life and Deaths of DDT," *The Wall Street Journal*, 14 June 2002, A12.

65. Thomas H. Jukes, "The Tragedy of DDT," in *Rational Readings*, 217-220

66. For more on the nature of arbitrary assertions and why they should be dismissed without consideration, see Leonard Peikoff, *Objectivism: The Philosophy of Ayn Rand* (New York: Meridian, 1991), 163-171.

67. These quotes were taken from Lomborg, *The Skeptical Environmentalist*, 254 and 256.

68. For more on emotionalism, see Peikoff, *Objectivism*, 161-163.

69. For more examples, see Lockitch, "Fighting the Hydra."

70. I owe the basic point in this paragraph to Schwartz, "The Philosophy of Privation," 236-237.

71. I am not saying it is impossible for the majority of people to rationally assess environmentalism. They can. However, they will have to learn how to use the tools of reason in order to do this, if not through their formal education then on their own.

72. See Immanuel Kant, *Critique of Pure Reason*, trans. Norman Kemp Smith (New York: Palgrave Macmillan, 2003), 29.

73. More specifically, a consistent application of the valid ideas of the Renaissance and Enlightenment must occur for destructive ideological movements, such as environmentalism, to be rejected once and for all. This means the philosophy of Objectivism (the philosophy of Ayn Rand) must be fully integrated into our culture. For discussion on the subjects mentioned in this paragraph, see the following sources: on the nature of reason, see Peikoff, *Objectivism*, 152-160; on the rise and fall of reason, see Peikoff, *Objectivism*, 182-186 and Leonard Peikoff, *Ominous Parallels: The End of Freedom in America* (New York: Stein and Day, 1982), 101-139; and on the link between reason and capitalism, see Reisman, *Capitalism*, 19-21. On the history of the battle between reason and its antithesis, see Peikoff, *Objectivism*, 453-458.

74. For more on this, see Schwartz, "The Philosophy of Privation," 222.

75. Theodore Kazinski (a.k.a., the Unabomber), "Industrial Society and Its Future," *Washington Post*, 19 September 1995, SS1.

76. For an example, see Kirkpatrick Sale, "Unabomber's Secret Treatise: Is There Method in His Madness?" *The Nation* 261, no. 9 (25 September 1995): 305.

77. Southern Poverty Law Center, "Fringe Eco-Radicals Growing More Violent," *Intelligence Report*, no. 112 (Winter 2003): 3.

78. See Graber, "Mother Nature as a Hothouse Flower."

79. The only reason we have not seen such destruction yet is because, fortunately, environmentalism has not yet been integrated into our culture fully and consistently enough.

80. An even more fundamental problem people must overcome to clear the fog is the bad epistemological ideas they have accepted. Namely, the rejection of reason as man's only means to knowledge. On this subject, see the section in this chapter titled "Environmentalism and the Abandonment of Reason" and the references provided there.

Chapter Seven

Economic Inequality

Introduction

Some people complain that the free market produces a distribution of wealth and income that is "unfair" and "unjust." It is not fair or just, they claim, that some people are so rich while others are poor. They also complain that the opportunities available to people in the market are "unequally distributed." They claim that all people should be able to start with the same opportunities in life so that each person has an equal chance to succeed. Hence, the market has failed to adequately distribute "society's" supply of income and opportunities, and the government must intervene to correct the situation by, among other things, redistributing income through a graduated income tax and provide some people with greater opportunities by, perhaps, supplying them with an education paid for by taxpayers. Inequality with respect to wealth, income, and opportunities are the issues that will be discussed in this chapter.

Wealth and Income Inequality

Causality and Inequality

Wealth and income inequality in a free market are instances of the law of causality—of causality in production. Some people are more talented, more ambitious, or will save more, and thus will earn higher incomes and accumulate more wealth than other individuals who are less talented, ambitious, or who save less. Egalitarians (those who want equality with regard to income, opportunities, and other things) want to deny the law of causality—a fundamental law of reality—by calling for wealth and income redistribution. This is an attempt to

171

wipe a metaphysical fact (a fact inherent in the nature of reality) out of existence. Any attempt to do so must fail because it is an attempt to rewrite reality. It must lead to disaster because one cannot change the nature of reality. Reality requires that one put forth effort to provide some good or service to others in order to earn an income. Some people will be better at this than others. This fact will remain so no matter how hard egalitarians attempt to wish it (and legislate it) out of existence. Reality is what it is regardless of what one might want it to be. In any war against reality, reality will always win. That is exactly why wealth and income redistribution have led to disastrous results when put into practice (as the history of socialism attests).

In addition, egalitarians often speak of a "distribution of income" as if there is only so much "income" out there somewhere and that someone hands out this limited amount of income to everyone. Egalitarians act as if there is no causal factor determining the income someone receives. According to them, some people just happen to randomly receive more income than others, and this is unacceptable.

In connection with this point, it is important to note the self-reinforcing effects of redistribution. Redistribution (i.e., the taking of income from those who have earned it in the marketplace to give it to those who have not) makes it appear that wealth and income come from nowhere and thus *are* causeless. This makes it appear as if no one deserves any more income than anyone else.

The problem with the above theory is that *income is not distributed, it is earned.* Redistribution of income undermines this knowledge. It undermines one's understanding of the fact that *the causal factor in the production of wealth is the individual human mind.* An individual earns a higher income to the extent he uses his mind to think, gain some skill or an education, and figure out how to produce and sell a product or service. Or, he earns more income by using his mind to think and act in a long-range fashion by saving and investing more money (and making better investments) for his future. The principle here is, the more rational the individual, the more he will tend to earn.

Further, when one person earns more income under capitalism, this does not mean that others must earn less income. This is true because, under capitalism, one earns greater income by being more productive. This leads to a higher productive capability and thus a growing abundance of wealth in the economy. This, in turn, leads to more goods being available and a higher standard of living, which means higher income levels for everyone in the economic system. One person's gain under capitalism is not another person's loss. This only occurs under socialism and the welfare state, where the government takes wealth and income from some people to give it to others. Under capitalism, one person's gain is everyone else's gain because success in a free market is achieved by producing wealth and engaging in voluntary trade.[1]

The Economics of Wealth and Income Inequality

The Incentive to Produce

Economically, income inequality is needed in order to provide an incentive to produce wealth. This can be shown in a simple example.[2] Imagine that an individual has the ability to gain some new skill and, on the basis of this new skill, earn an additional $1,000 in annual income. If there is no income redistribution, he has the full economic incentive to gain the skill. This is true because he keeps the entire $1,000 in additional income. Hence, the productive capability and the average standard of living in the economy rise on the basis of the new skill this individual acquires, thanks to the incentive of earning a higher income.

Now imagine that income is redistributed over, say, ten people, perhaps his immediate family and friends. This individual still has a fairly strong economic incentive to acquire the new skill. He still gets to keep 10 percent, or $100, of the additional income, and the rest of the income goes to people he knows and cares about. Therefore, the productive capability and standard of living still rise.

However, the above is not true if the additional income is redistributed over a growing number of people. If it is redistributed over 100, 1,000, or 1,000,000 people, if it is redistributed over the entire population of the United States or the entire population of the earth, the individual will have virtually no economic motivation to gain the new skill. This is true because to the extent that the additional income is redistributed over a larger number of people, the fraction of additional income the individual in question actually receives approaches zero. The principle here is as follows: *to the degree to which complete income equality is achieved, the lower is the economic incentive to produce.* If complete income equality is achieved, people have virtually no incentive to produce because they cannot use their talents and abilities to further their own lives. This, of course, would lead to an extremely low productive capability and standard of living for everyone.

With complete income equality, not only is there no incentive to increase one's ability to produce, there is actually a strong incentive to decrease one's productive activities. It is easy to see why by making a change to the above example. Imagine that, instead of being able to gain a new skill to earn extra income, the individual considers doing something that would decrease his income by $1,000 per year (perhaps by working less). Again, if there is no income redistribution, the individual feels the entire effect of the lost income, since his income falls by $1,000. Therefore, he has the highest possible economic incentive to avoid doing whatever it is that decreases his income.

However, if the loss of income is redistributed over a growing number of individuals, his income decreases by less and less. If the loss is redistributed over ten people, he loses only $100. If it is redistributed over 100 people, he loses only $10. If it is redistributed over 1,000,000 people, or the entire population of the United States or the world, he loses essentially nothing.

Therefore, he has a strong incentive to decrease the amount of work he does. In fact, if complete income equality is achieved, he has an incentive not to work at all precisely because his income will decrease by virtually nothing. The principle here is as follows: *to the degree that complete income equality is achieved, the greater is the incentive not to produce.* Therefore, in general, to the degree that income equality is achieved, the productive capability and standard of living will be lower.

Redistribution and Poverty

Forcibly imposing equal incomes on people might make everyone's income the same; however, it will also make everyone's income extremely low. Even poor people will have lower incomes when income equality is imposed on an economic system. Their incomes may be higher relative to that of rich people (because now there are no rich people); however, poor people's incomes, in terms of the goods and services they can purchase, will be lower relative to what their incomes would have been had the rich been able to keep the incomes they earn. Why is this so?

Here, one must, again, keep in mind how someone becomes rich in a capitalist society. One does so by being more productive; i.e., by inventing new products, improving upon old ones, using better methods of production, and producing those goods for which people have a demand.[3] This means when income is taken from the rich and given to the poor, it is being taken from the most productive members of society and given to the least productive members of society. This means the productive capability of the economic system will be lower and the rate of economic progress will be lower. Over time, any one-time gain by poor people from income redistribution will be erased by the loss in purchasing power of their additional money income due to the lower rate of economic progress and thus the slower year-to-year increase in the standard of living. In other words, the poor may have more money to spend with income redistribution but because of the decreased incentive to produce, and because money is being taken from the more productive members of society, very little will be produced and thus there will be very little for the poor to buy with their additional money income. In a society with complete income redistribution, where everyone has the exact same income, everyone will be—equally— miserably poor.

So income redistribution is not in the interest of the poor, as many so-called humanitarians believe. In fact, income redistribution is positively against the self-interest of the rich *and* the poor. It is in the interest of everyone to have each individual's right to keep the income he earns protected, no matter how large or small that income. This is what is required to provide people with the incentive to produce and thus make possible a high and rising standard of living for everyone, rich and poor alike.

The Redistribution of Wealth
Redistributing the wealth that rich people possess (their homes, cars, businesses, etc.) has an even more harmful economic effect than redistributing their income because most of the wealth that rich people possess is tied up in productive assets (i.e., businesses). Therefore, redistributing such wealth would not only take away the incentive to produce more wealth in the future, and take wealth away from the most productive individuals, it would decrease the supply of wealth that is currently employed for the purpose of producing the goods and services that everyone consumes (i.e., it would decrease the supply of capital in the economy *today*). This would have an immediate and devastating impact on the productive capability and standard of living of everyone.

The Morality of Wealth and Income Inequality

To avoid any confusion, I must state that I am not attempting to suggest that the rich should be allowed to keep their wealth and income because they are the most productive members of the economy and therefore raise the income of poor people more than anyone else. This would be a defense of the "property rights" of the rich on an altruist base. This "defense" says, in essence, that because the rich serve others the most, it is okay for them to keep their wealth and income. This is not a proper defense of rich people's income because, as I have shown throughout this book, the altruist code of morality is destructive to human life and thus is not a proper standard to determine what is right (or good).

A proper defense of the property rights of the rich is based on the morality of egoism. This defense says that rich people, and all other people, have a right to their own lives and thus a right to the income they earn. No one has any right whatsoever to sacrifice rich people to poor people through income redistribution. This violates the rights of the rich and is immoral because it stands in opposition to the requirements of human life.

The desire to redistribute wealth and income is based on the corrupt altruist code of morality. According to this moral theory, it is unjust for some individuals to have more wealth and income than others. It is a sign that an individual has not sacrificed himself to others enough and thus is morally obligated, according to altruism, to give some of his wealth and income to others. In fact, having great wealth and income, according to altruism, is a sign that an individual has actually sacrificed others to himself. This is what allegedly makes it possible, according to the creed of sacrifice, for individuals to obtain the wealth they possess. The individual is therefore obligated to "give back" (i.e., sacrifice himself) to others because he has allegedly taken from others.

This is the case with the morality of altruism. Based on this moral code, one is led to believe that life requires sacrifice. The only choice available, according to this morality, is to sacrifice oneself to others, and thus others gain at one's own expense, or to sacrifice others to oneself, and thus one gains at the expense of others. Advocates of altruism do not understand that these are not the only alternatives. They do not understand that under a system based on voluntary trade (i.e., a free market or laissez-faire capitalist society) everyone gains. As I have stated in previous chapters, *no one is sacrificed under capitalism* because each participant in a voluntary trade gains from the exchange.[4] Further, as I have also stated, there are no conflicts of men's rational self-interests under capitalism. There is a harmony of men's rational self-interests under capitalism because the success of each man promotes the well-being of all men, as the earlier discussions in this chapter on how one earns a higher income and grows rich under capitalism illustrate.[5]

One does not become rich under capitalism by *taking* wealth from others; one becomes rich by producing or *creating* wealth. Nothing could be more just because to have justice one must get what he deserves or *earns*. This is exactly what happens when a man grows rich through production and trade under capitalism. A man earns the right to keep his wealth when he produces it, and he earns the business of others by getting them to voluntarily buy his product over the alternatives available. Hence, the claim by advocates of altruism that it is unjust for some people to have large amounts of wealth and income, when others have much less, is false. On the contrary, it is unjust to redistribute wealth and income because, when this is done, one is taking it from someone who has earned it and giving it to someone who has not.

It is only under socialism, the favored economic system of the advocates of altruism, that people must be, and routinely are, sacrificed. As was discussed in chapter 1, such a system is based on the morality of self-sacrifice. One can see this explicitly in the socialist slogan "from each according to his ability, to each according to his need." Here it is claimed that those who have the ability to produce are to be sacrificed to those who are needy. If this slogan was actually put into practice, the only result that would be achieved would be to make everyone needy, as has actually occurred wherever it has been implemented, such as in socialist nations.[6]

During the entire history of its existence in philosophy, advocates of altruism have never been able to answer one question: "Why should men sacrifice themselves to others?" No rational answer has ever been given to this question because there is no rational reason to sacrifice oneself. As I have stated, sacrificing oneself to others is self-destructive and therefore irrational. To the degree that altruism is consistently practiced, it will destroy one's life. Therefore, the rational thing to do is to reject the morality of self-sacrifice and embrace a code of morality that furthers one's life and well-being. The proper, or moral, thing to do is to act in one's rational self-interest. This is what one must do to live. So, if one is tempted to ask the question, "Why should one be selfish?" The answer is: "Because your life depends on it!"

One final point on the issue of wealth and income redistribution. As I have said, imposing equal incomes violates individual rights because its achievement requires massive amounts of the initiation of physical force. This is inconsistent with the requirements of human life. In contrast, the existence of unequal incomes under capitalism is consistent with the requirements of human life because it results from protecting individual rights. Therefore, egalitarians should not be seen as humanitarians, based on any sensible meaning of that term. They should be seen as the enemies of human life that they are because, by standing in opposition to what human life requires, they are literally against humanity. For someone to be an actual humanitarian (viz., someone who actually promotes the well-being of humanity), he must be an advocate of capitalism. This *is* what human life requires.

Inequality of Opportunity

Causality, Economics, and Inequality of Opportunity

As I mentioned at the beginning of this chapter, egalitarians are not only concerned with achieving equality in wealth and income, they are often concerned with achieving equality with respect to opportunities also. However, *the key with respect to opportunities is to have freedom of opportunity, not equality of opportunity*. Freedom of opportunity means that one has the opportunity to pursue those endeavors one has both the means and ability to pursue, and one will not be stopped from doing so by the initiation of physical force. The freedom of opportunity recognizes the facts of reality. It recognizes that people start in different positions in life (whether financial or geographical) and have different ambitions, abilities, desires, etc. As with wealth and income equality, by trying to achieve equality in opportunities, egalitarians are acting in contradiction to the facts of reality. They are attempting to deny causality with respect to opportunities and are acting in opposition to the requirements of human life (since people must be free to pursue the opportunities available to them to further their lives and happiness).

To protect the freedom of opportunity, of course, one must protect individual rights. By doing this, an economy will be able to achieve the greatest rate of economic progress and highest standard of living that are possible. This is the case because by protecting the freedom of opportunity, people will not be held back in pursuing any opportunities that are open to them (based on their ability, education, financial resources, geographic location, etc.) regarding the production of wealth, and thus more wealth will be produced. If people are forcibly prevented from pursuing opportunities to produce wealth, less wealth will be produced.

The Logical Implications of the Equality of Opportunity

It will help in understanding egalitarianism to uncover some of the logical implications of it. If egalitarians were serious about attempting to erase all inequalities in human beings, and have complete equality of opportunity, they would have to call for some very extreme measures to do so. For instance, they would have to push for the abolition of the institution of marriage, the raising of children in mass orphanages, genetic engineering, and prevent anyone who tried to improve themselves, in any way, from doing so. This, in fact, is the only way to even attempt to make everyone equal in every respect.

The above is true because the only way to get rid of genetic differences in people is to engage in the genetic engineering of humans. In other words, everyone would have to be a clone of one set of genes. Further, the only way to get rid of differences in the upbringing of children is to prevent individual parents from raising their own children. Hence, one would have to raise them all in mass orphanages. Also, no one could be allowed to get married because when people fall in love and get married they often want to have children and raise them on their own. One could not allow such desires to be acted upon, or even allow them to come into existence, if all differences are to be erased. In addition, egalitarians would have to keep everyone at the level of the most ignorant and laziest person to prevent anyone from rising above the crowd. Of course, attempting to achieve equality would require massive amounts of the initiation of physical force and would lead to misery and poverty.

It must be noted here that although egalitarians are rarely consistent enough to advocate—let alone attempt to achieve—the above, if they were actually to attempt to do so they would still not be able to succeed in making everyone equal. This is the case because human beings have free will and, despite the environmental and genetic influences that may affect them, humans are able to choose whether they want to attempt to achieve something or not. To have free will means to have the ability to choose to think or not; it means to choose to use one's mind or not. This is something that each individual chooses to do or not, on his own, regardless of how similar his genetic makeup and upbringing are to others. This is why people with a similar upbringing or an identical genetic code so often lead very different lives. For instance, identical twins might choose to have different friends, wear different types of clothes, and choose different careers. Or, two siblings who grow up in a poor neighborhood could choose radically different paths. One might choose to skip school and watch television all the time (and therefore remain poor), while the other might choose to work hard in school and pursue a career to lift himself out of poverty. Hence, any attempt to achieve complete equality must fail because it contradicts the fundamental nature of human beings.

Although egalitarians are rarely consistent enough to attempt to achieve complete equality, this discussion helps to expose the actual nature of egalitarianism. It illustrates, in the starkest terms, what would be necessary to achieve the egalitarians' goals and thus gives one an idea of the essence of an egalitarian. Such a person is one who wants dictatorial control over people's lives to force them to do whatever he wishes. This illustrates, more forcefully, that these alleged humanitarians are no supporters of the human race and, in fact, are among the lowest representatives of the species one could find.

Conclusion

As one can see, the critique of the market based on its lack of equality, like the others, is no critique at all. It simply shows, once again, that people are capable of accepting false, and sometimes vicious, ideas. It is the altruist code of morality that leads people to believe in the desirability of economic equality. It is this belief that leads people to think it is morally right for those with greater wealth, income, or ability to be sacrificed to those with less. Ultimately, it is this idea that must be rejected if we are to rid ourselves of such vicious attacks on the market and on human life. We must embrace the morality of egoism to free human existence, once and for all, from the chains of altruism. If we do this, we can all grow richer together under capitalism.

In addition, the discussion in this chapter provides another illustration of the link between individual rights and economics. It shows that when individual rights are violated, such as through wealth and income redistribution or in the measures necessary to achieve equality of opportunity, the productive capability and standard of living are lowered. Likewise, when individual rights are protected, such as by protecting the right of an individual to keep the wealth and income he earns and pursue the opportunities he has the means and ability to pursue, the productive capability and standard of living are raised.

Notes

1. For more on why capitalism is a "win-win" situation for everyone, see the sections titled "The Morality of Rational Self-Interest and Capitalism" and "Capitalism" in chapter 1.

2. This example is based on an example presented in George Reisman, *Capitalism: A Treatise on Economics* (Ottawa, Ill.: Jameson Books, 1996), 145-146. For another example, see Henry Hazlitt, *Time Will Run Back: A Novel About the Rediscovery of Capitalism* (Lanham, Md.: University Press of America, 1986), 88-91.

3. This statement is not contradicted by those who might become rich through inheritance. Here, the heir must still earn the wealth he has obtained in the sense that, in order to remain rich, he must wisely invest the wealth he has inherited. If he does not, he will, more than likely, become poorer in real terms (i.e., in terms of the actual wealth he possesses). At a minimum, he will become poorer relative to other members of society.

4. Of course, if a person wanted to voluntarily sacrifice himself to others, no one would stop him under capitalism. He would be free to choose to waste his life in this manner. However, no one would be forced to sacrifice himself to others because the initiation of physical force is banned under capitalism.

5. Also, see the discussions in chapter 1, on this same topic, in the sections titled "The Morality of Rational Self-Interest and Capitalism" and "Capitalism."

6. I owe this point to Harry Binswanger. Hear it in the audio taped debate of Harry Binswanger and John Ridpath versus Jack Clark and Jim Chapin, *Socialism versus Capitalism: Which Is the Moral System?* (Gaylordsville, Conn.: Second Renaissance Inc., 1989).

Chapter Eight

Public Goods

Introduction

Another argument against the market, which makes the claim that the market fails to provide an adequate supply of goods, is the "public goods" argument. Different, sometimes contradictory, definitions have been given by economists for the term "public good."[1] Hence, I will use the one that best captures what economists generally mean when they use the term. It will help in understanding what a "public good" is if one first understands what a "private good" is, since the two are considered to be opposites. Therefore, before presenting the definition of a public good, I will present the definition of a private good.

Public versus Private Goods

A private good is said to have two characteristics. First, it is said to be subject to the exclusion principle. This means that only those people who have the ability to pay for the good can purchase and consume the good, while those who do not have the ability to pay can be excluded from consuming the good. This applies to a good such as a Big Mac because it is very easy for McDonald's to prevent anyone from consuming a Big Mac if the individual has not paid for it. A lighthouse is often used as an example of a good to which this does not apply because once a lighthouse exists, ships passing by in the night can benefit from the lighthouse regardless of whether the ships' owners have helped to pay for the construction of the lighthouse. Hence, it is claimed to be difficult, if not impossible, to exclude those from using a lighthouse who have not helped to pay for its construction.

Private goods are also said to be subject to rivalry in consumption. This means that if one person consumes the good another person cannot. For example, if I consume a Big Mac, everyone else is prevented from consuming it. However, if I consume the services provided by a lighthouse, this does not prevent others from doing so. Other ships can pass by and use the lighthouse at the same time I do. Therefore, this good is not subject to rivalry in consumption.

As I stated earlier, a "public good" is the opposite of a "private good." Therefore, because a "private good" is said to be subject to both exclusion and rivalry in consumption, a "public good" is said not to be subject to both exclusion and rivalry in consumption. "Public goods" are goods that many people can consume simultaneously and with respect to which it is hard to exclude people from consuming. "Private goods," of course, include the Big Mac, mentioned above, as well as goods such as automobiles, homes, computers, oranges, and many, many more. "Public goods" are said to include goods such as the lighthouse, mentioned above, as well as national defense and sometimes roads and highways, among a few other goods.

National defense is considered to be a public good because once an army is paid for, when it defends a specific geographic region, it defends individuals in that region whether or not they have helped pay for the military. Therefore, national defense is said to be non-excludable. Also, an army can defend many people in a particular region at the same time. Hence, national defense is said not to be subject to rivalry in consumption.

Roads and highways are sometimes considered to be public goods because, up to a point, they are not subject to rivalry in consumption. This is the case because many people can use a road or highway without interfering with each other's ability to drive on it. Further, it is harder to make roads and highways subject to exclusion because it is more difficult than with "private goods" to keep people who have not helped pay for the construction of roads and highways from using them.

Public Goods and Market Failure

Why Markets Allegedly Fail Due to Public Goods

How does the existence of so-called public goods allegedly cause the free market to fail? It is claimed they do so because it is allegedly difficult or impossible to exclude people from the consumption of public goods. Because of this, it is said that such goods lead to a "free rider" problem when they are provided through the market. The free rider problem exists when people can benefit from a good without paying for it. This was shown, for example, with respect to lighthouses above. Because it is possible for an owner whose ship passes by a lighthouse to benefit from the lighthouse even though he did not help pay to build it, the ship owner is able to get a "free ride" off of those who did pay for it.

The "free rider" problem is said to result from the nature of a public good and therefore applies to all public goods. Because of this "problem" the market is said to provide too few of these goods. This is allegedly the case because if people can "free ride" off of others, fewer people will purchase the services that public goods provide and therefore fewer of these goods are likely to be produced and supplied in response to this lower level of demand. In fact, by the logic of the free rider argument, if everyone attempts to get a free ride off of others, no one will pay for the services these goods provide and therefore none of these goods would be produced in a free market. Hence, some extremely vital goods would go unproduced. The solution to this alleged problem is to have the government step in and provide the goods.

Another way to think about the issue of "public goods" is to recall the "externalities" argument against the market discussed in chapter 4. If one recalls this argument, one will recognize that the "public goods" argument is similar to the "positive externality" argument against the market. This latter argument said that because some goods (such as immunizations and lighthouses) provide external benefits, the market will provide too few of them. If one remembers, an external benefit is a benefit bestowed upon an individual not involved in the purchase or sale of a good and for which the individual does not pay. The market allegedly provides fewer goods that create external benefits than would be provided if everyone was required to pay for the benefits they received from these goods. Hence, it is claimed that the government should intervene to make sure the "optimal" amount of goods that create positive externalities is provided.

The "public goods" argument against the market is a subset of the "positive externalities" argument. All public goods allegedly create some positive externality. Because of this, the conclusion is that too few public goods would be provided by the market and thus, it is claimed, the government must step in and provide these goods or subsidize the industries that produce these goods so that an "adequate" amount will be provided. Therefore, whether one considers the "free rider" effect of public goods or one considers public goods as goods that create positive externalities, the only way to solve this alleged problem of market failure is to have some form of government intervention into the market.

Why Markets Do Not Actually Fail Due to Public Goods

As one might guess, because the "public goods" and "positive externalities" arguments are similar, some of the same criticisms that apply to positive externalities, and externalities in general, apply to public goods. Let's take a look at the criticisms of the public goods argument against the market to see why it does not provide a valid criticism of the market.

First, the concept "public goods" takes the focus off the fundamental issue one must be concerned with when determining whether a good (or service) should be provided through the market or by the government. That fundamental issue is whether the provision of a good involves the use of physical force or not. Some of the goods that are said to be public goods, such as national defense, should not be provided by the market even if they could be. However, this is not a question of the so-called free rider problem; it is a question of controlling the use of force. In order for force to be used to protect individual rights (i.e., to protect people from the initiation of force), it must be rigidly controlled. To do this, it is imperative that the use of force be relegated to self-defense by a government that is controlled by objective rules and procedures to determine exactly how force can and cannot be used. A proper constitution provides the basic set of rules a government must follow to insure that force is used appropriately. Such a document restricts the government to using force only in retaliation against those who initiate force.

If national defense, or any other form of force, was provided through the "market" it would lead to a massive violation of individual rights and would therefore be a threat to individuals. Imagine if everyone had to hire private police forces, which adhered to different sets of rules and laws, to protect themselves. Or imagine if everyone had to carry guns around to protect themselves, as in the old west. If this was necessary, the world would be a very unsafe place because this would lead to a proliferation of the use of force, not to its abolition.

For instance, imagine if a person comes home and finds that his television set has been stolen, and he walks around his neighborhood looking in the windows of houses to see if someone has his television. Imagine that this person finds a home with a set that he thinks is his. So he calls his police force, say police force A, to apprehend the individual. However, the accused individual does not recognize the authority of police force A (or the government they represent), so he calls his police force, say police force B, to protect himself. Now one has two groups of armed men facing each other in a standoff. It does not take much imagination to understand what would happen next.[2]

The private provision of police protection or national defense would lead to anarchy and gang warfare. Far from protecting individual rights, it would lead to greater violations of individual rights. The world would be a very dangerous place, and our standard of living much lower, because one would have to fear being attacked or apprehended by others, or their police forces, for any arbitrary reason.[3]

Concerning the application of the criticisms of "positive externalities" to "public goods": as I stated in chapter 4 in connection with positive externalities, people should be required to pay only for those goods they voluntarily contract to receive. They should not be forced to pay, through government imposed taxes, for goods that they would not have purchased voluntarily. Forcing individuals to pay for goods or services they do not choose to purchase represents a violation of individual rights and decreases the satisfaction and well-being of individuals in the economy. This latter, as stated in chapter 4, occurs because the voluntary purchases people make are the ones that bring them the most satisfaction. Therefore, when individuals are forced to purchase a particular good, they are often being forced to purchase something they would rather not have purchased.[4]

Furthermore, there are ways to exclude people from consuming many so-called public goods or get people to pay for the provision of such goods in the first place. For instance, people can be excluded from the use of highways through the use of tolls. Tolls make it possible to require individuals to pay for their use of the highway based on the number of miles and type of vehicle they drive. With today's technology, the provision of toll roads would not even necessarily involve drivers having to stop to pay tolls at a toll booth. It is possible for cars to have transponders installed, and their movements tracked, so it can be determined exactly where each driver enters and exits the highway. This makes it possible to automatically charge drivers the correct amount. Such technology is already used in many places.

Providing highways privately, with the incentive of the profit motive, would vastly improve the ability to provide the roads that are desperately needed in America. The increase in the number of highways that would occur, along with the fluctuation of tolls during the time of day and week with the volume of traffic, would greatly reduce traffic congestion in the major cities in a relatively short period of time. Here, the incentive would be in place to build the highways that people demand and to get people to use the highways during off-peak times. No such incentive exists today because the government, which provides virtually all highways today, does not (and should not) act on the profit motive, and thus has much less incentive to provide the roads that people demand and set up a toll structure that would more evenly distribute the use of highways over time.[5]

Lighthouses could be provided privately as well. As was stated in chapter 4, this is how it was done in Great Britain for two centuries.

The market would be able to provide the right amounts of those "public goods" that it is appropriate for it to provide because individuals have a self-interest in the provision of such goods. Private individuals would be responding to the profit motive with respect to the provision of these goods, and this would give them the selfish incentive needed to provide the right amounts. So-called public goods that involve the use of force, such as national defense, must be provided by the government in order to protect individual rights and establish and maintain the existence of a market. No sign of market failure is visible here. If one has an understanding of the nature of the goods involved, and the nature of the free market, one sees only another success of the free market because individual rights are protected, the standard of living is raised, and the ability of individuals to further their lives and happiness is improved.

A Deeper Look at the Concept "Public Goods"

As with the externality argument against the market, there are more fundamental criticisms that can be made against the public goods argument. Like the "concept" externality, the concept "public goods" is an invalid concept. This is the case because it groups fundamentally different things together under the same concept. As stated in previous chapters, in order to form a valid concept, one must not do this. The concept "public goods," for instance, groups together services related to the use of force (such as national defense) with goods completely unrelated to the use of force (such as highways and lighthouses). By grouping fundamentally different things together under the same concept, one obliterates the crucial distinction between them and causes people to forget or ignore this distinction.[6] Without the recognition of this fundamental difference, it is much easier for people to believe that the government should provide all "public goods."

Furthermore, rivalry and excludability exist to a greater or lesser degree with virtually all goods and services. For instance, anyone who has driven on a highway during rush hour in virtually any major city knows all too well that rivalry exists on the highways. In addition, as was discussed above, it is not that difficult to exclude people from using highways if they do not pay. Further, while rivalry does not exist in the consumption of lighthouses and it is difficult, if not impossible, to exclude people from using a lighthouse, it would be possible for lighthouse owners to collect fees from shippers at nearby ports so that users of the lighthouse would be required to pay for their use of it.[7]

As for national defense, rivalry in consumption exists here because if a division of the army or a fleet of ships (or an individual soldier or ship) defends one geographic region of the country, it cannot at the same time defend another region of the country. For instance, a naval fleet cannot at the same time defend the east and west coasts of the United States. Further, although it would be harder to keep people who have not paid for the army from benefiting from it, such people could be publicly denounced (as they should be) and urged to pay because it is in their self-interest to do so. In addition, if the people in a large enough region of a country refuse to pay for national defense, the government might choose to withdraw troops from that region. Those regions that do pay could receive a larger number of troops, army bases, naval ports, etc.

Also, as with the "concept" externality, the "concept" public good is a collectivist term used to justify forcing individuals to live for some group (or collective). It attempts to claim that goods belong to "society" and therefore "society" must pay for them. Such a term is used to justify forcing individuals to pay for highways, national defense, lighthouses, etc., regardless of whether individuals would benefit from such things or not and regardless of whether people want to pay for these things or not. As stated in previous chapters, collectivism is destructive to human life because the individual—particularly each individual's judgment about what is in his rational self-interest—is sacrificed to the desires of some group.[8]

No distinction should be made between "private" and "public" goods. Ultimately, all goods are private in the sense that they are owned and/or paid for by individuals or private organizations owned by individuals. Even goods owned by the government are paid for by individuals: viz., taxpayers. Therefore, just as with the term "externality," the term "public good" should be thrown out. It should not be used in intellectual discourse or debate because it leads to confusion and false conclusions, as all invalid concepts do. The term "public goods" leads to confusion over what is the proper function of a government and causes misunderstanding about how specific goods and services could be most efficiently and effectively provided.

The real distinction to make in this case is not between "public" and "private" goods and services, but between those goods and services that are associated with the use of force and those that are not. The latter distinction is fundamental because of the dramatically different effects these things can have on human life. Things associated with the use of force, like the police and national defense, must be objectively controlled and thus provided through a government limited by a proper constitution, so that force is used only to protect individual rights (i.e., so that everyone [including the government] is prevented from initiating physical force). Things not associated with the use of force, such as highways and lighthouses, should be provided by private individuals through the market.

Conclusion

Once again we see that the market does not fail. The failure that occurs with respect to so-called public goods is that those who accept the validity of such a term fail to understand the proper method of concept formation and thus fail to reject this invalid and misleading concept. Further, they fail to see that individuals cannot be yoked to some collective because this goes against the fundamental fact that human beings are *individuals*. The fundamental unit of value with regard to human beings is the individual and attempting to force individuals to live for some collective stands in opposition to the requirements of human life. The use of force stands in opposition to human life because it prevents people from being free from the initiation of physical force so they can use their minds to think, act on their own rational judgment, and take the necessary actions to further their lives and happiness.

The failure of collectivist methods of providing so-called public goods can be readily witnessed in the abysmal job the government has done in the provision of goods such as highways. This evidence consists of the gridlock that exists in virtually all of America's major cities. To correct this failure of collectivism, one must restore the profit motive to the provision of this and all goods that are bought and sold within the context of voluntary trade.

Notes

1. For an example of these contradictions, see the definitions of "public good" presented in Roger A. Arnold, *Microeconomics*, 5th ed. (Cincinnati: South-Western College Publishing, 2001), 426-427 and Walter Nicholson, *Microeconomic Theory: Basic Principles and Extensions*, 6th ed. (Fort Worth, Tex.: Harcourt Brace College Publishers, 1995), 815.

2. I owe this example to Ayn Rand. See her *The Virtue of Selfishness* (New York: Signet, 1964), 132.

3. Rand, *The Virtue of Selfishness*, 127-128.

4. Based on this paragraph, some might wonder how the proper functions of the government are to be financed if people should not be forced to pay for government provided services. For a discussion of this topic, see the "Epilogue."

5. Of course, to completely solve the transportation problems that exist in major cities today, all so-called public transportation systems (including bus, train, and rail) would have to be privatized in order to allow the profit motive to create the incentive for suppliers to provide the proper amounts of these services. This would include allowing for the complete elimination of one or all of these services if sufficient demand does not exist to make their provision profitable. Further, the environmentalist movement would have to be prevented from hampering plans to expand the highway system and any other transportation systems.

6. For more on this topic, see the section titled "An Important Epistemological Discussion: The Nature of Concepts" in chapter 2 and the section titled "The Invalid Nature of the Concept 'Externality'" in chapter 4.

7. See the section titled "The Solution to Positive Externalities" in chapter 4 for more on the subject of lighthouses.

8. See the introduction and chapters 1 and 4 for more on the destructive nature of collectivism. In chapter 1, see the sections titled "Socialism" and "The Mixed Economy." In chapter 4, see the sections titled "The Solution to Negative Externalities" and "The Altruist and Collectivist Nature of 'Externality.'"

Chapter Nine

Asymmetric Information

What Is Asymmetric Information?

With respect to information, it is claimed that the market fails due to the existence of "asymmetric information." Asymmetric information is a term used by contemporary economists to describe a situation where either the buyer or seller in a market exchange has some information that the other does not have. For example, the seller of a used car has much more knowledge about the condition of the car than the buyer. Information in this situation is said to be asymmetric because it is not the same on both sides of the trade. The seller has more information about the car than the buyer.

Why Markets Allegedly Fail Due to Asymmetric Information

Inadequate Information

Asymmetric information is said to lead to market failure for a few reasons. One claim is that the market allegedly provides inadequate information to consumers and thus causes them to act differently than they otherwise would have acted had they possessed more (or "symmetric" or "perfect") information. For instance, the alleged lack of information provided by the market might lead a person to purchase a good or service that he would not have otherwise purchased, or it might lead him to not purchase a good or service that he would have otherwise purchased. This, in turn, would lead to a decrease in the satisfaction and well-being of individuals in the economy from what it otherwise would have been had the individual possessed more information about the product and thus made a more informed decision.

"Adverse Selection"

Asymmetric information is also said to lead to two other problems that allegedly result in market failure: "adverse selection" and "moral hazard." Adverse selection is said to occur when the parties on one side of a market exchange, who have information not known to parties on the other side, "self-select" (i.e., choose whether or not to remain in the market) in a way that adversely affects the parties on the other side of the exchange. This problem, it is claimed, can lead to the complete breakdown of a market.

The most famous description of the alleged ability for markets to break down due to "adverse selection" is the so-called lemons problem in the used car market, first put forward by the economist George Akerlof.[1] What is claimed to happen in this market is that buyers have limited information about the used cars on the market and therefore do not know for sure whether a car they want to buy is a "lemon." Because of this uncertainty, buyers will be reluctant to pay as much money for any particular car when compared to a situation in which they know for certain that a car they are buying is not a lemon. Therefore, the demand for used cars will decrease from what it would have been had buyers possessed greater information about the cars being sold. As a result, the average price of used cars will decrease.

Of course, sellers of used cars know that buyers without "symmetric" information are not willing to pay as much for used cars because of the risk of getting a lemon. This is said to provide an incentive for those sellers with the highest quality used cars to withdraw their cars from the market. They allegedly do so because the prices they can get for their cars, presumably, are below what they consider to be acceptable due to the existence of asymmetric information and the lower average selling price that prevails as a result of such information. This leaves a greater percentage of lower quality cars or "lemons" on the market.

According to supporters of this argument, the process does not stop here. Buyers, supporters of this argument say, know that the highest quality cars are pulled off the market due to the lower average selling price of a used car. This further increases one's chances of getting a lemon. Because of this increased risk, the prices used car buyers are willing to pay decrease further, as demand for the product falls. Of course, sellers of the highest quality cars left on the market at this point know this and thus are not willing to sell their cars at the lower prices. Hence, they pull their cars off the market. This leaves an even greater percentage of low quality cars on the market and thus an even greater chance of buying a lemon. This process could continue, according to its supporters, until there is nothing but lemons left in the used car market. Only those sellers with the lowest quality cars would be willing to sell their cars for the extremely low prices that people are willing to pay (presumably these sellers would be happy to get any price for their cars to avoid the cost of towing them to the junkyard). Therefore, buyers may not be willing to buy any used cars. In other words, the used car market completely breaks down.

As absurd as this argument is, many economists actually believe it. Evidence for its wide acceptance is provided by the fact that the original "lemons" article written by George Akerlof is widely read and cited, and by the fact that a section on the "lemons problem" is often included in contemporary economics textbooks. Its wide acceptance is also evidenced by the fact that this argument is considered by many economists to be a profound insight into used car markets and similar markets. Finally, evidence for its wide acceptance is provided by the fact that this argument helped Akerlof win the Nobel Prize in economics, instead of getting him laughed out of the profession for putting forward such a nonsensical theory.

Using adverse selection, one can follow the same procedure, as illustrated above in the used car market, to show that insurance markets, such as automobile and health insurance, have the potential to break down. Here, instead of the sellers "self-selecting" in a way that adversely affects the buyers, which is supposed to occur in the used car market, the buyers of insurance are suppose to make choices that adversely affect the sellers.

The story goes as follows: because there is a risk of insuring unhealthy people or bad drivers, due to the fact that insurers do not have "perfect information" about people's health or driving records, insurers are suppose to raise their rates relative to what they would be if the insurers had perfect information about people's backgrounds. This, in turn, allegedly drives the most healthy people and best drivers out of the market because they are the ones least likely to need the insurance and therefore are less likely to be willing to pay a higher price for it. Of course, this increases the risk of insuring unhealthy people and bad drivers. This, in turn, drives rates up further and drives more low risk customers out of the market. Eventually, rates are supposed to rise so high that only the most unhealthy people and worst drivers are left to buy insurance. They are willing to pay the high rates because they know they will get their money's worth. Except now, insurers leave the market altogether, knowing it is a losing venture, and the market breaks down.

The same is alleged to be possible in loan markets. Here, due to the risk of borrowers defaulting on loans, creditors are suppose to charge higher interest rates relative to what they would charge if they possessed "perfect information" about the credit worthiness of borrowers. Because of this, it is claimed, the most credit worthy borrowers leave the market. This increases the proportion of borrowers in the market who are not credit worthy and thus increases the interest rate that creditors must charge to compensate for the greater risk of making bad loans. Again, the process occurs until only those individuals who are least likely to pay back the loan, i.e., the greatest default risks, are willing to take out loans. Since creditors know this, they are very unlikely to make loans or are only willing to make them at very high interest rates to compensate for the very high risk of making a bad loan. The end result is that no loans are made and the loan market breaks down.

Advocates of the "adverse selection" argument do not necessarily claim that a market will completely break down. They may claim that a market will only partially break down because far fewer trades will take place due to the existence of asymmetric information. Either way, however, it is claimed to be a failure of the market.

One must realize that the claim that markets will break down due to adverse selection is not limited to the above markets. Based on the logic of the argument, most markets should have a tendency to breakdown because in most markets the two sides to the transaction have different information about the product or service being bought and sold (whether it be computers, homes, the services of a plumber, and many other things). Hence, one would expect to see the widespread breakdown of markets if this argument was valid.

"Moral Hazard"

"Adverse selection" is suppose to prevent trades from ever taking place. The other problem that asymmetric information is alleged to create, "moral hazard," occurs after a trade has already taken place. Moral hazard is said to exist when one party to a transaction changes his behavior in a way that is hidden from and costly to the other party. This is suppose to be a major problem in the insurance market. For instance, if a person buys health insurance, it is claimed that he will not take very good care of his health since he knows he will have to pay little or nothing for any healthcare services he may need. This, of course, is detrimental to the health insurance company because it increases the number of claims made and thus increases the cost of providing insurance. The same is said to be true with automobile insurance, fire insurance, and other types of insurance. People will be less careful once they have the insurance, supporters of this argument claim, since they know it will cover all or most of the cost of any damage done. Since insurers know this, they will charge higher premiums to those wanting to purchase the insurance. This could lead to an adverse selection problem, where only those people who represent the greatest health, accident, or fire risk will seek insurance. Hence, the moral hazard problem could help to cause these markets to breakdown.

Loan markets can also allegedly fall victim to the moral hazard problem because borrowers may make risky investments with money they receive from a loan. For example, to obtain a loan a borrower might say he is using the loan to build up his inventory of a product he currently sells. However, once he receives the money he could use it to invest in a completely different line of business, and it would be difficult for the lender to know. This could lead to a greater number of defaults and the raising of interest rates by creditors to cover the higher costs they face. This, in turn, could lead to the adverse selection problem and the break down of these markets.

Why Markets Do Not Actually Fail Due to Asymmetric Information

How Markets Provide Adequate Information

Now that I have shown the case against the market based on asymmetric information, let's see why markets do not, in fact, fail in this case either. Although it is true that there are differences in the information possessed by buyers and sellers, this does not cause markets to break down. This is the case because the profit motive gives businesses a strong incentive to provide adequate information about their products to consumers. Those businesses that do not provide the information that customers want put themselves at a competitive disadvantage relative to those businesses that do. If a company wants to get customers to purchase its product, it must provide customers with adequate information about the product. Otherwise, customers will not purchase the product or will purchase it from someone who does provide adequate information. As a result, those businesses that do not provide adequate information will become less profitable, while the ones that provide adequate information will become more profitable.

Further, there are many different means available for consumers to acquire information about products and ensure they are getting a good product. For instance, businesses often stand behind their products to show that they think the products are worth buying. They use warranties and guarantees to protect customers from defects and to insure that customers are satisfied. Brand names also provide information about the quality of a product. Companies gain a reputation with respect to the level of quality of the products they produce. For instance, Honda and Toyota have a reputation for building high-quality, long-lasting automobiles. A customer knows when he walks into a Honda or Toyota dealership he is more likely to get a high quality car than at the dealerships of other automobile manufacturers.

Advertising also provides information to consumers about products. Likewise, independent assessors, such as Consumers Union and Underwriters Laboratories Inc., help to provide information about products. Finally, word-of-mouth recommendations by friends, family, and other trusted individuals also help to provide information.

Fraud, of course, is illegal under capitalism. This is true because, as stated in previous chapters, fraud is an indirect form of the initiation of physical force since, through an act of fraud, someone attempts to take something from an individual against his will (usually his money). Therefore, anyone who knowingly gives false information is violating the principles on which a free market is based: namely, the prohibition of the initiation of physical force. Hence, acts of fraud are not a case of market failure because they are situations where the free market has been violated. The key to insuring that fraud is minimized is to have a court system that swiftly and adequately punishes the wrongdoer. In other words, the prevention of fraud requires the preservation of a free market, not its abolition.[2]

One implication of the asymmetric information argument against the market is that the government should forcibly require companies to provide information to consumers about their products in order to ensure that "adequate" information is provided. Requirements with regard to food ingredients, nutritional information, and the pricing of automobiles are just three examples of this type of regulation. However, based on the discussion in chapter 5, it should be apparent that the government has no way to know, or at least less ability to know, what information consumers care about getting because the government does not act on the basis of the profit motive. Therefore, the government will not necessarily provide information consumers want (or it will provide information that consumers do not consider worth the cost) because the government does not have the incentive that businesses have to determine what type of information consumers actually want. As with the regulation of safety and quality, the type of information the government requires businesses to provide is typically what politicians and/or pressure groups want, not what consumers want.[3]

The incentive for businesses to acquire information about customers and suppliers (including employees) is just as strong as it is to provide it. Again, the profit motive insures this. Knowing who your customers, and potential customers, are and what products they want provides a business with better information that it can use to better serve its customers and expand its business. This will help a business earn greater profits. For example, businesses use marketing surveys, such as focus-group studies, to acquire information concerning what products customers prefer. Of course, it also pays for businesses to acquire adequate information about their suppliers to insure that the businesses are getting good products and services. With regard to the hiring process, for example, businesses look at resumes, conduct interviews, and contact references to insure they are obtaining good employees.

Why Markets Do Not Break Down

It is absurd to think that markets, such as used car markets, will break down. The most obvious piece of evidence against this claim is the fact that such markets do not break down. These markets exist and there is a large number of transactions that take place within them. Markets, in general, do not break down because the profit motive gives sellers an incentive to sell a good product and provide adequate information. If an individual wants to build a successful business, he must provide a high quality product and deal honestly with individuals to build a good reputation. This will help him gain the repeat business of his customers and will help him gain business through his customers' good recommendations.

Even when sellers are making only a one-time sale of a product (such as when individuals sell their own cars) and thus do not have the incentive of developing and maintaining a good reputation to get them to sell a high quality product, markets do not break down. This is true because many of these sellers will act with honesty and integrity simply because these are virtues. Being honest and acting with integrity are virtues because they are requirements of human life. Most people are not so short-sighted and concrete-bound that they must have the incentive of gaining a good reputation to act virtuously. Rational people will forego a short-run gain that can be made by being dishonest or acting hypocritically because they know such action is not in their rational self-interest.

To be honest means to refuse to fake reality; it means to refuse to pretend that the facts are other than what they really are.[4] If an individual attempts to fake reality, such as by lying to get a person's business or to obtain some other value, eventually he will lose. He may get away with it once, or even a few times, but the more he does it, the greater the chances are that he will be caught. If a person acts this way consistently, he will not confine such actions to one isolated incident. He will end up engaging in such behavior in many or all areas of his life: his job, with his family, his friends, etc. The principle is that *to the degree that an individual attempts to fake reality, he harms himself.*

Even if an individual attempts to fake reality only once, he will harm himself because it will be harder for him to deal with reality and thus it will be more difficult for him to further his life and happiness. For instance, a person may tell one lie to a friend and not get caught. However, now this person must remember what the lie was every time he talks to his friend, so that he does not contradict his lie. Also, he must deal with any guilt he might feel for lying to his friend. Further, if his friend ever does discover the lie, it will damage his friendship. If it is a minor lie, the harm done to the liar will be minor. However, this does not deny the validity of the principle that attempting to fake reality harms an individual because even with a small lie the harm is still there. The principle says that *to the degree* one attempts to fake reality one will be harmed. Therefore, the bigger the lie one tells to obtain a value, the more harm one will inflict upon oneself, and the greater the number of lies, the greater the harm that will be done.[5]

It is never in one's self-interest to fake reality in any manner because life requires one to recognize the facts of reality so that one can deal with them and take the necessary action to further one's life. Fortunately, many people grasp this principle, at least implicitly, and therefore do not attempt to provide false information or withhold crucial information about products they sell. This is one reason why markets exist for individuals wanting to sell their cars and one reason why markets are able to exist in general.

In addition, with regard to used car markets, it is possible for a person to obtain a great deal of information about the cars being sold. One can obtain much information about a car just by test driving it, and the more cars one drives, the more information he gains about which car is the better buy. If this is not enough information to satisfy an individual, he could get someone who knows something about cars, perhaps a friend or relative, to give his opinion about the car. Also, he could hire a mechanic to give his opinion. People are not as ignorant and short-sighted as contemporary economists who put forward the "lemons" argument make them out to be. If a person wants to buy a used car, there are things he can do to make sure he is getting a good one. It is in his self-interest to do so.

With regard to the insurance business, insurance companies have ways to provide people with an incentive to be careful. Using deductibles, requiring the use of smoke detectors as a pre-condition to purchasing fire insurance, or requiring annual medical exams are just a few ways. Moreover, it is absurd to think that just because people have insurance they will be less concerned about harming themselves or their property. Even if a person has insurance, he still suffers great losses if he becomes ill or his house burns down. The financial losses may be less, but the danger to his life, possibly the loss of the ability to earn an income, the negative emotions one would experience, and the inconveniences these situations would create all represent losses or costs of one form or another. Again, people are not so short-sighted and irrational, as contemporary economists who put forward the moral hazard argument believe, that as soon as the potential financial loss of some calamity is removed people act in a manner that is detrimental to their lives and property.

Finally, with regard to loan markets, creditors have means of acquiring information about the financial history of loan applicants. This is how they determine the credit worthiness of a loan applicant. With regard to any industry, if information is necessary in order for the proper provision of the good, as long as there is a profit to be made, the information will be provided or obtained by the appropriate party and the market will not break down.

More Fundamental Criticisms of Asymmetric Information

Asymmetric Information and the Division of Labor

To believe that asymmetric information is harmful and that we should attempt to get rid of it or reduce the level of "asymmetry" that exists is to believe we should get rid of the division of labor because asymmetric information is an inherent feature of such a society.[6] However, getting rid of the division of labor would be devastating to the survival of man because of the enormous benefits it bestows upon mankind. In such a society, individuals specialize and become more knowledgeable about the jobs they perform and the products they produce. Therefore, as such a society develops, it will lead to more asymmetric information. However, such a society also leads to an enormous increase in the productive capability and standard of living. It does so for a variety of reasons.

Probably the greatest benefit from the division of labor, as discussed in chapter 1, is the increase in knowledge it allows a society to possess with regard to production. It increases the amount of such knowledge in direct proportion to the number of specializations. This radically improves the productive capability of the economic system relative to what it would be without the division of labor. If one recalls from chapter 1, without the division of labor, we would all be self-subsistent farmers incapable of producing any significant amount of wealth.[7]

In addition, the division of labor increases the efficiency of learning. It does this in one way by making it possible for people to specialize in what they are best suited for and perfect that one task. It does this in another way by increasing the ratio of the time spent using knowledge to the time spent acquiring knowledge. For example, imagine that someone wanted to fix a leaky pipe in his own home. If he tried to do this on his own, he would have to spend a great deal of time learning about plumbing relative to the time he would spend actually fixing the problem. A professional plumber, however, spends far more time fixing leaky pipes relative to the time he spends learning how to fix them and this dramatically decreases the cost of performing the task.

Finally, through the division of labor, everyone in an economy can benefit from the existence of productive geniuses, such as Thomas Edison and Bill Gates. In a self-subsistent society, such people spend their time doing what everyone else is doing: producing only food, clothing, and shelter. They may be much better than everyone else at producing these things, but they too spend their lives toiling at a level of bare subsistence. In a division of labor society, however, they spend their time inventing new products and raising the productivity of all the members of the economy. For instance, thanks to the productive genius of Bill Gates, all of us are now more productive at work due to the existence of better computer software. The division of labor not only increases the amount of knowledge that a given number of people can possess, it brings that knowledge and the methods of production that everyone uses up to the standard of the most intelligent members of the society.

Based on this discussion, one can see that getting rid of all asymmetric information, or even just a substantial portion of it, would undermine the division of labor and cause a massive decrease in the standard of living. Furthermore, based on our knowledge of the division of labor, one can also conclude that the way to raise our standard of living and improve the well-being of mankind is not to eliminate asymmetric information but to increase the amount of it. This is the case because as a division of labor society becomes more intense (i.e., more specializations are created within it), the knowledge about how to produce wealth that exists within such a society increases. As a consequence of this increase in knowledge, the productive capability and standard of living rise. However, as a side effect, a more intense division of labor also leads to a greater amount of asymmetric information, since people become more specialized and thus know less about the growing number of specializations. Therefore, in this sense, there is not enough asymmetric information.

Asymmetric information is not a problem in a free market economy because in such an economy trade is voluntary. If people did not benefit from specialization and trade because they were being harmed by asymmetric information (in other words, if they did not benefit from the division of labor), they would choose not to trade. Instead, they would choose to be self-subsistent. The reason why people do not do this, but instead choose to specialize and trade, is because of the enormous gains they can obtain from specialization and trade. Hence, the market succeeds. The market succeeds in allowing people to raise their standard of living and thus it improves their ability to further their lives and happiness to a much greater degree than would otherwise be possible. Far from being a sign of market failure, asymmetric information is actually a sign of market success.

If one will recall from chapter 1, a free market is the only type of economic system that is compatible with the nature of a division of labor society and thus is the only economic system that enables people to take advantage of all the enormous benefits that can be derived from the division of labor.[8] Therefore, the free market succeeds on two counts with respect to the division of labor: 1) it succeeds by making the division of labor possible and thus by tremendously raising the standard of living of everyone through the division of labor, and 2) it succeeds by providing the incentive for specialized producers in the division of labor to acquire and disseminate the appropriate information. With respect to this latter, it gives the incentive to producers to provide information about their products that consumers actually want, and it also gives the incentive to producers to obtain information about their customers that the producers need to efficiently and effectively sell their goods and services. In other words, all parties tend to be informed only to the degree that it is necessary for them to make rational decisions. Hence, information tends to be neither under- nor over-provided in a free market. Furthermore, by achieving this result, the free market enables the so-called adverse selection and moral hazard problems to be overcome. Therefore, these "problems" are not a problem in a free market either.

A Philosophical Analysis of Asymmetric Information

The asymmetric-information argument against the market represents an attempt to rewrite reality. It is based on the arbitrary belief that asymmetric information is not good and that people must have "perfect information" concerning the goods they consume. Economists who do not like asymmetric information do not like some aspect of reality (specifically, some aspect of the division of labor) and want to get rid of this aspect of reality. Since they cannot do this, they bemoan the allegedly harmful effects of asymmetric information.

However, one cannot change the nature of reality. One cannot wish asymmetric information out of existence, and one cannot wish perfect information (i.e., omniscience) into existence. One cannot *rewrite* reality.[9] One must accept reality as it is and use the nature of reality to his advantage to enable himself to further his life and happiness. This is exactly what a division of labor society in the context of a free market allows people to do.

Further, as with many arguments against the market, the asymmetric-information claim against the market is based on egalitarianism and, beneath that, altruism.[10] To someone who subscribes to egalitarianism, any differences that exist between people, including differences in information they possess, are unacceptable. Therefore, as with economic inequality, egalitarians who dislike information inequality call for government intervention to correct the situation. I have shown the destructive nature of egalitarianism in chapter 7. There I showed how egalitarianism attempts to deny the law of causality. This is no less true with respect to information. For instance, egalitarians want to ignore or deny the fact that because producers specialize at what they do and must have the expertise to produce and/or sell goods, they will have more information about the products than those who consume the products.

I also showed in chapter 7 how implementing egalitarian policies would require a massive initiation of physical force and how egalitarianism stands in opposition to the requirements of human life. The same is no less true for the implications of egalitarianism with respect to information. The government would have to force businesses to provide information and thus force consumers to pay for it. Such a policy ignores the rational judgments of individuals with regard to what information they should disseminate and acquire.

Attempting to eliminate asymmetric information would require the sacrifice of those who have the ability to gain knowledge through their own thought and effort to those who do not have the ability. In addition, one can see here another manifestation of the link between morality and economics, as well as between politics and economics, that I have discussed previously. Bad (i.e., false) moral and political theories lead to economic destruction when put into practice. Likewise, good (or true) moral and political theories lead to economic prosperity when put into practice. That is, implementing government policies based on altruism, such as by forcibly requiring everyone to have the same information, would violate individual rights and thus have economically harmful results, since it would lead to the elimination of the division of labor and therefore to a much lower productive capability and standard of living. Likewise, implementing government policies based on egoism, such as by protecting the freedom of individuals to acquire and use information, protects individual rights and thus has economically beneficial results, since it leads to a more intensive division of labor and therefore a higher productive capability and standard of living.

Many people, including many economists, have a pre-existing hatred of the market based on their belief in altruism. Altruism leads people to believe that one person can gain only by sacrificing others, including by taking advantage of those who have less information. However, this belief is not true. Advocates of altruism simply look for ways to rationalize why the market allegedly fails from an economic standpoint to corroborate their (false) moral views. It should be clear by now that altruism is a thoroughly corrupt and destructive code of morality. The actual failure here, as with all claims against the market, is not the failure of the market but the acceptance of false and destructive ideas like altruism.

Notes

1.George A. Akerlof, "The Market for 'Lemons': Quality Uncertainty and the Market Mechanism," *Quarterly Journal of Economics* 84, no. 3 (August 1970): 488-500.

2. For more on fraud, see the sections titled "Capitalism" in chapter 1 and "What Will Happen Without Regulation?" in chapter 5.

3. See the section titled "How to Achieve Higher Levels of Safety and Quality" in chapter 5 for how this applies to the regulation of safety and quality.

4. This definition was obtained from Leonard Peikoff, *Objectivism: The Philosophy of Ayn Rand* (New York: Meridian, 1991), 267.

5. Notice that I say lying *to obtain a value* is harmful to the liar. This does not mean that lying, as such, is always harmful or inconsistent with the virtue of honesty. Honesty does not mean adhering to the commandment "Thou shalt not lie." This is invalid as a principle and should not be practiced. For instance, if a criminal breaks into your house and during the robbery asks if there are any children in the home, even if your children are upstairs, it would be proper to lie and tell the criminal, "No." Lying in this case is consistent with the virtue of honesty. Honesty, properly understood, is the rejection of the unreal. In this case, you are rejecting the criminal's desire to violate your rights and the rights of your children. His desire is "unreal" because it has no basis in the facts of reality—it clashes with reality because it stands in opposition to the requirements of human life—and thus should be rejected. Here, one sees that lying *to protect one's values* from a criminal is beneficial to the liar and is a virtue. For more on this issue, and the subjects of honesty and integrity generally, see Peikoff, *Objectivism*, 259-276.

6. I owe this point to Richard E. Wagner, professor of economics at George Mason University, personal conversation.

7. See the section titled "Capitalism" in chapter 1.

8. See the sections titled "Capitalism" and "Socialism" in chapter 1.

9. For more on the subject of rewriting reality, see the section titled "Network Effects" in chapter 2 and the section titled "Causality and Inequality" in chapter 7 and the relevant references given there.

10. On the relationship between altruism and egalitarianism, see the section titled "The Ethical Basis of Perfect Competition and Economic Monopoly" in chapter 2.

Epilogue

What Should One Have Learned from this Book?

This book has been a journey through some of the more prominent arguments made by economists and other intellectuals against the free market. What should the reader have learned from this journey? The most important knowledge, besides the obvious fact that markets do not fail, is that the issue of market failure or success goes much deeper than economics. At its deepest level, it is primarily a moral and epistemological issue. One needs a proper view in these areas to ultimately understand why the market succeeds.

The refutation of the arguments against the market has involved exposing the epistemological, ethical, and economic errors made by the enemies of the free market. The criticisms of the market are based on inappropriate standards of judgment, such as altruism and collectivism. They are also based on the acceptance of invalid concepts and the misuse of valid concepts. To understand why markets succeed, one must reject these improper standards and embrace appropriate ones, such as egoism and individualism. One must also understand how to properly form and use concepts so one is not misled by invalid or inappropriately used concepts.

Epistemologically, I have discussed how there is a right and a wrong way to form concepts. Concepts are specific cognitive tools and thus have a specific nature. Based on their nature, concepts must be formed and used in a specific way, just as one must build and use any other tool, such as a chain saw, in a way that is appropriate to its nature. If concepts are formed and used in ways that are inconsistent with their nature, as with the chain saw, disastrous results can follow. The difference between the misuse of concepts and a chain saw, however, is that with concepts, the results have the potential to be much worse—and much more bloody. Why is this so?

This is the case because the inappropriate formation and use of concepts leads to ignorance and false conclusions. Such ignorance and false conclusions then provide, in part, the basis on which people mistakenly condemn the market as a failure and adhere to irrational and destructive ideas, such as socialism and environmentalism. In order to properly judge the market, or anything else, one must have the appropriate epistemological tools to do so. If one has the appropriate tools and properly applies them one will come to the correct conclusion, a conclusion based on the facts of reality, including the requirements of human life, and see that the market succeeds because it allows human life to flourish. Likewise, one will also see that socialism and environmentalism fail because they destroy human life.

Another epistemological issue I have briefly discussed is the importance of reason to man. In order for people to be able to further their lives and happiness, they must embrace reason as their means to knowledge. Reason makes it possible for individuals to understand the nature of the world and, among other things, makes it possible to form and use concepts appropriately and understand the validity of capitalism. All this, in turn, leads to successful results and greater prosperity for everyone. This has been proven by capitalism and all the scientific advances achieved by man.[1]

Economically I have shown that voluntary trade, which is consistently achieved only under capitalism, is beneficial to all parties involved. I have shown that capitalism protects individual rights, provides an incentive to produce, provides the means of coordinating the activities of millions of people, and thus leads to a growing standard of living for everyone. I have shown that capitalism is the only political/economic system consistent with the require-ments of human life. Hence, economically, the only proper conclusion is that markets succeed.

Next I want to discuss, in more detail, the moral arguments against the market. These are often closely linked to people's hatred of the free market. They are also widely accepted and have great influence. These arguments are not only accepted by the enemies of the free market but are also accepted by many of its alleged supporters, such as conservative economists.[2]

Some want to sacrifice the rich to the poor, some want to sacrifice adults to children, some want to sacrifice the young to the old, some want to sacrifice all humans to animals, plants, and rock formations, some want to sacrifice the healthy to the mentally retarded and crippled, some want to sacrifice other races to their own race, and some want to sacrifice employers to workers. The list could go on and on. The question to ask is, Who wins in this orgy of sacrifice? Who comes out ahead? The answer: no one. The only thing that occurs is that everyone is sacrificed.

In a society based on the morality of self-sacrifice, every person has his rights violated. Everyone is prevented, to a greater or lesser degree, from using his mind—his basic tool of survival—to further his life and happiness. Voluntary trade and the production of wealth are inhibited and in many cases completely prevented. When one puts the altruist code of morality into practice in politics, laws are passed that sacrifice some people to others. When people are forcibly prevented from living their lives for their own selfish benefit, the productive capability and standard of living in an economy decrease.[3]

It is irrelevant that the moral code of altruism has been the chosen code of morality by most of mankind for most of history. An idea does not become right just because it is old and it does not become right because a majority of the people feel it is right. An idea is right, regardless of how old it is and how many people believe in it, if it corresponds to the facts of reality. The morality of sacrifice is wrong *because* it is inconsistent with the facts of reality; it is inconsistent with the requirements of human life.

The field of ethics is not a playground for mystics and subjectivists.[4] What is moral, or good, is not determined by God and it is not based on one's feelings. Ethics is a science and is necessary because of the nature of human life. Human life is not automatic; people must make the right choices to further their lives. It is the field of ethics that is supposed to help men make the right choices in this endeavor. This is the field that defines a code of values to guide man's choices and actions. Man needs a proper code of ethics in order to survive. Such a code must be defined in a rational, objective manner, taking into account the nature of reality, the nature of man, and man's relationship to reality. This is what the moral code of egoism does. If a code of ethics does not take into account these factors, it will lead people to make the wrong choices and lead them down a path of destruction. This is what altruism does.[5]

Any attempt to defend the free market while accepting and espousing the morality of altruism is futile and destructive. In other words, if you are for altruism, then you are against capitalism. You may be for some of the economic aspects of capitalism; however, if you believe altruism is an ideal, you are undermining the fight for capitalism. "Supporters" of capitalism who believe altruism is a proper moral standard would do more good for capitalism by joining the cause for socialism. From an ethical standpoint, that is where they belong. If these "supporters" did this, it would clear the way for the real defenders of capitalism—those who understand the arguments for capitalism down to their ethical and epistemological roots—to provide a fully consistent and thus more powerful defense of it, one that is untainted by the toxins spewing from altruism.[6]

The economist Milton Friedman provides an excellent example of a pseudo-defender of capitalism. He is widely referred to as a supporter of the free market. However, he embraces the altruist code of morality and, as a logical manifestation of his belief in altruism, he supports government welfare programs. Further, he believes the government should provide city streets and highways, among other things, and that the government should intervene in the case of "externalities" when there is a "very clear balance of benefits over costs." He believes these types of government intervention should exist even though, as he admits, a defense of such intervention "can be interpreted to justify *unlimited extensions* of government power."[7] (Emphasis added.) Hence, he supports political ideas that, by his own admission, could lead to totalitarian dictatorship.

Now, Milton Friedman is not an advocate of dictatorship, but by supporting the principle that the government should initiate physical force in the economy *at all*, he opens the door for potential dictators and therefore does more to help them achieve their goals than they could have ever done on their own. He provides a moral sanction of his enemy's fundamental political ideas (i.e., he morally sanctions the government's use of the initiation of force) and thereby surrenders the power of morality to his enemy. In other words, he grants that it is *ideal* for the government to initiate force; he merely disagrees with the advocates of dictatorship over how much force the government should initiate. By doing this, Friedman makes it look like morality *is* on the side of the enemies of capitalism, since it appears that even its "defenders" admit that this is the case, and thus harms the fight for capitalism more than he helps it.

Why is advocating the right code of morality so important to the fight for capitalism? It is because morality is more fundamental than politics and economics. One's moral views determine what one believes to be ideal. As a result, the political/economic system that one considers to be ideal will be a reflection of one's moral views. This is why the complete and utter failure of socialism has not persuaded socialists to abandon their destructive beliefs. The miserably low standard of living and the corpses piled high under socialist regimes are not enough to convince socialists of the destructiveness of their beliefs. This is the case because they are morally committed to socialism; they believe it is an ideal.

One might ask at this point, why are there so many people who advocate some aspects of capitalism in economics but believe in altruism in ethics even though the two are incompatible? The answer is that people who believe in these incompatible ideas are being inconsistent. They either do not see or do not care that the ideas they support are inconsistent with each other. Ultimately, however, because these individuals are inconsistent, the arguments they give in support of the less fundamental ideas will be ineffective. It is like saying that action X is right, moral, good, and ideal, but you need to do the opposite. (In the present context, it is like saying that socialism or the welfare state is right, good, moral, and ideal, but one should support capitalism.) As long as action X is believed to be ideal, any arguments for the opposite action will lose their persuasiveness. Why should one do the opposite of X when X is the ideal? Typically, people rationalize this dichotomy by saying that acting morally is impractical and that one must be immoral (or, at best, amoral), at least occasionally, so that one can survive. This is how people justify advocating capitalism in economics while adhering to altruism in ethics. Nonetheless, they still admire and respect the ideal and use it as their standard for judging what is good, however inconsistently they may apply it.

It is important to note here that there is no break between what is moral and what is practical. What is moral appears to be impractical to most people only because most people accept an impractical code of morality: altruism. The moral-practical dichotomy acts as an epistemological sedative that numbs people's minds and causes them to ignore the destructive results of putting altruism into practice. This sedative causes people to ignore the impracticality of altruism. This is an example of rationalizing one false belief, altruism, with another falsehood, the moral-practical dichotomy. This is not a proper method of thinking.

The solution to this alleged dichotomy is to reject the false ethical view and embrace a proper code of ethics, one that represents a union between the moral and the practical because it is consistent with the requirements of human life. If one does this, and therefore embraces egoism, the apparent moral-practical dichotomy disappears. If one embraces egoism, one will see that capitalism is not only a practical system, it is also the *only* moral political/economic system. Capitalism represents a moral-practical unity because it leads to the production of an abundance of wealth (the practical), and it protects individual rights so that each individual can be free from the initiation of physical force to use his mind to think and further his life and happiness (the moral). In fact, based on a proper view of ethics, one understands that capitalism is practical *because* it is moral.

I urge readers to pursue knowledge in the field of ethics as one would do so in the field of physics or chemistry. The same objectivity is required. By remaining objective, one will come to the conclusion that egoism is the only proper moral code for mankind. Further, by embracing egoism, one will not only benefit oneself but, in the benevolent spirit of the morality of rational self-interest and capitalism, one will benefit the rest of mankind as well. Only when we have fully embraced egoism, right down to every thought we think and every action we take, will the path be clear, our purpose be a moral one, and our economic future be a bright one.

How Does One Create a Capitalist Society?

Spreading the Right Ideas

Given the philosophically corrupt state of our culture, the creation of a capitalist society is an extremely long-term pursuit. It is a goal that can only be achieved over several generations, at a minimum. To create such a society, one must begin by educating oneself so that one understands why capitalism is a goal worthy of achieving. This requires reading and understanding the arguments in this book. In addition, it requires a thorough understanding of the economic superiority of capitalism over alternative economic systems. This can only be gained by reading the works of the economist George Reisman. More fundamentally, it requires a complete understanding of the only fully integrated, reality-based philosophy: Objectivism. The best places to learn about this philosophy are from its creator, Ayn Rand, or from the person she designated as her legal and intellectual heir, Leonard Peikoff. From here, one can expand his knowledge on the nature of capitalism by reading various authors that have identified many important truths with regard to the subject.[8]

Once an individual has educated himself sufficiently, he can then proceed to educate the public on the nature of capitalism. Educating the public is a step that must be taken before any serious political action can be taken to implement capitalism. Without a good understanding of capitalism, any attempt to create the political institutions necessary for a capitalist society must fail because one will be confronted with a public that is opposed to such institutions. Since people's actions are based on the ideas they accept to be true, only after sufficiently large numbers of people are educated and understand the validity of capitalism, and pro-capitalist philosophy, will any political action be possible. Only then can sufficient support be garnered to change the political institutions of the country.

Educating the public does not necessarily mean becoming a teacher, although that is one very good option. Educating the public simply means expressing your ideas on any scale you are able to reach. It can be done by becoming a writer for a newspaper, writing opinion pieces or letters to the editor, or by something as simple as discussing rational ideas with your friends and family. Whatever you do, you must always keep in mind that the battle for a rational culture is a selfish battle. You are fighting for the type of society that is beneficial to you and that will allow you to pursue your own happiness. Therefore, the battle must be fought through means that are consistent with that purpose.[9]

Creating the Government of a Capitalist Society

I have given a brief description in other parts of this book of the characteristics of a government in a capitalist society. However, I have not stated explicitly what would have to be done in order to move from the type of government that exists in America today to the type of government that would exist in a capitalist society. As I stated in the introduction and chapter 1, a government in a capitalist society would be limited to protecting individual rights; that is, it would be limited to protecting people from the initiation of physical force. To do this, the government must be limited to three functions: the police, the military, and the courts. Given that these are the functions of a proper government—a government that is a supporter of human life—how does the government we have today need to be changed in order to achieve this goal?

In terms of brief essentials, the power of the government, in its legislative, judicial, and executive branches, must be radically reduced. Virtually all of the alphabet agencies would have to be abolished, including the FDA, EPA, FAA, SSA, FCC, CPSC, IRS, OSHA, and many, many more.[10] All these agencies, to a greater or lesser degree, initiate physical force against citizens. For instance, the

FCC regulates the ownership of radio stations. It has the power to determine who will be allowed to own radio stations in each region of the country. Therefore, the FCC has the power to forcibly prevent someone from owning a station even if he has the means and desire to do so. Even if the FCC forcibly prevented a large company from acquiring all the radio stations in a specific geographic region, as long as the company was attempting to acquire these assets through voluntary trade, the FCC would be initiating physical force against the company; i.e., it would be violating the individual rights of the company's owners.

Any of the above agencies that could perform legitimate functions in private hands, such as a private organization providing recommendations concerning drug and medical safety (a private "FDA"), could be sold off to the highest bidder or handed over to private individuals in some other manner. These individuals would then have to obtain voluntary funding for the organization and solicit users of its products and services in a voluntary manner. However, the rest of the agencies must be shut down.

Further, in a completely free society, there would be no Federal Reserve. In such a society, what people chose to use as money, how they chose to produce the money, and any other monetary institutions that arose (such as banks) would be established based on voluntary trade. People would voluntarily choose what money to accept, and not accept, in trade. Further, the characteristics of the institutions necessary for facilitating the use of money (again, such as banks) would be determined based on the voluntary choices of individuals to do business with those institutions that have the desired characteristics. There is no need for the government in this process and, in fact, any intervention on the government's part leads to greater instability of the monetary and financial system, as can be witnessed throughout America's history.[11]

In addition, the executive branch must have its cabinet-level departments reduced from the current fifteen to four: the departments of state, justice, defense, and the treasury. These are the only legitimate departments. They are the only ones that help the government defend individual rights and perform the administrative functions necessary to achieve this end. Also, the Constitution must be amended to eliminate inconsistencies with the government's proper function of protecting individual rights. For instance, the power of Congress to regulate trade must be eliminated.

It goes without saying that many of the laws that now exist must be abolished. These include welfare legislation, legislation favoring labor unions, minimum wage laws, legislation based on environmentalism, and many more. In order to abolish the necessary agencies and laws, one final government agency should be established—the agency to end all agencies and laws that violate individual rights. This agency would have the task of determining which agencies and laws must be abolished, in what manner they should be abolished, and over what time frame. Such an agency may also be given the actual authority to abolish the relevant agencies and laws or it may just provide recommendations to Congress (and Congress would have the final authority over what agencies and laws to abolish and how to abolish them). However, this agency must not be given the power to create any other agencies or laws. It should only be given the power to eliminate existing laws and agencies that violate individual rights.

Some of the agencies that would remain in the government, which would help it to perform its proper functions, include the Federal Bureau of Investigation, the Central Intelligence Agency, and the National Security Agency. These agencies perform functions necessary to protect the rights of citizens. Essentially, the government's role under capitalism would be that of a night watchman, with whom the peaceful, law-abiding citizen would rarely come into contact. The government would loom large only in the lives of criminals and foreign aggressors.

Based on the above discussion, if the IRS is to be abolished, some might wonder how the proper functions of the government will be financed. Such financing could be based on a system of voluntary taxation and/or a system of fees on contracts. These fees would pay for the privilege of having disputes with regard to those contracts arbitrated in a court of law and the remedies legally enforced. The fees could be paid to the court system as a type of insurance. People could still choose to engage in contractual relationships without paying the fees; however, the contracts would not be legally enforceable.

Some might think a system of voluntary taxation would not work. In the context of today's government, where funds are used to finance a myriad of activities that are wasteful and destructive to taxpayers (such as building golf courses and stadiums, subsidizing businesses, financing dubious scientific research projects, providing welfare handouts, and providing funds to governments that are hostile to the United States), this belief is correct. In today's context, a system of voluntary taxation most certainly would not work because it is not in the self-interest of taxpayers' to support so-called pork-barrel projects and hostile governments. However, in a completely free society, where the government is pared back to its proper function of protecting individual rights, people would be willing to pay voluntarily for the protection the government provides because it would be in their self-interest to do so. It is especially in the self-interest of wealthy individuals and businesses, which have large amounts of property that need to be protected. In fact, many businesses would probably require employees to pay a small percentage of their paycheck to the government as a condition of their employment. This, of course, would be a voluntary agreement between the employer and his employees.

Based on the discussion in the above paragraph, one must recognize that establishing the proper method of financing the government of a capitalist society is the last step to take in creating such a society. The first step is to properly educate the public. The second step is to pare the government back to an appropriate level. Once these have been accomplished, then it will be possible to implement a system of voluntary taxation.[12]

I have given only a very brief overview of some of the issues associated with the establishment of the government of a capitalist society. I have not provided more detail because the purpose of this book is not to provide a detailed plan about how to establish the government of a capitalist society. The purpose is to show why markets do not fail, but in fact succeed. Let these remarks serve as an indication of what needs to be done.[13]

Conclusion

The achievement of a capitalist society is possible *and* practical. It is practical because it has the ability to lead to success in practice: the practice of people furthering their lives and happiness. Such a society is practical regardless of the number of people who may be opposed to it. Even if the overwhelming majority of people are opposed to capitalism, this simply shows that the overwhelming majority of people are impractical. This is the case because if the ideas of those who are opposed to capitalism are put into practice, whether they are backed by a majority of people or not, they will lead to failure in practice. An idea does not become practical simply because a majority of people believe in it. Likewise, an idea does not become impractical because no one believes in it. No one, including a majority of individuals, can change the nature of reality and make an impractical idea practical or vice versa.

Furthermore, capitalism is possible *because* it is practical. However, the road ahead is a long one. Each step along the way the battle must be fought with the ultimate goal of achieving a free society in mind. If one keeps this ideal shining as a beacon to guide one's actions, no matter how distant the realization of the ultimate goal may seem, the beacon will serve as an inspiration to continue the battle and make the realization of such a society possible. Further, if one keeps clearly in mind that man's means to knowledge is his reason, and understands all that that implies, one will have the conviction of the rightness—and righteousness—of his cause and will take great pride and joy in acting to achieve the ultimate goal.

Notes

1. On the link between reason and capitalism, see the section titled "Environmentalism and the Abandonment of Reason" in chapter 6 and the references given there. In addition, if one is thinking that the use of reason and the scientific advances it has created have not always lead to better results, such as with the potential use of nuclear weapons by dictators, this is a mistaken conclusion. It is not the use of reason and nuclear technology that has led to potential destruction at the hands of evil dictators but the acceptance of irrational ideas such as communism and socialism, i.e., the *abandonment* of reason, that makes these evil acts possible.

2. My statements here regarding the moral arguments against the market should not be taken as a denial of the fact that the more fundamental, epistemological arguments are

not widespread, influential, and accepted by both the enemies and alleged supporters of capitalism. They are. However, I choose here to focus more attention on the moral arguments because these have been, and continue to be to this day, used more explicitly against the market. I leave a more detailed discussion of epistemology and its link to fields such as economics to philosophers.

3. Even the people who sacrifice others, such as dictators, lose in the orgy of sacrifice. This is true because if everyone is busy trying to sacrifice others, any "victory" will probably only be short-lived. Therefore, it will not be long before the sacrificers become the sacrificed. Further, a society where everyone spends their time and energy attempting to sacrifice others is an extremely stagnant and poor society. There is little to no incentive to produce, since rights are not protected, and most of the resources that exist are wasted trying to sacrifice others instead of being used to produce wealth. Hence, everyone loses in the long run because there is no economic progress and the standard of living is low. This is readily apparent when compared to a society based on egoism, such as a capitalist society, where the rate of economic progress is high.

4. I owe this observation to Leonard Peikoff.

5. I owe the observations in this paragraph to Ayn Rand. For more on egoism versus altruism, see the section titled "An Important Discussion on Moral Theory: Egoism versus Altruism" in chapter 1 and the references given there.

6. If the alleged supporters of capitalism do not believe in altruism, but believe in some mix of altruism and egoism, to clear the way for the real defenders of capitalism these "supporters" should openly renounce their alleged support for capitalism and explicitly join the cause for the mixed economy or welfare state.

7. For the quotes and Friedman's other views mentioned in this paragraph, see Milton and Rose Friedman, *Free to Choose: A Personal Statement* (San Diego: Harcourt Brace Jovanovich, 1990), 30-32, 109, and 189.

8. For a good source of authors, see the bibliographies in George Reisman's *Capitalism: A Treatise on Economics* (Ottawa, Ill.: Jameson Books, 1996), 993-998 and Ayn Rand's *Capitalism: The Unknown Ideal*, (New York: Signet, 1967), 338-340. Also, many of the works listed in the bibliography at the end of this book are good sources of pro-capitalist economic thought.

9. For more on this topic, see Ayn Rand, *Philosophy: Who Needs It* (New York: Signet, 1982), 199-204.

10. For those readers who are not familiar with the government agencies I have named, they include, respectively, the Food and Drug Administration, Environmental Protection Agency, Federal Aviation Administration, Social Security Administration, Federal Communications Commission, Consumer Product Safety Commission, Internal Revenue Service, and Occupational Safety & Health Administration.

11. Here I am neither going to provide the details of the instabilities created by the government's intervention in money and banking, nor the details of the stability created by a free market in money and banking. However, for a source of these details, see Reisman, *Capitalism*, 895-966 and passim.

12. My discussion on financing the government of a free society is based on Ayn Rand, *The Virtue of Selfishness*, (New York: Signet, 1964), 135-140.

13. For those who want more detailed guidance about how to establish a capitalist society, see Reisman, *Capitalism*, 969-990.

Bibliography

Akerlof, George A. "The Market for 'Lemons': Quality Uncertainty and the Market Mechanism." *Quarterly Journal of Economics* 84, no. 3 (August 1970): 488-500.

Arnold, Roger A. *Economics*. 5th ed. Cincinnati: South-Western College Publishing, 2001.

Ayn Rand Institute. *Earth Day vs. Man: In Defense of Industry and Technology*. Marina del Rey, Calif.: Ayn Rand Institute, 2000.

Binswanger, Harry, ed. *The Ayn Rand Lexicon: Objectivism from A to Z*. New York: Meridian, 1986.

Binswanger, Harry, et al. *Socialism versus Capitalism: Which Is the Moral System?* Gaylordsville, Conn.: Second Renaissance Inc., 1989. Audiocassette.

Blackburn, John D., Elliot I. Klayman, and Martin H. Malin. *The Legal Environment of Business*. 4th ed. Homewood, Ill.: Irwin, 1991.

Bryant, Peter J. "The Age of Mammals: Evolution of Mammals." *Biodiversity and Conservation*. 2002. http://darwin.bio.uci.edu/~sustain/bio65/lec02/b65lec02.htm# MAMMALS accessed August 31, 2004.

Campbell, Noel D. "Exploring Free Market Certification of Medical Devices." Pp. 313-44 in *American Health Care: Government, Market Processes, and the Public Interest*, edited by Roger D. Feldman. Oakland: The Independent Institute, 2000.

Coase, R.H. "The Lighthouse in Economics." *The Journal of Law and Economics* 17, no. 2 (October 1974): 357-376.

Colander, David C. *Microeconomics*. 5th ed. New York: McGraw-Hill/Irwin, 2004.

Courtois, Stéphane, et al. *The Black Book of Communism: Crimes, Terror, Repression*. Translated by Jonathan Murphy and Mark Kramer. Cambridge: Harvard University Press, 1999.

Eggleston, Edward. *A History of the United States and Its People*. Lake Wales, Fla.: Lost Classics Book Company, 1998.

Emsley, John, ed. *The Global Warming Debate*. London: The European Science and Environment Forum, 1996.

Friedman, Milton and Rose. *Free to Choose: A Personal Statement*. San Diego: Harcourt Brace Jovanovich, 1990.

Gieringer, D. H. "The Safety and Efficacy of New Drug Approval." *Cato Journal* 5, no. 1 (1985): 177-201.

Goldsmith, Donald. *Nemesis: The Death-Star and Other Theories of Mass Extinction.* New York: Walker & Company, 1985.

Graber, David M. "Mother Nature as a Hothouse Flower." *Los Angeles Times Book Review*, 22 October 1989.

Gwartney, James D. and Richard L. Stroup. *Microeconomics: Private and Public Choice.* 8th ed. Orlando: Harcourt Brace & Company, 1997.

Harberger, Arnold C. "Monopoly and Resource Allocation." *American Economic Review* 44, no. 2 (May 1954): 771-787.

Hayek, F. A., ed. *Capitalism and the Historians.* Chicago: The University of Chicago Press, 1963.

Hayek, F. A. *Individualism and Economic Order.* Chicago: The University of Chicago Press, 1948.

Hazlitt, Henry. *Time Will Run Back: A Novel About the Rediscovery of Capitalism.* Lanham, Md.: University Press of America, 1986.

Healey James R. and Jayne O'Donnell. "Deadly Air Bags: How a Government Prescription for Safety Became a Threat to Children." *USA Today*, 8 July 1996.

Hirshleifer, Jack and David Hirshleifer. *Price Theory and Applications.* 6th ed. Upper Saddle River, N.J.: Prentice Hall, 1998.

Kant, Immanuel. *Critique of Pure Reason.* Translated by Norman Kemp Smith. New York: Palgrave Macmillan, 2003.

Kazinski, Theodore (a.k.a., the Unabomber). "Industrial Society and Its Future." *Washington Post*, 19 September 1995.

Klein, Daniel B. and Alexander Tabarrok. "The Drug Development and Approval Process." 2003. http://www.fdareview.org/approval_process.shtml accessed August 30, 2004.

———. "History of Federal Regulation: 1902-Present." 2003. http://www.fdareview.org /history.shtml accessed August 30, 2004.

———. "Theory, Evidence and Examples of FDA Harm." 2003. http://www.fdareview. org/harm.shtml accessed August 30, 2004.

———. "Why the FDA Has an Incentive to Delay the Introduction of New Drugs." 2003. http://www.fdareview.org/incentives.shtml accessed August 30, 2004.

Kohler, Heinz. *Economic Systems and Human Welfare: A Global Survey.* Cincinnati: South-Western College Publishing, 1997.

Kopel, David B. *Antitrust After Microsoft: The Obsolescence of Antitrust in the Digital Era.* Chicago: The Heartland Institute, 2001.

Lehr, Jay H., ed. *Rational Readings on Environmental Concerns.* New York: Van Nostrand Reinhold, 1992.

Liebowitz, Stan J. and Stephen E. Margolis. *Winners, Losers, & Microsoft: Competition and Antitrust in High Technology.* Oakland: The Independent Institute, 1999.

Locke, Edwin and Stephen Sapontzis. *Do Animals Have Rights?* Gaylordsville, Conn.: Second Renaissance Inc., 1990. Audiocassette.

Locke, Edwin A. *The Prime Movers: Traits of the Great Wealth Creators.* New York: AMACOM, 2000.

Lockitch, Keith H. "Fighting the Hydra: The Futile Battle of the Skeptical Environmentalist." *The Intellectual Activist* 16, no. 12 (December 2002): 6-18.

Lomborg, Bjorn. *The Skeptical Environmentalist: Measuring the Real State of the World.* Cambridge: Cambridge University Press, 2001.

Maduro, Rogelio A. and Ralf Schauerhammer. *The Holes in the Ozone Scare: The Scientific Evidence That the Sky Isn't Falling.* Washington, D.C.: 21st Century Science Associates, 1992.

Maurice, S. Charles and Christopher R. Thomas. *Managerial Economics*. 7th ed. New York: McGraw-Hill, 2002.

Mises, Ludwig von. *Human Action: A Treatise on Economics*. 3rd ed. Chicago: Contemporary Books, Inc., 1966.

Mohl, Bruce. "U.S. Advises Car Makers on Dangers of Rear Air Bags." *Boston Globe*, 15 October 1999.

Nemtzow, David M. "More Power to You: On Bjorn Lomborg and Energy." *Grist Magazine*, 12 December 2001. http://www.grist.org/advice/books/2001/12/12/to/index .html accessed October 28, 2004.

Nicholson, Walter. *Microeconomic Theory: Basic Principles and Extensions*. 6th ed. Fort Worth, Tex.: Harcourt Brace College Publishers, 1995.

Peikoff, Leonard. *Objectivism: The Philosophy of Ayn Rand*. New York: Meridian, 1991.

———. *Ominous Parallels: The End of Freedom in America*. New York: Stein and Day, 1982.

Peikoff, Leonard, ed. *The Voice of Reason: Essays in Objectivist Thought*. New York: Meridian, 1989.

Pimental, David. "Skeptical of the Skeptical Environmentalist." *Skeptic* 9, no. 2 (2002): 90-94.

Ralston, Richard E., ed. *Why Businessmen Need Philosophy*. Irvine, Calif.: Ayn Rand Institute Press, 1999.

Rand, Ayn. *Atlas Shrugged*. 35th anniversary ed. New York: Signet, 1992.

———. *Introduction to Objectivist Epistemology*. 2nd ed. New York: Meridian, 1990.

———. *Philosophy: Who Needs It*. New York: Signet, 1982.

———. *The New Left: The Anti-Industrial Revolution*, Revised edition. New York: Signet, 1975.

———. *Capitalism: The Unknown Ideal*. New York: Signet, 1967.

———. *The Virtue of Selfishness*. New York: Signet, 1964.

———. *The Intellectual Bankruptcy of Our Age*. Gaylordsville, Conn.: Second Renaissance Inc., 1961. Audiocassette.

———. *For the New Intellectual*. New York: Signet, 1961.

———. *The Fountainhead*. New York: Signet, 1952.

Ray, Dixy Lee, with Lou Guzzo. *Trashing the Planet: How Science Can Help Us Deal with Acid Rain, Depletion of the Ozone, and Nuclear Waste (Among Other Things)*. Washington, D.C.: Regnery Gateway, 1990.

Reisman, George. "News Report: California's Blackouts Caused by Demons." 2002. http://www.capitalism.net/articles/News%20Report%20California's%20Blackouts% 20Caused%20by%20Demons.html accessed August 25, 2004.

———. "California Screaming, Under Government Blows." 2000. http:// www.capitalism.net/GovernmentBlows.htm accessed August 25, 2004.

———. *Capitalism: A Treatise on Economics*. Ottawa, Ill.: Jameson Books, 1996.

Sale, Kirkpatrick. "Unabomber's Secret Treatise: Is There Method in His Madness?" *The Nation* 261, no. 9 (25 September 1995): 305.

Schell, Jonathan. "Our Fragile Earth." *Discover* 10, no. 10 (October 1989): 44-50.

Scherer, F. M. *Industrial Market Structure and Economic Performance*. 2nd ed. Boston: Houghton Mifflin, 1980.

Schwartz, Peter. "The Philosophy of Privation." Pp. 219-44 in *Return of the Primitive: The Anti-Industrial Revolution*, Ayn Rand. Edited and with an introduction and additional articles by Peter Schwartz. New York: Meridian, 1999.

Southern Poverty Law Center. "Fringe Eco-Radicals Growing More Violent." *Intelligence Report*, no. 112 (Winter 2003): 3.

University of California, Berkeley, Museum of Paleontology. "What Killed the Dinosaurs? The Invalid Hypotheses." *DinoBuzz: Current Topics Concerning Dinosaurs.* 2004. http://www.ucmp.berkeley.edu/diapsids/extincthypo.html accessed August 31, 2004.

Wakeland, Jack. "California's Green Brownout, Part 2." *The Intellectual Activist* 15, no. 5 (May 2001): 11-31.

———. "California's Green Brownout, Part 1." *The Intellectual Activist* 15, no. 3 (March 2001): 15-30.

Wall Street Journal. "The Life and Deaths of DDT." 14 June 2002.

Zinsmeister, Karl. "MITI Mouse." *Policy Review*, no. 64 (Spring 1993): 28-35.

Index

About the Author

Brian P. Simpson is assistant professor at National University in La Jolla, California. He is the lead economics faculty and faculty advisor for the Bachelor of Business Administration program. He has recently created a minor in economics that focuses on free market economics and the philosophical foundations of a capitalist society. He has presented papers at scholarly conferences and his writing has appeared in such periodicals as the *Los Angeles Times*, *Orange County Register*, and *San Diego Union-Tribune*. He has been interviewed for articles in publications such as the *Baltimore Sun* and *Stocks, Futures & Options Magazine*. Before pursuing a career in economics, he was an aerospace engineer performing rigid body dynamic separation analyses in the Delta Launch Vehicle Division of McDonnell Douglas Space Systems Company in Huntington Beach, California. He holds a Ph.D. and M.A. in economics from George Mason University, an M.B.A. from Pepperdine University, and a B.S. in aerospace engineering from Syracuse University. He enjoys watching movies, weight lifting, and hiking.